WALKING
with
GOD
through
DEEP VALLEYS

Register This New Book

Benefits of Registering*

- ✓ FREE **replacements** of lost or damaged books
- ✓ FREE **audiobook** – *Pilgrim's Progress*, audiobook edition
- ✓ FREE information about new titles and other **freebies**

www.anekopress.com/new-book-registration

*See our website for requirements and limitations.

WALKING
with
GOD
through
DEEP
VALLEYS

Lessons on finding contentment
when life is hard

Rev. Dr. Stephen A. Gammon

We love hearing from our readers. Please contact us at www.anekopress.com/questions-comments with any questions, comments, or suggestions.

Walking with God through Deep Valleys
© 2020 by Stephen A. Gammon
All rights reserved. Published 2020.

No part of this book may be reproduced, stored in a retrieval system, or transmitted in any form or by any means – electronic, mechanical, photocopying, recording, or otherwise, without written permission from the publisher.

The Holy Bible, English Standard Version (ESV) is adapted from the Revised Standard Version of the Bible, copyright Division of Christian Education of the National Council of the Churches of Christ in the U.S.A. All rights reserved.

Cover Design: Robert Hatcher
Editor: Sheila Wilkinson

Printed in the United States of America
Aneko Press
www.anekopress.com
Aneko Press, Life Sentence Publishing, and our logos are trademarks of
Life Sentence Publishing, Inc.
203 E. Birch Street
P.O. Box 652
Abbotsford, WI 54405

RELIGION / Christian Living / Inspirational
Paperback ISBN: 978-1-62245-690-1
eBook ISBN: 978-1-62245-691-8
10 9 8 7 6 5 4 3 2 1
Available where books are sold

CONTENTS

Introduction ix
On Walking With God 1
On The Sweet Gift Of Family 4
On Dealing With Disappointments 7
On Resting Well 9
On Having No Fear Because Our God Is With Us 11
On God Remaining Faithful 13
On Knowing Reinforcements Are On The Way 16
On Being Okay When Life Is Hard 18
On The Joy Of Being Home 20
On Believing God Is With Me Now 22
On Thankfulness Even When Life Is Difficult 24
On Gratitude For Chemotherapy 27
On Continuing To Rest Well 29
On Feeling Good Today 32
On Reminders That This Is Temporary 35
On Divine Appointments Continuing 37
On Learning Contentment 40
On Being Real 43
On Being Blessed To Be A Blessing 46
On God's Light Shining Into Our Darkness 49
On Making Progress With God's Help 54
On Experiencing Deep Satisfaction 58
On A Life Of Knowing And Trusting God 61
On Being Together Forever 65
On Strength In Life's Ups And Downs 68
On Lessons Learned When Short Of Breath 72
On Disappointment To Delight 76
On Admitting Our Nervousness 79
On Prayer And Praise 82
On Enduring Gratitude 84
On Treasures To Hold On To When Struggling 88
On Finding Contentment In Our Deepest Valleys 91
On What To Do When We Feel Like We Are Losing It 94
On How God Blesses Us In The Midst Of Our Struggles 99
On The Wonderful Grace Of Jesus 104
On Hard Struggles And True Faith 108
On Helping Somebody By Praying 111
On Waiting Well 114
On Promised Rewards Exceeding Temporary Risks 119
On Finding Calm In A Lingering Storm 125
On Not Journeying To Difficult Places Alone 130
On What To Do When Facing A Daunting Task 134
On Believing In God And Eternity 138
On Always Being Ready To Preach, Pray, Or Die 142

On Trusting God When We Cannot See	148
On The Blessing Of Being With Family	150
On Finishing Our Course Well	154
On What To Do When Fear Pursues Us	158
On Our Promised Upgrades: A New Resurrection Body	162
On Shedding Discouragement With God's Help	167
On Trusting God For Discernment To Do His Will	171
On Receiving All That We Need	175
On Waiting When We Would Rather Not	179
On Dreaming Of Heaven	182
On Admitting Our Struggles And Sharing His Suffering	186
On Trusting God Through Our Transitions	191
On Going Home Soon	194
On Saying Goodbye	199
On Receiving Strength Through Faith And Persistent Prayer	202
On Coping With Pain With God's Help	206
On God's Watch Care Over His Children	210
On Noticing Grace	213
On Incarnational Ministry	218
On Celebrating God's Gifts In The Face Of Our Trials	222
On Facing Confusion With Hope	225
On Leaning Upon God's Strength When We Are Weak	229
On Vulnerabilities To Victories	232
On Finding God's Peace When His Plans Have Changed Ours	236
On Being Sick Of Being Sick	240
On Answered Prayers Amidst So Many Cares	244
On Seeing No One But Jesus	247
On Accidents And Providence	251
On Dealing With Unexpected Delays	255
On Encouragement For Our Discouragement	259
On Being Forever Family	264
On Staying Positive When Feeling Negative	267
On Wandering Aimlessly Or Purposefully	271
On Coming To Jesus For All That We Need	274
On God's Restoration Of What Is Broken	279
On Making The Most Of Social Distancing	284
On Praying Like Jesus	293
On Running To The Finish Line	300
On Uncertainties And Certainties In Times Of Storm	307
On Praying Today For God's Will Tomorrow	312
On Rejoicing In Answered Prayer	314
On Easter And Everlasting Joy	317
On Knowing We Are Not Alone	322
On Peace Amidst Uncertainty	324
On Enduring Trials With Joyful Anticipation	328
On Never Bearing A Crucible Alone	332
On Enduring The Struggle To Experience The Miracle	336
On Setting God-Pleasing Goals	339
On Dying In Christ	345
Acknowledgements	353
About The Author	355

INTRODUCTION

Sometimes life is hard, as though we are walking through difficult, deep valleys. It has been this way for me for some time now, as I have been sick, sometimes very sick. The primary physical battle I am fighting is multiple myeloma, which is a cancer of bone marrow and blood plasma cells. Because of immune deficiencies, I have experienced many infections, which have consumed considerable time and effort to fight.

If you have known prolonged illness, painful loss, great disappointment, or a difficult challenge in life, perhaps you too have battled discouragement and discontentment. In this broken world, such struggles are common. As publication of this book approaches, our nation and our world are facing a true pandemic because of the coronavirus infection called COVID-19.

This prolonged challenge has affected everyone in some way, and painful effects may long endure. It has affected us all financially, socially, and in so many more ways. In the face of our struggles, people around the world wonder how to cope when life is hard. Some may be wondering if contentment and joy are even possible.

Disappointments and delays have come to us all. Regarding the effects from the pandemic on our own lives, we can struggle with questions about how to cope, much less thrive again. Along the way we may have many fixed questions in our minds: When will school reopen? When will travel restrictions be lifted? When can we safely gather again? Will our finances return to normal? All beyond our control, expected dates keep changing, and we must adjust and cope with the delay. We can easily face all of this with increasing discouragement and discontentment.

Finding contentment in life is never automatic. It can be especially hard when our circumstances are difficult. Two people may face similar hard circumstances with one being joyful, relatively contented and at peace while the other is miserable and filled with discontentment. Have you noticed this? Have you wondered how one can experience contentment and peace, even when life is hard?

If we should climb to the summit of a mountain and enjoy an awesome view or feel the gentle breezes and behold the grandeur and beauty of a lush valley, we would still lack contentment if our focus is on the next conquest, our difficult circumstances, or our disappointment in not achieving what we want. Finding contentment and peace in this life can be especially tough when we are trudging through long and deep valleys of sickness, pain, uncertainties, grief, or loss.

Through my own struggles, God has been teaching me much about how contentment is found when walking through the difficult and deep valleys of life. The journey through my deep valley of illness and the ripple effects from it has been hard for me and for people that I love. But by God's sweet grace, I know whom to turn to, and that is what I have been doing. And oh the joy of walking with God through a deep valley!

At every juncture, in every challenge, and in every time of distress, disappointment, loss, pain, and fear, I have heard my Lord calling me to trust Him and to lean upon Him now by faith. As I have done so, I have sensed His presence. I have heard His voice and received His comfort and peace. I have experienced His contentment by walking with Him through my deep valley. For this I give Him praise.

In October 2018 I was diagnosed with active multiple myeloma. At that time I served as Bishop/Overseer/Senior Pastor of a local congregation in Coventry, Rhode Island. With the diagnosis, I began a chemotherapy regiment that drained me physically and lowered my energy level; my compromised immune system required me to avoid crowds, so I resigned from my pastoral office. After four decades of front line ministry in Christian service, I grieved this change deeply.

But because I had walked with my Lord for so long and found Him faithful in every season and situation, I knew He would be with me through this challenge too. Still, I struggled. I hated being sick, and I grieved that I could no longer serve as a shepherd of God's flock. I also wrestled with the required isolation because of my illness. I experienced much discontentment because my circumstances were so far from what I wanted them to be.

So I did what all of God's children are blessed to do. I asked God to help me. He always answers this prayer. In great grace and unfailing love, God began teaching me important lessons about finding ultimate contentment – not in our circumstances but in personal relationship with Him. The lessons I learned while walking with God through the deep valley of illness and leaning upon my Lord are sweet treasures to me now. They have caused me to regard my struggles not as merely bearable but as worthwhile and even purposeful to my Lord.

Where have you looked in your lifetime and where are you now looking for your happiness and contentment? Have you been prone to think that peace and joy can only be found when your circumstances are what you desire them to be, when life has become easier for you, or when whatever you have longed for is at last yours? Is this really the path to enduring contentment? No, for the Lord teaches us otherwise.

As little children we presumed we would be happy and content when we were given whatever candy, treat, toy, game, fun experience, or gift that we desired. Who among us has not heard a little child scream or cry with a persistent demand? And if a child does receive whatever it was they demanded, though they might have expected to be content, they soon wanted something else. Circumstance-based contentment and happiness does not long endure.

As we approach adulthood, we might presume that we will be content when circumstances turn out the way we want them. If we are liked by a certain group or by a particular person we are attracted to, or if we acquire the cell phone, clothes, car, or whatever material thing we most desire, we expect to find contentment. We might think we will be content when we have made the team or won the trophy we worked for, acquired the job we wanted, achieved our academic goals, or when we received the letter of acceptance from the university of our choice.

But again, circumstance-based contentment does not long endure. Perhaps in His grace God will allow us to experience unpleasant circumstances for a while when we are young, so we might learn that lasting contentment in this life is not to be found in these areas. Rather, we are to look to Him.

As adults, we may continue to carry childish presumptions about finding contentment. We might still presume that when our circumstances are finally to our liking, we will be content. So we might look for it in our successes, or achievements, or advancements, or acquisitions, or in whatever recognition to which we have aspired.

We might even presume we will find enduring contentment by marrying the person we want, or having our dream wedding. We might think living in our dream house, having children, or watching our children achieve what they want will bring contentment. We could think that electing our preferred candidates and experiencing desired political changes will produce contentment. Acquiring wealth, traveling the world, and having grand adventures might also appear to be what we need. Then, we think we will be content! But of course, circumstance-based contentment is fleeting. It will not endure, for in this broken world, circumstances will never be all we want them to be. Has this been a primary lesson from COVID-19 and from other deep valleys we have walked? Are you and I learning now where true contentment comes from?

Every new and exciting experience eventually fades. Every new promotion, achievement, or exciting romance becomes familiar and loses its luster with time. Every shiny new car eventually becomes an old clunker. And every young and energetic body eventually ages and becomes weaker or infirmed. This is what I have been experiencing. Perhaps you are too. If not, stand by, for you will.

The Bible, God's inspired Word, reveals that God loves us much more than our finite minds can grasp. As amazing as it seems, our heavenly Father longs for us to know the depths of His love. Our God longs for us to believe, receive, and treasure the best gift that has ever been given – the inestimable gift of His only begotten Son, the Lord Jesus Christ.

Jesus is the Lamb of God who takes away my sins and yours and the sin of the world. God's salvation, which is offered through faith in the Lord Jesus Christ, brings to all who will believe and receive Him complete forgiveness with the promise and certainty of everlasting life.

INTRODUCTION

This means that we are enabled by God to live every moment of our lives in personal relationship with Him – for all of today, tomorrow, and forever.

The sacrificial death, burial, and resurrection of the Son of God, the Lord Jesus Christ, made this priceless gift available to us. Our part is to believe and then receive Him – just as we are, with humble repentance and faith, determined to trust Him as our Savior, to follow and serve Him, and to walk with Him in personal relationship as our first love, best friend, and Lord.

God wants us to learn that true contentment and lasting peace in this life is not found by having pleasant circumstances. Rather, He wants us to experience the lasting peace and true contentment that is found in knowing and loving God and living in personal relationship with Him. He is the One who made us and who loves us now and forever. We can live in right relationship with God for time and for eternity through faith in the Lord Jesus Christ. This is true no matter the depth of our struggles or circumstances.

So how will we learn this critical lesson? How will we learn where enduring contentment is found? How will we learn that real and lasting contentment and peace are always derived in personal relationship with the eternal God who made us, who loves us more than we know, and who is with us even now? How will we fully realize our Lord's amazing promise to be with us always – today, tomorrow, and forever? The Bible has much to say about this.

One of my favorite passages on this theme is found in Paul's letter to the Philippians. The apostle wrote this letter from a prison cell where he did not deserve to be and surely did not want to be. We can presume that he experienced loneliness and discomfort, as he missed his friends and wanted his circumstances to be different.

Yet by God's grace, Paul was able to write this inspired letter, filled with joy and encouragement. He wrote, *I have learned in whatever situation I am to be content. I know how to be brought low, and I know how to abound. In any and every circumstance, I have learned the secret of facing plenty and hunger, abundance and need. I can do all things through Him* [Christ] *who strengthens me* (Philippians 4:11-13).

Notice the apostle said, *I have learned in whatever situation I am to be content*. Like us Paul had enjoyed some great circumstances. He had also endured some difficult circumstances. But through it all, Paul learned the life-changing secret that helped him in the struggle of his imprisonment and suffering. What exactly did he learn? He learned that he could *do all things through Christ who strengthens me.*

This is the lesson we most need to learn. When we have learned it, no struggle or hard circumstance can cause us to despair. Paul's personal testimony was that contentment is ultimately found, and grace and strength are received, through faith and personal relationship with the Lord Jesus Christ. Paul learned this lesson in and through his adversity. We can learn the same.

This is my testimony. I have known so many blessings in my life, and along the way I have faced many trials. I have learned far more in the trials, for the trials required my dependence on God. Whenever I have called upon my Lord, He has always met me; He has always taught me; He has always held me; He has always loved me. Always.

The blessings I have known in walking with God through life have been innumerable. As I recount a few of them, I encourage you to remember His blessings in your life too. The list of His blessings to us is long indeed.

By God's grace I was born into a loving Christian home. As none of us choose our family of origin, I know this was God's blessing to me. As a little boy I came to childlike faith, believing and loving the Word of God and accepting Jesus as my Lord and Savior. When I was a young boy, He was very real to me, as real as my parents and five siblings.

At nineteen, by God's grace I began to grasp the Lordship of Jesus, and I surrendered my life to Him, determined to go wherever He would lead me, to do whatever He would have me do, and to say whatever He would have me say. At twenty-one, I married Helen, the most beautiful and amazing woman who has been my fantastic life partner.

When I was twenty-five, I graduated from seminary, and Helen and I were led of God to serve Darlington Congregational Church in Pawtucket, Rhode Island. Our nine years there were blessed. I loved serving my Lord and shepherding His church. During those years God blessed us with our three precious children: Carl, Amy, and Jonathan. How I loved being a husband and dad.

Then the Lord surprised us by leading me into military service. For more than seven years, I served on Active Duty as a chaplain in the United States Navy. Our family lived in Virginia where I served in Norfolk aboard USS Emory S. Land (AS-39). Then we moved to Kaneohe, Hawaii, where I served primarily as Chaplain of 3rd Battalion, 3rd Marines, a U.S. Marine Infantry Battalion, with whom I did two Western Pacific deployments. Then we moved to Connecticut, where I served as Staff Chaplain at the U.S. Navy Submarine School.

I loved military service, for those years were filled with many divine appointments. But in 1996, after seven years of active service, Helen and I discerned that God wanted us back in civilian ministry. I accepted His call to serve as Senior Pastor of Trinity Evangelical Church in Peterborough, New Hampshire. I continued to serve as a chaplain in the U.S. Navy Reserves, which required two days per month and twelve days per year of military service. Our years in New Hampshire were sometimes challenging, but we experienced tremendous blessing there.

In 2001, soon after the attack against America on September 11, I was recalled to Active Duty service in the U.S. Navy. I received a call at 10:15 p.m. on October 3 with orders to report the next day. I was away from my family and congregation for a year, serving as a Navy Chaplain. That year was filled with many divine appointments for me, and I loved it. But when the year was completed, I was excited to return home to my family and resume my responsibilities as a shepherd of God's flock.

In late 2002 and early 2003, the faith group in which I served was looking for a new executive director, a position called *Conference Minister* in the Conservative Congregational Christian Conference (CCCC). To my surprise I was invited to be a candidate for that position, and to my greater surprise I was called to serve the Lord and the CCCC in this leadership role.

In the summer of 2003, as our oldest son Carl was living in Colorado, and our daughter Amy was attending college in Oklahoma, Helen and I moved to Minnesota with our youngest son Jonathan. The eight years that followed were filled with many blessings, as I served the Lord by caring for His churches and pastors.

In 2011 I was again recalled to active duty service in the Navy with orders for one year. I listened and prayed, for I knew that stability was needed in the leadership role I held. Led by the Lord, I resigned as Conference Minister and trusted God to bless and lead the CCCC and to bless, direct, and provide for Helen and me.

In God's good plan, my one year on active duty became five and a half years, for the Navy repeatedly asked if I would continue serving. Each time Helen and I prayed and discerned that God would have me say yes. I served first with U.S. Fleet Forces Command with additional duties in Port Hueneme, California, and then San Diego, California. I then served with Commander Joint Task Force in Guantanamo Bay, Cuba, and finally for two years at Marine Corps Recruit Depot in Parris Island, South Carolina. In each step and location, we experienced God's blessing.

In the summer of 2016, when I retired from the Navy, the Lord led us once more to serve a local congregation. His call was to Church of The Apostles in Coventry, Rhode Island. I expected and hoped that Helen and I would be there for many years, but in the fall of 2018, after I had served this congregation for just two years, I resigned because I had received my diagnosis of multiple myeloma.

In sharing this overview of God's leading and blessing in my life, I hope to illustrate that when we entrust our hearts to the Lord and make ourselves available for His service, He faithfully pours His blessings upon us. He has surely done this for me.

I treasure the memories when I was formally ordained into pastoral ministry on February 22, 1981. On that day my eighty-seven-year-old grandfather, Pastor Morley Durost, put his hands on my shoulders, looked at me through his coke-bottle thick glasses, and with tears in his eyes he said with evident joy, "Stephen, I wish I was sixty years younger and in your shoes and could do it all again!"

After many years of knowing, loving, and serving my Lord, I understand now what my grandfather meant. There is great joy, blessing, and contentment in walking with God and serving Him. I have fervently prayed that you too will learn and experience this.

I can also attest that there is a great deal of struggle and hardship along our earthly journey. Some days we can hurt a lot. My testimony is that those are the days, and those are the seasons, when we can be most ready to learn and receive priceless lessons and precious gifts from the Lord that we might have otherwise missed. But to receive and learn these lessons while walking through deep valleys, we must be spiritually open to listen to what our Lord would teach us and to accept whatever He gives in our time of need.

So, how did this book come about? Due to my illness and immune deficiencies, I was homebound a lot, which was hard for me. I asked my Lord what I could do for His glory at this time. I know that as long as we have breath, our Lord has good works prepared for us to do for Him: *For we are His workmanship, created in Christ Jesus for good works, which God prepared beforehand, that we should walk in them* (Ephesians 2:10).

Because I was receiving requests from family and friends for health updates, I desired to have one place where I could post updates so that anyone who was interested could read it. I was then reminded about CaringBridge, which is a website where people who are ill can post health updates, and family and friends can read it; they can also post a personal reply if they desire. So this is what I determined to do.

Soon after, I heard from my friend Pastor Ken Winters who is also dealing with cancer and is a retired Navy Chaplain and CCCC minister. Ken said that he and his wife Connie had been blessed by a book authored by Steve and Sharol Hayner titled *Joy in the Journey – Finding Abundance in the Shadow of Death*.[1] Helen and I read this book together devotionally, and we were blessed by it.

Steve Hayner served as president of Columbia Seminary and was relatively healthy and fit when he was diagnosed with pancreatic cancer. Following his diagnosis, Steve and his wife, Sharol, began posting their updates and reflections on CaringBridge. Their posts were visited by countless friends and family who became part of their prayer support team. The posts by Steve and Sharol were honest, meaningful, and real, and they encouraged people by demonstrating how to live joyfully with God's grace in the midst of suffering and pain, even when facing death.

Many were blessed by the testimony of the Hayners, and with their encouragement after Steve's death, Sharol compiled their CaringBridge posts into this exceptional book to be published for the blessing of many others, including me. The book included some brief reflections

---

1   Steve and Sharol Hayner, *Joy in the Journey – Finding Abundance in the Shadow of Death* (InterVarsity Press, 2015).

and responses from people who knew Steve and Sharol, which I found to be very helpful.

God used the Hayners' book to motivate me to do something similar. I was urged by several readers of my CaringBridge posts that I should compile these posts into a book, for they believed these lessons could be helpful to many. Discerning that this was a leading from the Lord, I have written this book.

In this volume you will find the chronological posts that I put on CaringBridge and then shared on Facebook. Typically, these included a medical and personal update with lessons I was learning from the Lord that week, while walking with God through my deep valley of cancer and the lifestyle changes and challenges that came with it. Originally, I wanted to include comments from people I know and love and some from people I do not know, but space did not allow it. I thank all of you though for those encouraging words that carried me through this journey. I have included in each lesson a few reflective questions to help each of us consider the implications of this lesson for our own lives.

In writing these things and now publishing them, I have felt vulnerable. It feels risky and daunting to admit my weaknesses and struggles, but God has made it clear to me that I must do this for my own sake, for His sake, and for the sake of those who read this book. It has been my earnest prayer that what you read here might bless you by pointing you to the One who loves you so.

If you are walking, or in the future should find yourself walking, through a hardship and deep valley where you have not journeyed before or are wrestling because of personal hardships from the COVID-19 pandemic, I pray that you might remember in faith and know in the depths of your being that you do not walk alone God who loves you is with you now.

He is walking with you, and He is going to be with you in this moment, and today, tonight, tomorrow, all of your days, and forever. May we always remember that our God is with us in the deep valleys, and He is and will be forever faithful!

1

ON WALKING WITH GOD

October 13, 2018

Walking with God throughout my life has been the great blessing for which He created me. He created all of us to walk with Him for time and for eternity. Walking with God means we will never ever be alone; we are always protected, so we have no reason to fear. Walking with God means we have a loving, powerful, and lifelong friend who is always with us in every season and circumstance of life.

I rejoice that my Lord has been with me from infancy until now. I know with certainty that we continue to walk together until I breathe my last, and then forevermore. By faith I am entirely confident of this.

I have often prayed that many more throughout this world will hear and believe the good news of Jesus Christ and thus experience the peace that comes from walking with God through faith. This is His desire, so it is mine. I long to introduce others to Him and be used of the Lord for this purpose.

Walking with God does not mean that our path is always going to be easy. In fact, the Lord declared that following Him will include carrying a cross. He said, *If anyone would come after me, let him deny himself and take up his cross daily and follow me* (Luke 9:23). All who heard Jesus say this understood that a cross was an instrument of suffering and death. This hard declaration by Jesus caused many to run away from Him, for who would voluntarily choose such suffering?

But we who put our faith in the Lord Jesus Christ receive Him as our Savior and Lord. We humbly and gratefully receive the priceless treasure of salvation and the depths of His great love that He brings. We also receive by faith the sure promise and life-changing perspective that we are going to live with Him forever. Our Lord then anoints and enables us to embrace and enjoy the privilege of *Walking with Him* throughout our life journey, even in our seasons of trial. Our Lord is personally and intimately with us in the trials. Lately I have gained deeper appreciation for this lesson.

I have cancer. I hate that word and I hate what it does to people. Over the years I have pastored, prayed, cared, cried, and walked with individuals and families who were dealing with cancer and other serious health conditions. Now it is my turn. I have multiple myeloma, which is bone marrow and blood cancer, specifically cancer of blood plasma cells.

In August 2017 as my Dad was dying, I learned that he had multiple myeloma. The next month I learned that I had the precursor to this disease, which is called Monoclonal Gammopathy of Undetermined Significance (MGUS). By April 2018 my MGUS had progressed to early stage multiple myeloma (smoldering myeloma). And two weeks ago, on October 1, 2018, my doctor informed me that I now have active multiple myeloma and need chemotherapy. Treatments are scheduled to begin on Monday.

One of the sweet blessings of being part of a family is that when struggles come to us, we experience them together. Helen and I were blessed this past week to have all three of our adult children visit us – Carl, Amy, and Jonathan. We talked, prayed, and shared life-on-life and heart-to-heart.

Church family offers this same gift. How I thank God for the love and support of so many Christian family and friends, including Church of The Apostles in Coventry, Rhode Island, where I currently serve. Helen and I are grateful for the love, prayers, and expressions of support from our family. We thank you. The sweet blessing of *Walking with God* continues.

FOR REFLECTION

What does *Walking with God* mean? In what ways have you experienced this blessing? What blessings have you known by walking with God through times of trial? How does this lesson apply to your recent or current circumstances? What must happen within you for you to continually receive and notice strength from walking with God? Ask God to help you in this, and He surely will.

2

ON THE SWEET GIFT OF FAMILY

October 15, 2018

Last weekend our three children were all with us – Carl, Amy, and Jonathan, respectively from Minnesota, Alaska, and Texas. The last time just the five of us had been under one roof was eighteen years ago. They came to be with Helen and me and each other. That sweet time was wonderful. We kayaked together, enjoyed great meals together, worshipped God together, watched playoff baseball together, and just loved on each other.

Sharing heart to heart and life on life brought us much joy. As Helen and I travel the path that is before us, which includes dealing with this cancer, we are blessed to know that our family is with us on this path, praying, encouraging, listening, and loving. How we treasure the love and support of our children, siblings, and extended family. What a sweet gift of God!

As I enjoyed and reflected on this, I heard our heavenly Father whisper in my heart, "This blessing is for you a glimpse of the joy that my children bring to me when they gather with each other to love and worship me and to love each other, as we share life together as family. For my children, this is a foretaste of heaven."

I have experienced that foretaste of heaven in the local congregation I serve, Church of The Apostles in Coventry, Rhode Island. Being God's children, we are forever family. Yesterday I shared my current struggle with them, so they can bear it with Helen and me. I told them that I am about to begin chemotherapy, and I asked for their prayers. I have received many words, cards, and reminders of their love with assurances that they are praying for us and that we are not in this alone. I have been buoyed, supported, and held up by the love of family.

God wants all of His children to experience this. For friends and family who hold us up – thank you! For all who are prayerfully holding up other friends and loved ones who struggle – keep it up! God is glorified. His strength and love are flowing through you!

FOR REFLECTION

Do you know deep in your heart that through faith in the Lord Jesus Christ you are God's own child now and forever? Have you brought joy to your heavenly Father and blessing to yourself and to Christian brothers and sisters by gathering with His family for worship, fellowship, and sharing life? If your answer is yes, what blessings have these times brought you? Give God the praise. If your answer is no, will you prayerfully determine to make this a priority going forward? Ask God to help you in this, and He surely will.

Steve and Helen, with Carl, Amy, and Jonathan

Kayaking together as a family

3

ON DEALING WITH DISAPPOINTMENTS

October 16, 2018

I have faced more than a few disappointments in my life, and I expect you have too. Today was another one for me. I went to the hospital to receive my first chemotherapy treatment to begin attacking this cancer. I had been forewarned of various potential side effects of the drugs. These realities had been outlined multiple times by physicians and nurses and in printed literature that was given to me.

I realize that taking chemotherapy drugs can prove unpleasant for a while, but this offers the best hope of destroying the cancer cells that have invaded my bone marrow and blood. Then healthy life-giving blood cells can grow again. For this reason I wanted to begin treatments today. But it did not happen.

Because I have been coughing for a few days, I was given a viral antigen detection test at the hospital, which came back positive for a particular virus. So today's chemotherapy was canceled, and I was sent home for a week with explicit orders to rest. Because multiple myeloma has contributed to my immune deficiencies, my ability to fight off viruses and infections is already reduced. And because one side effect of the chemotherapy drugs is to further reduce my immune system, today my oncologist said it is unsafe for me to receive it until I am free of infection. Though this news was disappointing, and I am tempted with discouragement, I intend to choose a better way.

What will I not do? I will not be afraid, for I know He holds me close. I will not complain, because I know it is futile. I will focus on what I know – I know that God loves me, and I know that He does all things well.

What else will I do? I will pray, for I know He answers prayer. I will trust, because I know God is faithful and trustworthy. I will rest, because I know that in Him there is peace. I will hope, for I know that He is faithful to every promise He has made. And I will wait while He works within me, inviting and allowing my Lord to hold me close, for I know I can trust Him to care for me and for all whom I love.

On my drive home from the hospital, the Lord reminded me of these precious words from Isaiah 41:10, which I take to heart as medicine for my soul: *Fear not, for I am with you. Be not dismayed, for I am your God. I will strengthen you. I will help you. I will uphold you with my righteous right hand.* Holding on to the promises of God in the face of life's disappointments allows us to receive from the Lord all that we need.

FOR REFLECTION

When faced with discouragement, what choices are you prone to take? What major disappointments have you faced? What does Isaiah 41:10 say about how you can overcome disappointment in the face of trying circumstances? Ask God to help you in this, and He surely will.

4

ON RESTING WELL

October 19, 2018

On Monday of this week, my oncologist directed me to "go home and rest for a week." These might seem like simple directions that anyone could follow, but it has not been easy for me. The Holy Spirit has been reminding me of some important lessons on resting well, which I humbly share with you here, for this may also speak to you.

While resting physically this week, much of the time in bed because I am sick, I thought about resting. Because I am unable to do work that needs to be done, I thought about that too. Because I have been unable to start chemotherapy to kill cancer cells, I also thought about that. And because I am now unable to care for my congregation and family the way I long to, I thought about that too.

God has revealed to me that I have not been resting well, for there is much more to His rest than physical inactivity. The rest that our Lord desires for us includes trusting Him to hold us safely and completely no matter how we feel, similar to the way a tired child nestles comfortably and peacefully in Mommy or Daddy's arms. Trusting God and resting in Him means letting go of the burdens we have been carrying and letting God carry those burdens and carry us too. This brings us rest.

Again I have been hearing my Lord's invitation. He is saying to all who will hear and respond in faith, *Come to me, all who labor and are heavy laden, and I will give you rest* (Matthew 11:28). The rest that Christ offers will not be acquired by spinning our minds in incessant worry. He promises to grant us rest when we say yes to His invitation, thus coming to Him in faith. In this matter, I know I remain a work in progress. I am being reminded that His rest is a gift to me and to all who will stop striving and trust Him enough to settle comfortably into His strong and loving arms.

I have been reliving a memorable time just a few weeks ago when I was a very sick hospital patient, suffering from a blood infection. At one point, as I lay striving hard against discomfort and worry, the Holy Spirit met me up close and personal, giving me a vivid awareness that many were praying for me right then, and that He was hearing and answering their prayers. In those precious moments. I felt like I was being held tenderly in the arms of God, so I stopped striving, and in peace I rested. May the Lord who loves us, teaches us, and holds us close, help us to continually rest well in Him.

FOR REFLECTION

What struggles have you experienced with resting? What does the Lord require from you so you can continually experience His rest? How does this lesson apply to your recent or current circumstances? Ask God to help you in this, and He surely will.

5

ON HAVING NO FEAR BECAUSE OUR GOD IS WITH US

October 22, 2018

I have been meditating on God's assurance to His children that we must not fear, for He is here with us now, holding us perfectly safe and secure. I mentioned before the sweet promise of God in Isaiah 41:10. This is an excellent verse for God's children to memorize, that we might draw strength from it whenever needed. This is a great treasure to hold on to, for it is God's sure promise to all of His dear children. *Fear not, for I am with you; be not dismayed, for I am your God; I will strengthen you, I will help you, I will uphold you with my righteous right hand.*

This promise has led me to recall precious memories of when our children were young and I took them into the water to teach them to swim. I knew they needed to learn so they would be safe if they were ever in water over their heads. I still recall how sweet it was to feel them clutching to me. Though they were at first afraid of the water, I wanted them to know that they could trust me in it.

When the water was deep, they clutched me tighter and pleaded with me to not let go. I reassured them that they were safe in my arms, and with my help they could swim. I reminded them that I was not going to leave them, nor would I let them go under. I then let them swim toward me for a couple feet, and then for a few feet more. I caught them every time. When they became tired, I held them, and when they were rested, they swam a little more. My children learned to swim in deep water.

Lately our Father in heaven has been teaching me this same lesson. At times this week, I felt like I was swimming in deep water. I could not touch the bottom. I was tired, and at times I was tempted to be afraid. But when I stopped striving enough to listen, I heard my Father say, "I am right here. I will not let you go under. Swim toward me. Trust me. I will hold you while you rest."

I went to my oncology appointment today, which was scheduled for my chemotherapy treatments. Last week when I reported for this purpose, I was directed to go home and rest for a week. Today I was again told to go home and rest for yet another week before chemotherapy can begin. The reason for the extended delay is that I have not yet fully recovered from the upper respiratory and sinus infections I have been fighting. Because the chemotherapy drugs will further decrease my ability to fight illness, I must be free of infection before I begin.

Today when I heard of the extended delay, like a tired child swimming in deep water, I felt tired and afraid. But later in the day, I took much needed time to pray and listen. And do you know what I heard? I heard my Father saying again to me, "Don't be afraid. I am here with you. Swim toward me. Trust me. I will hold you while you rest."

Praise God that even in the deep waters, we are entirely safe in His arms. I testify that God always keeps His promises. He has always kept His promises to me, even today.

FOR REFLECTION

For a child in deep waters, how can being held affect his or her fear, and what is needed for the child to let go of that fear? When and how has the Lord taught you to release your fears and hold on to Him? What does the Lord desire of you now so you can experience strength from this truth? How does this lesson apply to your recent or current circumstances? Ask God to help you in this, and He surely will.

6

ON GOD REMAINING FAITHFUL

October 28, 2018

Does God remain faithful even when life is hard for us? Oh yes, He certainly does! Is He faithful even when we hurt? Yes, He surely is! Is God faithful even when storms come and our circumstances are not what we would choose? Yes, He absolutely is!

In his second letter to Timothy, writing from the suffering of his prison cell, Paul quoted a saying that was familiar among Christians in the early days of the church. He reminded Timothy that these words are trustworthy, for they describe the faithfulness of God: *The saying is trustworthy, for: If we have died with Him we will also live with Him; if we endure, we will also reign with Him; if we deny Him, He also will deny us; if we are faithless, He remains faithful, for He cannot deny Himself* (2 Timothy 2:11-13). I am forever glad that God *is* faithful and true. How about you?

These words reveal what many early Christians were facing. Living for Jesus Christ, they all faced death, and some died for His sake. To these disciples, the Lord's encouraging reminder was, *If we have died with Him, we will also live with Him*. What a glorious promise in the face of hardships, that even if our current struggle should end in death, we will forever be with the Lord, living eternally with Him.

The apostle Paul wrote this letter from prison to fellow Christians who were also facing hardship. Suffering himself, and anticipating his own imminent promotion to glory, Paul knew that in Jesus Christ we are called and enabled to endure, and that *if we endure, we will also reign with Him.* What a glorious promise, that in the end we will be part of our Lord's eternal kingdom. This confident expectation encourages us to look beyond our current struggles and to look forward in faith to what will be.

Paul understood, perhaps because he had experienced it himself, that in our struggles we may be tempted to think that God has forsaken us or that His promises are not true. Such perspectives can be temptations to faithlessness, denying the character and truthfulness of God. In times of struggle and pain, when my own faith has been weak, I have sometimes succumbed to faithlessness. Have you been there too? Even then we are reminded that *if we are faithless, He remains faithful, for He cannot deny Himself.* How wonderful to know that our God remains faithful to us, no matter what the level of our faithfulness.

This week my Lord reminded me of this truth, for He has always been, is now, and will forever be faithful in all things, in my life and in yours. As I reflect on the blessings I have known while walking with God these many years, I testify that I have experienced His faithfulness in every season, even in the hard times, even when I was not wholly faithful to Him. God has always been faithful to me and directed my steps daily, in season after season, with abundant provision for His service.

A few weeks before my grandfather was promoted to glory, he testified to me of the joy he had known in loving and serving the Lord. I have known the same joy. Through all the years of my life, God has blessed me. So I know that in this season of my life as I am now fighting cancer, and in every season to come, the Lord will remain faithful, for He cannot deny Himself. I hold on to this promise and trust God for my life and for all whom I love. I pray that you too may know the joy of trusting Him.

This week I have stood on the promise of God's faithfulness. For thirty-eight years I have served my Lord as a shepherd of His flock, wherever He has called me to serve. Prior to that, while in college and seminary, I also discipled others. This week, after four decades of ministry leadership in the kingdom of God, I resigned from my pastoral office; I submitted my resignation to the leadership team of Church of The Apostles.

My focus must now be fighting this cancer, which requires that I avoid crowds where I could be exposed to sickness. This morning I spoke to my congregation via live video feed and informed them of my resignation, effective immediately. I reminded them of the sure promise of God's faithfulness. Now I ask for your prayers – for me and for Helen and for Church of The Apostles. For all who are praying for us, from the depths of my heart, I thank you.

Does stepping away from pastoral ministry grieve me? Yes it does! Am I at peace about it? Yes I am, for I know this is the right decision. Can we simultaneously hurt and be at peace? Yes we can, for while we live in this broken world where there is cancer, frailty, illness, uncertainty, sorrow, and pain of various kinds, we who walk by faith and know the Lord Jesus Christ are graced to endure with His strength and eternal perspective. We know His promises and we believe in heaven. Until He calls us home to glory, we can choose in faith to trust the One who is forever faithful. I will trust the Lord.

FOR REFLECTION

How have you known God's faithfulness when life was hard? When have you experienced hurt and peace at the same time? What does God desire of you so you may experience His peace when life is hard? How does this apply to your current circumstances? Ask God to help you in this, and He surely will.

7

ON KNOWING REINFORCEMENTS ARE ON THE WAY

October 29, 2018

I praise God, for today I was judged well enough to begin chemotherapy. I am happy about this, because now at last the cancer cells in my body are facing attack. In addition to the chemo drugs I began taking today, two orally and one by injection, I also received intravenous immunoglobulin (IVIG) therapy, which is going to be administered every four weeks. IVIG introduces into my body healthy immunoglobulins gleaned from plasma donors, much like an army of reinforcements hired for my defense to strengthen my immune system for the ongoing battle against illness.

    God assures me that in the same way He is answering the prayers of His people for me. Far stronger than the chemotherapy drugs or IVIG treatment I received today, God reminds me that in answer to the prayers of His people, He is providing powerful spiritual reinforcements. He assures me that I am never alone, nor are any of us.

    Again, I want to express my deepest thanks for every kind expression of love sent my way and for every prayer offered for Helen and me. In these ways God has used you to bring spiritual reinforcements to us. For this I am forever grateful.

FOR REFLECTION

When have you felt weak or outnumbered but experienced God bringing spiritual reinforcements to you? How appreciative have you been for the prayers of others for you? How motivated have you been to faithfully pray for others who are struggling? What changes do you need to experience these truths? How does this lesson apply to your recent or current circumstances? Ask God to help you in this, and He surely will.

8
ON BEING OKAY WHEN LIFE IS HARD

November 3, 2018

After a couple difficult days and symptoms of yet another infection, I am now back in the hospital. Though this is admittedly hard for me, as life can be for all of us at times, ultimately I am okay. I am sensing His presence and enjoying His peace.

I am making a faith decision to not focus on the wind and waves but to fix my eyes on the Lord who is my sure foundation and secure anchor. He is always near and ever faithful, including here and now.

I hope and expect that this will be a short hospital stay. I also know that on this side of eternity more hardships will come to me and also to you. Such realizations point me heavenward.

Though my illness is admittedly hard, I want you to know that by God's grace I am okay. I am very grateful and immensely blessed by so many expressions of love and concern for Helen and me. Thank you especially for your prayers. I give thanks to God for His great faithfulness and for His continual presence.

FOR REFLECTION

How is it possible to look past our storms and struggles and to feel and be okay? What does the Lord require of you so you might experience this? How does this lesson apply to your recent or current circumstances? Ask God to help you in this, and He surely will.

9

ON THE JOY OF BEING HOME

November 6, 2018

I was released from the hospital last evening. A few days of intravenous antibiotics, bed rest, and medical attention, along with faith-filled prayers offered on my behalf, brought me an abundant measure of His healing touch. To all who have prayed for me, I thank you. I am so much better than when I entered the hospital and very glad to be home.

While in the hospital, I kept reminding myself that this was only an interim stop. I did not want to be there, and I did not feel well, but I knew that my location and condition were temporary; I would soon be going home. This perspective helped me a lot.

This outlook also helps me, and all of God's children, when we face the struggles of this life. We are always looking forward to the beautiful home Jesus is preparing for us in heaven. By faith we know that the hard situations we must confront along the way in this broken world and in our mortal bodies are all temporary. We look ahead with longing for our certain hope and the heavenly home we will see in the presence of the Lord God Almighty. Jesus Christ has made this promise to us, and at the cost of His life on the cross, He has provided the way for us to enter in.

The apostle Paul spoke eloquently of this sweet promise in 2 Corinthians 5:1-2. He wrote, *For we know that if the tent that is our earthly home is destroyed, we have a building from God, a house not made with hands, eternal in the heavens. For in this tent we groan, longing to put on our heavenly dwelling.*

In other words, we must not be too attached to these mortal bodies, for they are all like temporary tents. I have at various times slept in temporary tents, including during my years of service with infantry Marines. Tents are okay for a little while, but that is all. When we are living in tents, we do not want to stay there indefinitely, for we much prefer our permanent home. And when at last we arrive home, we are glad.

All who are in Jesus Christ through faith can have this heavenly longing, for when at last we lay aside these temporary bodies, we will be home where we want to be and where we belong. I want you to know that I am looking forward with longing to when I will receive the fulfillment of this promise.

But today it is great to be in the home I share with Helen. She has sweetly cared for me and nurtured me, as she reflects her Christ-like nature. After my discharge today, I went with her to an appointment, and we then went together to vote. Back at home I got a few things done, took prescribed medicines, and then rested. I enjoyed this day at home with Helen; I am reminded again that by God's grace the best is yet to come.

FOR REFLECTION

When have you experienced the joy of going home? How do you relate to having a joyful expectation of returning to the glorious home the Lord Jesus is preparing for you in heaven? What would enable you to experience such joyful expectation? How does this lesson apply to your circumstances? Ask God to help you in this, and He surely will.

10

ON BELIEVING GOD IS WITH ME NOW

November 11, 2018

Before He ascended to the glory of heaven, Jesus's final words to His disciples included these: *And behold, I am with you always, to the end of the age* (Matthew 28:20). I love that promise, and I firmly believe it. I have long experienced its truth and I know with certainty that my Lord's Word is always true. I give testimony again, in this season of my life, of the Lord's great faithfulness in keeping His powerful and hopeful promise.

Throughout my life I have been blessed with opportunities to walk with God and serve Him. I have done so in every state in the United States, and thus far, on every continent but Antarctica. I have encountered many difficulties, dangers, sorrows, and challenges that required me to lean upon my Lord in faith for His protection, wisdom, and peace.

I testify to you today that in every situation I have encountered my Lord has been with me, ever faithful to His promise. He has always given me everything I needed for each situation, and He has always shown me that His grace is more than enough for me. Whenever we walk in faith and realize our Lord is with us, then we can know His peace.

Our Lord brought this comforting truth to me again today, as I recognized again how much I need and treasure His presence. Today is Sunday morning; this day marks five weeks since I was last able to join my church family for worship and fellowship. I have been unable to attend because of illness and my compromised immune system.

Two weeks ago I resigned my pastoral position in the church, and last Sunday I was an inpatient in the hospital. Today Helen joins our church family for worship, fellowship, and learning, for which I am so glad, as I know many will bless her, and she will bless others too. I wish I could have joined her, and I look forward to when I may do so again.

But today I am home alone; though not really. My Lord reminds me that He is with me always. This is true. I encourage you to believe it too. Whatever you may be experiencing, you really are not alone. Our Lord is always with you. He is with you now, and He is with me. In this moment, and in every moment, our God is with us. Let us all recognize and believe it. How sweet is His presence.

FOR REFLECTION

When, in the face of personal struggles, have you been blessed by believing God's promise to be with you? How can you respond so you may continue to experience strength from this truth? How does this lesson speak to your situation? Ask God to help you in this, and He surely will.

11

ON THANKFULNESS EVEN WHEN LIFE IS DIFFICULT

November 18, 2018

M. Scott Peck began his best-selling book *The Road Less Traveled* with these words: "Life is difficult." Has your life experience confirmed this? Mine has. Multiple myeloma, infections, and other symptoms I have been experiencing due to this cancer with the likelihood of more struggles in the future and the effect of all of this on my life and ministry have pointed out to me again that life can be difficult.

The Bible explains that the ultimate reason for our difficulties is humanity's rebellion against God. We live in a broken world in which the consequence of sin includes discord, disease, disasters, depravity, depression, disappointments, and often deep pain. This does not mean that our difficulties should be simplistically regarded as punishment for our specific sins or the sins of others. The Lord Jesus specifically taught that this is not the case when He said. *It was not that this man sinned, or his parents, but that the works of God might be displayed in him* (John 9:3).

The context of Jesus's words indicates that He was about to show His love and power by healing a man who had been born blind. We know that our Lord is able to do this even now, for He is forever a miracle-working, prayer-answering God. I have been blessed to see God work miracles in our day: miracles of physical healing, emotional healing, material provision, restoration of broken relationships, clear direction, and (greatest of all) spiritual healing by the gift of salvation and everlasting life through repentance and faith in the Lord Jesus Christ.

On the day when Jesus healed that man who had been born blind, the man who could then see was understandably overflowing with gratitude, praise, and faith in the Lord. His testimony was powerful, profound, and contagious because of what Jesus Christ did for him in the difficulty of his blindness. This man boldly declared to all who could hear, *One thing I do know, that though I was blind, now I see* (John 9:25). We too can cry, "Hallelujah!" to the One who showed such love and mercy to one in such difficulty. Our Lord is the same today.

Let me ask you a question. Is it easier for you to be thankful when your prayers have been answered as you wanted and the healing that you desired has come or when you are still proverbially sitting on the side of the road begging? God's Word teaches that for His people it should make no difference. You and I have cause for thankfulness to God – whatever our circumstances may be. Though we might presume that our thankfulness should be greater when circumstances are to our liking, this is not so.

Our Lord calls us to treasure most what matters most, and nothing matters more than love and relationship with Him. Nothing matters more! Motivated by His infinite love and mercy, the sinless Son of God willingly endured extreme difficulty and took upon Himself the righteous judgment that our sins deserved. He willingly bore the sins of everyone in this world when He died on that cruel cross of suffering. This demonstrates how much He treasures us, and how much He longs for us to be in right relationship with Him now and forever. How much then are we valuing our relationship with Him?

The difficult situation I am facing now reminds me again to treasure Him above all else. Though my circumstances are not what I want them to be now, and though this cancer and the consequences of it are difficult, my reasons for gratitude are greater. Why? Because I know the Lord. I know that He loves me and that by His grace He has forgiven me. I know that He is with me now, and that I will be with Him forever.

In my life I have received more blessings than I can count, including the sweet blessing of my dear wife Helen and the blessings of faith, family, freedom, and all of God's provisions. I also know that there is *the crown of righteousness* in store for me (2 Timothy 4:8). I have the sure hope of everlasting life in the presence of my God with the saints of all the ages. These blessings put my difficulty in perspective.

This week as we are celebrating Thanksgiving in the United States of America, we should count our many blessings, for haven't we all been blessed in many ways? Let us thank Him in our difficulties too, for these point us to our need for the One who truly is our greatest treasure? The apostle Paul said it this way in 1 Thessalonians 5:18, *Give thanks in all circumstances; for this is the will of God in Christ Jesus for you.*

FOR REFLECTION

When has the Lord taught you thankfulness in the midst of difficulty, and how did it bless you or others? How does this lesson apply in you? How can you continue to be thankful, even when your life is difficult? Ask God to help you in this, and He surely will.

12

ON GRATITUDE FOR CHEMOTHERAPY

November 19, 2018

This morning when I returned to my oncologist, I prayed that I'd be well enough to resume chemotherapy. By God's grace, treatment was resumed! When I received this good news today, I sent a text message from the hospital to Helen and to my siblings informing them of my excitement. Helen's happy reply was, "Who thought one could get so excited about chemo?" Great question! The answer today is *me*.

Things that we might not typically regard as good news become for us great news and a cause for gratitude when we realize that they are an answer to prayer and precisely what we need now. I thank my God for this answer to prayer today and for countless times throughout my life when He has provided what I needed when I needed it, whether I realized it at the time or not. May God be forever praised.

Please pray with me now that I can avoid further infections and continue receiving the chemotherapy treatments I need. I am determined to trust Him every day, for I know in every situation my Lord knows what I need. He knows what you need too.

With a grateful heart, I continue to pray and depend on my Lord, and I ask you to pray with me that God will be glorified through all of this. Thank you so much.

FOR REFLECTION

When have you experienced true gratitude for something that seemed so hard on face value? What does God desire within you for you to experience such thankfulness? How does this lesson apply to your circumstances? Ask God to help you in this, and He surely will.

13

ON CONTINUING TO REST WELL

November 25, 2018

This week more than one friend urged me to rest well. Their words led me to pray and ponder again on what this means. God's intention for humanity includes that we rest. The creation story reveals that God rested on the seventh day (Genesis 2:1-3). Is this because God was tired? Surely not, for God is supreme and eternal, infinite in power and strength. Why then did God rest, except that He might ponder and enjoy all He had done?

So when God made us in His own image, He created within us a need for rest. Our need for rest is not because of sin or the fall described in Genesis 3. Rather, rest is part of God's intentional design in making us in His own image. Later God commanded observance of the Sabbath, so that among other reasons, we would regularly remember and rest (Exodus 20:8-11). We are created and called by God to rest well. So why do we find it so difficult?

Physically I need to rest now, for my illness demands it. But as I look back over the years of my life, I realize that I have often struggled with rest. Some of my recent struggles with rest are because of the need to let go of my work responsibilities, which is where I often found my purpose.

We who are in Jesus Christ are called to strive for excellence in all we do, but the Lord never said that work is where we are to find our ultimate meaning. Rather, our purpose is to be found in relationship with God through Jesus Christ. This requires that we rest well and enjoy times of inactivity and being still. My own struggle through the years included a faulty perspective about the profit of busyness; on my days off I often worked, and on vacations I brought work with me. Sometimes I failed to see that resting well is to be an act of worship and renewal for God's people.

My Lord reminds me that my current illness affords me another opportunity to rest well, and in this I find blessing. One of my favorite Scriptures on this theme is the invitation of Jesus recorded in Matthew 11:28-30. Jesus says, *Come to me, all who labor and are heavy laden, and I will give you rest. Take my yoke upon you, and learn from me, for I am gentle and lowly in heart, and you will find rest for your souls. For my yoke is easy, and my burden is light.* This is both an invitation and a promise. The invitation is for us to come now and find rest in personal relationship with Jesus Christ. And the promise is that we will find rest for our souls when we do this.

I testify that this promise is wholly true. These past months I have had to rest physically, for my body demands it. But I have had to rest spiritually far more as I lean on the Lord and enjoy Him, for my soul demands it. Though we may be prone to busyness and worry, God knows we need His rest and peace, which requires our trust. This experience and enjoyment of being in the safety of His arms is where we know His love and feel His heartbeat; this is where He invites us to come. Continuing to rest in Christ is like being a child comfortably asleep in Mommy or Daddy's arms. We are unphased and untroubled by all that is going on around us, because we are where we want to be – held in His loving arms. This is where I am resting. It is where I want to be.

Though I still struggle at times with frustration because of what I can no longer do, I understand that who I am in Christ transcends what I am able to do for Him. I will therefore be still, rest in His arms, and aim to do so continually.

Loving parents understand this. We appreciate what our children do for us, but this is not why we love them. A loving parent does not focus on what a child has given them or done for them. Nor does a loving husband or wife regard our spouse in this way. True love is a commitment that gives. It is neither conditional nor transactional (I will love you if you do some task for me). Real love is transformational and covenantal (I love you because I love you, and I always will). In such love we find rest.

When little children are sick, they want to be held. My mom told me that when I was a little boy and was sick, I wanted to be held. When I cried, if no one else could quiet me down, my grandfather could. When he took me into his arms, I would quiet down and fall asleep. Now I find such rest in my heavenly Father's arms. I do not struggle there. I find peace, trust, love, hope, and solace. I find sweet dreams for today and bright hope for tomorrow in His arms.

As friends have said to me, I also say to you, "Rest well, my friend. Rest well."

FOR REFLECTION

When and why have you struggled with finding rest? When and how did the Lord teach you to rest in His arms? How does this lesson apply to you? What does God desire within you that you may receive strength from these truths? Ask God to help you in this, and He surely will.

14

ON FEELING GOOD TODAY

November 28, 2018

A question I am often asked is, how are you feeling? Though this may be an easy question to ask, it is not always easy for me to answer, as there are many ways I could respond. When I consider how I am feeling physically at that moment, my answer varies day by day and sometimes hour by hour. When I am fighting an infection or feeling sick, or when I am feeling fatigued or experiencing the physical effects of chemotherapy, my answer might be, not so good.

But if I consider how it is with my soul, I know I am being sustained and uplifted by many in prayer (Thank You!). I am also experiencing my Lord's presence every day. So regardless of how I may feel physically, my answer is, it is well with my soul. Despite my physical struggles, because my Lord is ever faithful and always with me, I feel good.

This speaks to our choice of perspective, for we do have a choice. At various times we can all struggle with loss, grief, disappointment, and pain, for we live in a broken world where such things are common to humanity. None of us are exempt. But the most amazing and wonderful news is that God so loved this world, which includes every one of us, that He lovingly and sacrificially gave His only begotten Son to die for us.

The Lord Jesus was and is the perfect loving sacrifice for us, so that all who believe in Him will not perish but will have the promised and priceless gift of everlasting life as declared in John 3:16. For all who believe in the Lord Jesus and who thus respond to Him with love, faith, repentance, and obedience enjoy a life perspective that is forever changed, even in the midst of brokenness and suffering.

When we hurt, the devil may tempt us with discouragement, faithlessness, and despair; we are then prone to yield to such temptation if we focus on our pain. But we can make a superior choice. By God's great grace, we can choose to hold on tightly to our faith in the Lord Jesus Christ. The apostle Peter wrote to a suffering church. In 1 Peter 5:7, he urged hurting Christians to cast all of their anxieties and cares upon the Lord, because He cared for them. In the same way, He cares for us.

Peter also directed Christians to resist the devil's attempts to devour us by standing firm in our faith in the Lord Jesus, knowing that the sufferings we endure are not unique to us but are common to brothers and sisters throughout the world (1 Peter 5:8-9). Let us reflect on this truth, and let it remind us that we are in very good company, for our God is faithful in every generation and in every culture, to all of His beloved children throughout the whole world.

Peter then stated a glorious promise that we are called to believe and hold on to through all that we may now endure. *And after you have suffered a little while, the God of all grace, who has called you to His eternal glory in Christ, will Himself restore, confirm, strengthen, and establish you. To Him be the dominion forever and ever. Amen* (1 Peter 5:10-11).

May this promise permeate our perspective in the face of all temporary struggles.

Back to the question of how I am feeling. As I write this, my answer is, I generally feel good today. Physically I have felt better this week because I have now avoided infection for three weeks. I have also completed my first chemotherapy cycle, so this week I am off two of the chemo drugs to allow my body to regroup. I also received my monthly intravenous immunoglobulin (IVIG) treatment, courtesy of plasma donors, to strengthen my ability to fight infections. So today I feel pretty good physically, and in that I am rejoicing.

But I fully expect that as I proceed, there are going to be more ups and downs in how I feel, which is true for us all. I am determined, though, to do what Peter encouraged us to do. I will hold on in faith to the promises of God in Christ, which transcend my struggles. And no matter how I may feel, I will cast my cares upon the Lord, as I receive and enjoy His eternal perspective. For these reasons, by God's grace I am feeling good today. I am praying the same for you.

FOR REFLECTION

How are you feeling? When in the face of personal and physical struggles, have you looked past the way that you felt and experienced what it means to be well with your soul? How may you experience being well in your soul, no matter your situation? How does this lesson apply to your circumstances? Ask God to help you in this, and He surely will.

15

ON REMINDERS THAT THIS IS TEMPORARY

December 1, 2018

When in my last update I reported that I was feeling good physically, I knew that assessment would not endure. Since then I have felt well enough at times to enjoy some degree of normalcy, but at other times I have dealt with uncomfortable symptoms and was forced to inactivity. This has allowed me to reflect on the temporary nature of many things but the enduring effect of the Christian faith upon such awareness.

Perhaps we have all experienced various chapters in our lives in which things were the way we wanted them, and we were largely satisfied. I look back on several times in my life in which I have known such blessing, and I would have gladly remained there longer. But we can never hit the pause button in this life.

Whatever season of life we are in right now, we know that this is temporary, as are the changing seasons in New England where I live. Whenever the current season is hard, we are urged and enabled to lean upon the Lord and hold on a while longer, for we trust that a better season is coming.

We continually face reminders of the temporary nature of things.

Just look in the mirror and compare what you see to what you used to see. Remember your youthful energy, your young children, or people you loved who are no longer with us. Or recall events that suddenly happened and rocked your world.

Yesterday our daughter Amy, her husband, Joey, and our grandsons Levi and Luca were affected by a strong earthquake that struck their home in Alaska. Their house shook violently, and some things fell and broke. They were afraid as it happened, but by God's grace none of them were injured. They lost some things that could not endure but retained what matters most, which gave them cause for reflection and praise.

Faith in Jesus Christ brings perspective and hope. As for the afflictions we now endure, the apostle Paul urged Christians to remember that all of our struggles are temporary. We are to hold tightly in faith to what long endures: *For this light momentary affliction is preparing for us an eternal weight of glory beyond all comparison, as we look not to the things that are seen but to the things that are unseen. For the things that are seen are transient, but the things that are unseen are eternal* (2 Corinthians 4:17-18).

This perspective helps me these days. I know that however long I must deal with multiple myeloma, however I may feel day by day, or however easy or difficult the path becomes, these struggles will only be for a season. How very blessed we are to know the One who endures forever.

FOR REFLECTION

When and how in the face of your personal struggles have you come to understand and experience the sentiments expressed in 2 Corinthians 4:17-18? What does God desire within you so you may live these truths? How does this apply to your circumstances? Ask God to help you in this, and He surely will.

16

ON DIVINE APPOINTMENTS CONTINUING

December 4, 2018

My lifestyle has changed dramatically because of my illness. One difficult adjustment is that I am no longer in daily physical contact with many others. But, I can still see and treasure divine appointments that my Lord has prepared for me. Ephesians 2:10 makes this promise for all followers of Jesus. After the apostle Paul reminds us that we have been saved by grace and through faith, not as a result of our works lest we would boast, he adds, *For we are His workmanship, created in Christ Jesus for good works, which God prepared beforehand, that we should walk in them.*

After walking with God for so many years, I can assure you that I have seen this promise come to fruition again and again. To know that God continues to prepare divine appointments for me to walk in is reassuring to me in my current season of life. I know He will do this for me and for you as long as we live. Our responsibility is to recognize and respond to each one.

This week I experienced this truth again. For the first time in eight weeks, I attended Sunday worship service with my church family, Church of The Apostles. It was wonderful for me to be there. At Helen's insistence and my doctor's recommendation, I wore gloves and a mask, as low white blood count and low neutrophils put me at risk of infection. After a couple hours, I was physically wiped out, for my stamina is lacking. But despite the hassles of glove and mask and fatigue, it was good to be in the Lord's house again and in the company of dear brothers and sisters in Christ.

In addition to enjoying the blessings of corporate worship, I was blessed Sunday by several divine-appointment encounters in which I knew that God was ministering among us. I prayerfully encourage and hope that each of you may seek and experience this same joy and privilege by making it a priority of your life to enter into fellowship with God's eternal family in the Lord's church as commanded in Hebrews 10:25. This is our Lord's loving instruction to all, and it is for us a taste of heaven. In our obedience God prepares divine appointments, and for each one He prepares us to receive a blessing and to be a blessing for Him.

We of course have a personal part in each divine appointment our Lord prepares. Our part is to recognize and respond to them, being led by the Holy Spirit. For this reason my practice is to pray each day, "Lord, help me today to recognize and respond to every divine appointment you have prepared for me." When we see life this way, we see our Lord show up, often in surprising ways, and we become part of what He is doing.

Because my oncology appointments and chemotherapy treatments happen every Monday now, I bathe all of these encounters in prayer and ask God to help me give or receive whatever He intends in each divine appointment. Every time I go for treatments, I experience the fulfillment of this prayer. Yesterday was no exception, as I had heart-to-heart conversations with four other patients who were also there for treatment and blessed conversations with several nurses and staff.

I receive my chemotherapy treatments in a room with other patients who are also dealing with the challenges of cancer. Some are new in their diagnosis, and others have been ill for some time. Some are distraught about their future. Some have faith in the Lord and some do not. I have a better understanding of where they are now, and God stirs my heart to care. He reminds me of His love for each one, that He wants them to know they are not alone, and He invites them to look to Jesus in faith and lean on Him.

We share our stories with each other, but when people learn that I am a retired Navy chaplain and a member of the clergy who also has cancer, the door often opens wide to discuss spiritual matters. For this I give praise to God.

Would you please pray with me that the Lord continues to help me be faithful as His light in every divine appointment He has for me? I will pray the same for you.

FOR REFLECTION

Reading and reflecting on Ephesians 2:10, can you look back on divine appointments that you know the Lord prepared for you? How have you been doing lately in your current season of life at recognizing and responding to divine appointments? What changes can you make so you may respond to each divine appointment He prepares for you? Ask God to help you in this, and He surely will.

17

ON LEARNING CONTENTMENT

December 9, 2018

Some lessons in life are hard to learn. This week I have struggled again with contentment. I fought with various uncomfortable physical symptoms and feeling miserable. Even more difficult than physical discomfort is a sense of isolation, as my social contacts have been reduced.

A fitting word to describe the cumulative effect of all of this is *depressed*. I do not find it easy to admit this designation. Recently after an oncology social worker interviewed me, she recorded in my medical record that I am depressed. When I read this, my initial reaction was denial. "No, I am not!"

But upon honest reflection, I have come to understand and agree. "Yes, I am!" It *is* depressing to feel the way I feel some days and to miss my children and grandchildren, as I cannot safely travel to visit them. It *is* depressing to miss regular fellowship with my church family and the many blessings while serving my Lord as a shepherd of His church. And it *is* depressing to realize that these situations may not be resolved soon.

Because we can hide nothing from God, and He asks us to be humble, *casting all your anxieties on Him, because He cares for you* (1 Peter 5:7), I know that I need to stop any pretense and be real with Him about my struggles. By doing this, I will be able to receive the fullest blessings and learn the hardest lessons that God will teach me.

One lesson is the secret of contentment. Are you learning it too? The apostle Paul admitted his own hardships. While Paul faced untold personal difficulties, God equipped him to speak effectively to struggling Christians. From the isolation of his prison cell, Paul described what the Lord had taught him. He said, *I have learned in whatever situation I am to be content. I know how to be brought low, and I know how to abound. In any and every circumstance, I have learned the secret of facing plenty and hunger, abundance and need. I can do all things through Him* [Christ] *who strengthens me* (Philippians 4:11-13).

Paul learned this lesson the hard way, just as we must learn it; He learned how to be at peace in any and every situation. We learn this lesson when we lean upon the Lord in our difficult times and experience firsthand the reality that God completely satisfies in all situations. How is learning this lesson even possible? Paul knew what I have come to know: Jesus Christ reigns no matter the chaos in this broken world or in our personal circumstances.

Paul says that he *learned to be content*. This implies that it did not happen automatically or quickly; it took time. He did not learn from a sermon or seminar or book but in the challenges of real life. I am now blessed to be in such company as the apostle Paul, for I am learning this same lesson. We cannot learn true and lasting contentment by the strength of our own will. It is learned only *through Christ who strengthens me* (Philippians 4:13).

As I love the Lord most of all, I can enjoy the depths of His love. As I lean on Him in faith, I can trust Him today in this day and in this situation. In all of this, I am learning the secret of contentment. I appreciate and I thank you for your prayers, as I admit to my struggle in the school of contentment. How very blessed we are to have such a patient and loving teacher.

FOR REFLECTION

Reflecting on Philippians 4:11-13, how did Paul learn the secret of contentment? How and when have you learned such lessons in difficult circumstances? In what way can you grow so you may experience His contentment no matter what your circumstances are? How does this apply to your current situation? Ask God to help you in this, and He surely will.

18

ON BEING REAL

December 16, 2018

At times this week I have felt reasonably okay but at other times not well at all. Sometimes I have had a positive outlook and felt encouraged, and at other times I have felt down and discouraged. As I write this on Sunday morning, I am physically tired, and I grieve because I cannot join Helen and our church family for fellowship and corporate worship. These struggles are real to me.

All of our lives include victory and defeat, celebration and disappointment, joy and sorrow, hope and foreboding, accomplishment and regret, good weather and violent storms. It is foolish to pretend otherwise, but sometimes we do. We may as well be real.

When people ask, how are you, we sometimes give an automatic response like, fine, thank you, even when it is not true. Why do we do that? Are we simply saying what we think they want to hear? Or do we think they don't really care, so we don't want to tell them? Or are we in denial about our struggles, perhaps hindered by embarrassment or pride? At various times over the years, Helen has challenged me with, "Steve, don't say you are fine when you are not!" This is good counsel.

Lately I have heard the Lord speaking to me again about being real with myself, with others, and with Him. Being real with myself includes owning my struggles, for if I cannot admit to myself when I am struggling, how will I admit it to God or anyone else? If we have experienced broken trust, being real with another person involves taking a risk, being vulnerable, and speaking truth..

To be real with God, we must know and trust His character; we must believe He loves us and He is wholly trustworthy. It also means saying yes to His invitation to come. Hebrews 4:16 says, *Let us then with confidence draw near to the throne of grace, that we may receive mercy and find grace to help in time of need.* This presumes awareness and admission of our need and a faith decision to be real before God's throne. It is coming to God as we are with our joy and praise, and with our worries and struggles.

I have been hearing afresh the personal invitation of Jesus: *Come to me, all who labor and are heavy laden, and I will give you rest* (Matthew 11:28). Jesus knows when we are *heavy laden*, and when this happens, He wants us to come to Him. I feel privileged to exercise the great opportunity that is afforded to all of Jesus's disciples as expressed by the apostle in 1 Peter 5:7 to *cast all your anxieties on Him, because He cares for you.* My Lord has reminded me that *all* really does mean *all*. Being real with God means bringing to Him whatever is happening in our lives, including our joys and our struggles. It is coming to Him just as I am in this moment. Whenever we do this, God meets us – every single time.

In August 2016 our family gathered in Maine to celebrate our dad's ninetieth birthday. I often remember this sweet event when I look at the picture that was taken on that beautiful day – a picture of our smiling family of eight: Mom and Dad and their six children. Three of the eight persons in that picture have since been promoted to heaven. In December 2016 it was my brother Dr. David Gammon; in August 2017 it was my father Pastor Glendon Gammon; and in April 2018 it was my mother Marjorie Gammon.

Though I miss each of them very much and grieve their absence, at times with watery eyes, I am happy for them, for I know by God's grace that they are now in the glorious presence of God where there is everlasting joy and no more sorrow, crying, or pain. I have come to the Lord in joy or sorrow, for He is always the One I need.

While I now deal with my own mortality and various struggles, my

Lord reminds me that *He is Lord of all.* He is Lord of all my circumstances, all my victories, all my struggles, and all of me. Because this is true, He invites and blesses me to come to Him day after day and moment after moment and be entirely real with Him.

As I do this, He meets me every time. He reminds me that He knows me completely and cares for me deeply, and He can do infinitely more than I can even ask or imagine (Ephesians 3:20). I am blessed to be real with God, which is where I want to be. Such blessing is offered to all who will receive it. Are you receiving it?

FOR REFLECTION

When have you struggled with being real with God or with others? When have you learned what it means to be real with God, and how did you learn it? What is the connection between being real with God and being real with your spouse or with anyone else? What does God desire within you to help you experience being real with Him as a way of life? Ask God to help you in this, and He surely will.

19

ON BEING BLESSED TO BE A BLESSING

December 18, 2018

Whenever we have been greatly blessed in this life, we may be stirred by gratitude and love, and find ourselves longing to bless others. By God's grace this has been my story. I have been blessed along my earthly journey by loving parents, siblings, and extended family. I have been blessed by my amazing wife Helen, our children, their spouses, and by our grandchildren. I have been blessed by the family of God, the body of Christ, and by many dear friends through the years. And most powerfully, I have been blessed by the Lord.

As a young man, by God's gracious touch, I was filled with His love. I knew I wanted to love and serve the Lord with my life. I wanted to proclaim His truth and show His love to others, wherever and to whomever He would lead me. I can now look back over the many places I have gone and people I have met in His service, and I marvel at the joy and adventures. The journey continues.

When cancer reared its ugly head and I had to redirect my focus to chemotherapy treatments and fight this disease, I suddenly had to step aside from my regular pastoral responsibilities. This decision was painful to me for several reasons, one of which was my sense that I would lose treasured opportunities to be God's instrument of blessing in people's lives. But that perception was entirely untrue.

I recall conversations I had with my mom on this theme after she had moved into a nursing home and could no longer attend her church or live her life as she had known it. She too was at first depressed by the undesired changes in her life, especially the death of her husband, my dad. But she had long walked with God, so she chose to believe that God had a good plan for her where she was, and she saw opportunities that He was entrusting to her.

I saw my mom live this perspective, and she became a blessing to many. Whether she moved slowly with her walker, sat in her chair, or lay in her bed, she shared the good news of Jesus. She expressed His love and hers as she shared with those around her. She added to her long list of family and friends for whom she faithfully prayed, and she prayed for staff and residents of the nursing home. She motivated me then, and in heaven's glory she motivates me still.

My personal prayer has long been that God will always lead me and help me recognize and respond to every divine appointment that He has prepared for me in accordance with Ephesians 2:10. In this way I might be a blessing to others for Him. The Lord used an incident yesterday to remind and encourage me that we can all be His instruments of blessing when we see and seize the opportunities He affords us.

In my chemotherapy session, I enjoyed fellowship with four other patients and with my physician and nurse. I thanked God for their precious lives and for the blessing they were to me, and I asked that He would help me to listen well, reflect His love, and speak His truth. Though we may often be unable to see the lasting effects of our availability or the extent to which we have blessed someone, we can always entrust the results of our encounters to the Lord, and we can continue praying.

Clearly the Lord knew that yesterday I needed a personal word of encouragement on this theme, for even in my trying circumstances, He is still blessing me to bless others. As my chemotherapy session was nearing the end, the assigned oncology nurse came in to administer medications. I knew from previous encounters that she also loves the Lord, and that she is a beautiful example of His love to everyone she cares for, including me. I had told her this previously, hoping to encourage her in the Lord.

Yesterday as I prepared to leave, she spoke to me with emotion and in such a way that everyone in the room could hear her words. She offered praise to God and then said that without using my name on Sunday, she shared with her entire congregation how God had used me to bless and encourage her with my words of affirmation and gratitude and by assuring her that I was praying for her. Today the Lord used her to bless me.

I was humbled by her words and by my Lord's sweet reminder that He continues to use me and you and all believers who are available to bring glory to Him and to be His blessing to others. We are blessed to bless others. I pray that as long as we have breath, we will live this privilege.

FOR REFLECTION

When and how have you learned this lesson that you are blessed by God to be a blessing to others? What inner change do you need to experience this joy of being His instrument to bless others, even as He is blessing you? How does this lesson apply in your current circumstances? Ask God to help you in this, and He surely will.

20

ON GOD'S LIGHT SHINING INTO OUR DARKNESS

December 23, 2018

This year's celebration of Advent and Christmas has felt strange, because it is the first year in a long time that I have not preached or led worship of *Immanuel, God With Us* (Isaiah 7:13-14; Matthew 1:22-23). I have therefore been recalling recent Christmases. Five years ago, I led worship for troops at Guantanamo Bay, Cuba. Four years ago and three years ago, I did the same for Marine recruits at Parris Island in South Carolina. And I treasure memories of the last two years with Church of the Apostles, my church family in Coventry, Rhode Island, especially two years ago when all of our children and grandchildren were with us in our new home. Having no such privilege this year, it feels like something is missing. Helen and I are grateful, however, that this year we will share some of Christmas Day in Connecticut with Helen's cousin Cindy Richter.

I have also reminisced about wonderful Christmases of long ago with parents, siblings, and sometimes grandparents. And I have enjoyed precious memories of years when Helen and I were raising our children. But this year is different; something is missing. Because my illness prevents us from traveling, our children cannot be with us, and my compromised immunity precludes me from being in crowds, I am feeling these losses.

As Christians we hear and celebrate the announcement declared by angels on that night long ago of *good news of great joy that will be for all the people. For unto you is born this day in the city of David a Savior, who is Christ the Lord* (Luke 2:10-11).

This is *good news of great joy*, and we can revel it, for God fulfilled His promise to us, sending His son, and our savior But I will admit that due to personal losses in my life and the impact of cancer my joy this season of joy has been tempered by sadness. The Lord has used this struggle to help me become more aware that many hurt through the Christmas season, even many people of Christian faith.

If your heart is aching for some reason, on our Lord's behalf I urge you to remember what He has urged me to remember. In this broken world, pain is common to all, but the Christ whose coming we celebrate entered this broken world as was prophesied. He became *God with us* (Isaiah 7:14-15; Matthew 1:23). He came to share our pain and bring us His salvation of hope, healing, help, and everlasting life.

What losses have you suffered? Are you grieving the loss of a loved one, a dream, your own health, a broken relationship, or of life as you longed for it to be? If so, prayerfully consider what I have heard the Lord saying to me lately.

In my struggle I have sometimes felt like I am walking in diminished light. I have never felt like I was walking in utter darkness, for I know the Lord is always with me. But sometimes the light seems dimmer than I need it to be. Whenever this happens, I know the problem is mine and not God's.

Today I was again reminded of how gracious and loving God is, for I awoke reflecting on these inspired Scriptures about the light of Christ shining into my darkness and yours:

> *The people who walked in darkness have seen a great light;*
> *those who dwelt in a land of deep darkness, on them has*
> *light shone* (Isaiah 9:2).

ON GOD'S LIGHT SHINING INTO OUR DARKNESS

> *The light shines in the darkness, and the darkness has not overcome it. There was a man sent from God, whose name was John. He came as a witness, to bear witness about the light, that all might believe through him. He was not the light, but came to bear witness about the light. The true light, which gives light to everyone, was coming into the world.* (John 1:5-9)

> *Again Jesus spoke to them, saying, "I am the light of the world. Whoever follows me will not walk in darkness, but will have the light of life.* (John 8:12)

The prophet Isaiah described the world of his day and of ours as *a land of deep darkness*. What an apt description. By the inspiration of God, Isaiah prophesied of the great light that was to come into this world and shine in the darkness. The apostle John, one of Jesus's closest disciples, testified that the Lord Jesus Christ is *the true light which gives light to everyone*.

Jesus affirmed this assessment when He declared, *I am the light of the world*. He said that anyone who follows Him will no longer walk in darkness, for we will have the light of life with us. This is the message of Christmas, as we celebrate the good news that He shines over us and dispels the darkness from our lives. This phenomenal news is true for me and for you, even when our life is hard.

The Lord gave me a visual reminder of this when I awoke today. It was still nighttime, but when I looked outside, I was amazed to see light. The light of the moon shone brightly, as it reflected the light of the sun. I beheld this scene, and the Lord reminded me, "Though there is darkness in your world now, I am shining over you." Blessed by this thought, I put on my coat and went outside in the back yard for a better look. I worshipped the Lord while gazing upon the light from above that dispelled the darkness. Today I am giving praise that the Lord Jesus has done this in my heart; He has shone over and dispelled the darkness of my pain.

Reflecting on this, I realize that if I had not awakened early today or failed to notice the heavenly light that shone in the darkness, it would still have been there, but I would have missed the blessing of it. It shone brightly, whether I noticed it or not. Thus the Lord reminds me that the light of His glory is also shining over us and over the darkness of this world, regardless of whether we take notice. I have often been brought to repentance for the times when I have failed to notice the miracle of His marvelous light by focusing on the darkness.

No matter what may be happening now in the darkness of your world, I hope you will let the wonder of Christmas bless you. It is extraordinary news that Almighty God has come to us in the incarnation of His Son, the Lord Jesus Christ. We celebrate this in the history of our Lord's incarnation and first advent, and we look forward with joyful anticipation of His second advent. May we have confident assurance of the promise that we who in this life have trusted in Jesus Christ as our Lord and Savior will soon behold Him in the brilliance of His glory.

As the Scriptures have declared, *The sun shall be no more your light by day, nor for brightness shall the moon give you light; but the Lord will be your everlasting light, and your God will be your glory* (Isaiah 60:19). *And the city has no need of sun or moon to shine on it, for the glory of God gives it light, and its lamp is the Lamb* (Revelation 21:23).

Looking back to our Lord's first advent and looking ahead with expectation to His second advent requires that we open our spiritual eyes to see who He is and to choose to put our trust in Him. This will profoundly change our world view, and Christmas becomes more than a religious holiday to observe glorious events of human history or a time of hopeful anticipation of future events that will surely come.

Christmas faith is to be experienced here and now. It is seeing that our Lord shines over us today. It is enjoying the penetration of His light into our darkness and pain today. It is allowing Him to comfort us and give us hope in our current circumstances, even when life is hard. Our Lord's light is shining over us now, whether we notice or not. How much better to notice and offer Him our praise.

I want to thank you again for your prayers for Helen and me. God is answering your prayers. We are also praying for you. I pray that you may have a blessed Christmas, filled with joy in Jesus, who is the Light of the World.

FOR REFLECTION

When and how have you experienced God's light shining into your darkness? What are your reflections on the concept that God's light shines over us and dispels darkness, whether we take notice or not? How can you learn to experience and reflect His light in the darkness of this world? How does this lesson apply to your current circumstances? Ask God to help you in this, and He surely will.

21

ON MAKING PROGRESS WITH GOD'S HELP

January 1, 2019

Can we tell if we are making progress? Sometimes that is an elusive measurement. At other times, signs of progress are noticeable and bring us much encouragement. Such is my update on progress toward beating back cancer cells that have been destroying my bone marrow and blood and contributing to my susceptibility to sicknesses.

Progress in this kind of cancer battle is primarily measured through blood counts. I have had blood drawn weekly, and sometimes more often, to measure the levels of various types of cells, particularly white blood cells that are called neutrophils, which help in fighting infection. These levels are used to determine if it is safe for me to receive chemotherapy that week or if any other treatment may be needed. If the neutrophil count becomes too low, chemotherapy must temporarily be halted. I am pleased to report that until now, although my neutrophils have at times been low and close to the cut-off point, they have not been so low as to preclude treatment.

Specific blood labs that measure myeloma cells and various other cancer markers are called Serum Protein Electrophoresis (SPEP). These cancer cells and markers are measured every three to four weeks. The last two SPEP results have shown a steady decline in myeloma cells, which means the chemotherapy is destroying cancer cells. For this I rejoice, and because many are praying for me, I especially wanted you to know this.

I am so grateful for the oncology care I am receiving at the Providence VA Medical Center. The doctors, nurses, social worker, and entire staff are skilled, compassionate, and caring providers. I thank God for them and often express my appreciation to them.

From time to time I consult with a multiple myeloma specialist at the Dana Farber Cancer Institute (DFCI) in Boston. It was DFCI that confirmed my diagnosis of active multiple myeloma and recommended that I begin chemotherapy now. I declined their invitation to commute to Boston weekly for treatment, because I preferred to pursue treatment at the Providence VA, which is much closer to my home. We agreed that I would consult with DFCI quarterly for their assessment on my progress and recommendations on next steps. Last Friday I traveled to Boston for such a consultation.

The assessment by the DFCI multiple myeloma specialist indicated that I am making good progress with my current chemotherapy regimen. They hope that by March, after just six three-week chemo cycles, the myeloma cells may be substantially decreased. Then, if I meet all physical requirements for proceeding, they recommend a bone marrow transplant using my own stem cells as the next step in treatment.

We scheduled an appointment to return to DFCI on March 1 to measure progress and consult with a stem cell replacement specialist. Because I am nervous about this option, I am glad that I still have time to decide. As you pray for me and with me, and as I know God is faithful to grant wisdom to all who ask Him, I have confidence that He will provide direction in this matter. *If any of you lacks wisdom, let him ask God, who gives generously to all without reproach, and it will be given him. But let him ask in faith, with no doubting, for the one who doubts is like a wave of the sea that is driven and tossed by the wind.* (James 1:5-6).

My point is that God answers our prayers, though not always in the ways we expect. I have seen God bring immediate healing in answer to the faith-filled requests of His children, for He is loving and able. At other times I have seen the Lord bring gradual healing as He works for His glory through a process. And sometimes I have seen the Lord answer prayers in ways we would not have chosen, but He reminds us that He is with us in our pain, and we can trust Him, for He is Lord of all and we are not.

We who are in Jesus Christ are to become like Him. This is our desire, and it is His grace within us. Our deepest longing is to mature beyond a primary focus on what we want God to do for us. Our greatest aim is to be much less about us and much more about Him and His glory. When this happens, we will reflect His example by laying down our lives in sacrifice, suffering, and death. We will pray as our Lord prayed, *Father, glorify Your name* (John 12:28) and, *Father, if You are willing, remove this cup from me. Nevertheless, not my will, but yours, be done* (Luke 22:42).

More and more as time goes by, this is what I long for. I think the best opportunities for learning to trust and pray like this occur when we are in a place where we must pray this way. In doing so, we become enabled to experience the sweet release of His liberty and the calm of His peace. We are then blessed by God to taste the satisfying joy of drinking deeply from the well of living water that our Lord promised and provides.

Monday of this week was a chemotherapy day for me. Two others shared the room with me for their treatments. One was another multiple myeloma patient with whom I have had many conversations, for we are walking together on this path. Another patient entered whom I had not met before, and who was accompanied by his wife. I soon discerned that they were Christians, and he has been dealing with cancer for several months, enduring strong chemotherapy. They told me they have been praying and inviting others to pray with them for God's deliverance through it all.

As we spoke, the oncologist entered and gave to him and his wife the startling news that his recent PET/CT Scan surprisingly showed no cancerous tumors whatsoever. She said, "The tumors that were previously there are now entirely gone." Praise was offered to God in our chemotherapy room that day, for He deserves all the glory.

However God may choose to glorify His name through me, I will give Him glory. This is my joyful aim, and in Christ this is our shared privilege now and forever. Again I thank all who have prayed for Helen and me, as you are our partners on this journey. I feel the power of your prayers, and I rejoice in them. This journey is indeed hard at times, but it is good. God is glorified, for by His grace and in His will, I am making progress. In this I rejoice.

God sent us another reason to rejoice this week. Helen and I were blessed by a visit from our brother-in-law Gary Pardun who is married to Helen's sister Carol. Gary is not only our brother-in-law, he is also a brother in Christ with a true servant heart. He flew from South Carolina to Rhode Island to encourage and love on us, and with tools in hand, he skillfully repaired or remedied many things in our home that needed attention. What a wonderful demonstration of love in action.

God can use many things to remind us of His loving care. Sometimes we are blessed to do what Gary did, to be His instrument to provide His loving care to others. When we are given such opportunities, we must not miss them. At other times we are blessed to be recipients of God's care through others. Whether we are giving or receiving, when we do it in our Lord's name and through His grace, we are blessed. In this we can rejoice.

FOR REFLECTION

To what degree have you been longing for God to receive glory in and through your life, even when your way is hard? What are some ways God has reminded you lately of His loving care for you? What does God desire for you to make progress in your walk with Him? How can you apply this in your current circumstances? Ask God to help you in this, and He surely will.

22

ON EXPERIENCING DEEP SATISFACTION

January 12, 2019

Jesus promised us that when we come to Him in faith we will be satisfied. To the woman at the well, He said, *Everyone who drinks of this water will be thirsty again, but whoever drinks of the water that I will give him will never be thirsty again. The water that I will give him will become in him a spring of water welling up to eternal life* (John 4:13-14). He also said, *I am the bread of life; whoever comes to me shall not hunger, and whoever believes in me shall never thirst* (John 6:35).

God has been speaking to me about this lately, for He promised that those who come to Him will be satisfied. I have been reflecting on this in the context of the misery so prevalent in this world and the longing for something better. Regarding my own struggles, I have heard Him speak of the deep satisfaction He lovingly gives.

We sometimes make the mistake of thinking that God promised all of our circumstances will be pleasant, our paths will be easy, or that if we have sufficient faith, everything will be just the way we like it. But God did not promise this. In this broken world, haven't we all faced disappointment, difficulty, and loss? We have, and we will again. This week I have experienced insomnia, fatigue, and at times debilitating back pain, each of which have tempted me with discouragement.

But our God gives us deep satisfaction, as I have been reminded by reading the two-volume biography of J. Hudson Taylor who was used of the Lord to bring the good news of Jesus Christ to inland China. Nearly every time I have opened these books, I've been moved to tears and biblical conviction. J. Hudson Taylor loved the Lord with all of his heart, and he gladly sacrificed all for obedience.

Suffering much for the gospel, Hudson Taylor's losses included the deaths of three children and of his beloved wife Maria. He also suffered frequent illnesses while carrying the tremendous burden and responsibility of leading pioneer missionary efforts into inland China. But what has struck me most is that through all of this, Hudson Taylor was not despondent, nor did he ever entertain the temptation to quit. Rather, he did what God invites every disciple of Jesus Christ to do. He came in faith to the Lord, and he was satisfied in Him.

He grasped and experienced the power of our Lord's promise that *Whosoever drinketh of the water that I shall give him will never thirst* (John 4:14 KJV). The present tense of the Greek verbs in this passage flooded it with new meaning for Hudson Taylor, so in his time of great need he wrote to a friend, "Do not let us change the Savior's words... It is not, 'Whosoever has drunk,' but 'whosoever drinketh.' It is not of one isolated draught He speaks, or even of many, but of the continuous habit of the soul. Thus in John 6:35 the full meaning is, 'He who is habitually coming to me shall by no means hunger, and he who is believing on me shall by no means thirst.' The habit of coming in faith to Him is incompatible with unmet hunger and thirst."[2]

Hudson Taylor wrote to another friend, "Where many of us err is in leaving our drinking in the past, while our thirst continues in the present. What we need is to be drinking – yes, thankful for the occasion which drives us to drink ever more deeply of the Living Water."[3]

I understand better now what J. Hudson Taylor meant. As he was being very real about his own struggles and losses, so can we be real

---

[2] Dr. and Mrs. Howard Taylor, *Hudson Taylor and the China Inland Mission; the Growth of a Work of God*, 2 vols. (London: Morgan & Scott, L.D., 1920), 213.

[3] Taylor, *Hudson Taylor and the China Inland Mission*, 213.

about ours. Taylor's relationship with the Lord was an infinite treasure to him and brought him hope, comfort, peace, and love sufficient for his needs even in the face of his great losses; in Christ Jesus he remained deeply satisfied. So can I and so can you experience deep satisfaction in our Lord, no matter what our circumstances may be, as we come often to drink deeply of Him.

Because I have walked with the Lord Jesus for so long, I can attest firsthand that this is true. No matter what we may face along our life journey, our Lord satisfies. How often I have come to the spring of living water and received from His hand the cup that quenches my thirsty soul. So today, I offer my thanks to the Lord for this illness, for it is driving me to drink even more deeply of Him. Yes, He satisfies deeply.

FOR REFLECTION

Reflecting on the explanation of J. Hudson Taylor about our Lord's invitation to us to be always thirsty and to be drinking deeply of Him, what occasions has the Lord used in your life to bring you to drink more deeply of His Living Water? What does God desire so you may find your thirsty soul quenched in Him? How does this lesson apply to you? Ask God to help you in this, and He surely will.

23

ON A LIFE OF KNOWING AND TRUSTING GOD

January 23, 2019

God has blessed me through the years with the privilege of knowing and trusting Him. I came to know Him when I was a young boy, and I surrendered my heart to Him when I was a young man. Through the years I experienced the great joy and blessing of what it means to follow and serve Him, as I walk with my God wherever He has led me. There is no greater joy in life than this.

I can only begin to describe how blessed I have been. This blessing continues daily and forever, for personal relationship with God through Jesus Christ is not only for time but also for eternity. My current illness and the physical limitations I face now afford me the divine perspective that comes from the joy of God's faithfulness in the past and the anticipation of the future with the same sweet assurance.

I needed the confidence of such faith in every season of my life, especially last week when I faced yet another physical challenge. In addition to various repercussions of multiple myeloma, including reactions to chemotherapy, I live with limitations of a compromised immune system and back pain from a herniated disc. Then last week

I experienced a Transient Ischemic Attack (TIA), which sometimes is called a mini-stroke.

This scared me; I suddenly had excruciating head pain and double vision. These symptoms lasted less than an hour, but I made a visit to the emergency room where I underwent various tests. Thankfully, these ruled out a stroke with permanent damage, though additional tests are still forthcoming.

I must again face a question that I expect you have encountered too – maybe even now: In my times of uncertainty and confounding struggle, how will I respond? Will fear be my default response? Or will trust and faith in my Lord hold me solid? I want to share with you what I have come to experience over and over: God is forever faithful, and He can always be trusted. I will therefore put my trust in Him.

The biography of J. Hudson Taylor has reminded me of the blessings of trust and God's faithfulness. Several times I have paused in my reading with tears, deep conviction, and great rejoicing in the faithfulness of God through every generation.

James Hudson Taylor was born in England in 1832, and he was promoted to glory in 1905. He lived his life knowing and trusting God. As a young man, he surrendered to the Lord, and how God used him in His service! J. Hudson Taylor modeled what it means to live a life of knowing and trusting and walking with God.

He trusted in a great God:
Departing alone for China in 1853 at the age of twenty-one, J. Hudson Taylor carried God's vision for reaching inland China in his heart. Hundreds of millions of people lived there who had never heard the good news of Jesus Christ. He had no idea how to do it, but in light of the Lord's Great Commission revealed in Matthew 28:18-20, he knew it was the Lord's clear command, so he trusted that God would accomplish it.

After many years of fruitful ministry and open doors to reach China with the good news of Jesus Christ, he prayed for God's vision and believed in what God could do. For example, in 1897 he and the mission leaders in China prayed, believing God for reinforcements of a hundred more missionaries to come that year. They had no idea how this would happen, but they had faith in God. One hundred and two new missionaries arrived that year, for God made a way where there was no way; He answered prayers of faith.

When a Christian man confessed to J. Hudson Taylor, "I need greater faith," Taylor's reply was, "No. What you need is faith in a greater God." In a time of great opposition in China when many Christians suffered and died for the cause of Christ, Hudson Taylor reminded the church that "Satan is mighty, but God is Almighty!"[4]

Do you also believe that God is a great God and nothing is too difficult for Him? Do you hear Him calling you to trust Him? You may need to shift your focus from having more faith to placing the faith you have in the infinitely great God. This may be evident in your present trials as stress is lessened by knowing that God is able.

He trusted in a loving Father who provides for His children:
As he referred to his role as a father, J. Hudson Taylor described how he never stopped thinking about or caring for His dear children, nor could he ever. He then declared that we can know with more certainty that our Father in heaven never stops thinking about us. He will surely see that we are well cared for and that our needs are fully supplied.

Because he believed this, Taylor refused to ask people directly for money; he preferred instead to present his needs to God and trust Him to provide. On one occasion after preaching to a large audience in England, the people wanted to immediately take an offering for the work, but Taylor forbade it, because it lacked opportunity for people to first pray and discern what God would have them do. Rather than take an offering at that time, he told the people to go home, pray, and then do as the Lord directed them. This is what they did, and God abundantly provided.

Some gave thousands of British pounds to advance the kingdom of God in China, and some gave hundreds. Many gave whatever they could, and some gave all they had, like the poor widow described in Mark 12:41-44, who gave two small copper coins. A Chinese pastor's wife joyfully gave all of her jewelry and dowry to be sold to provide enough resources to reach a particular village with the good news of

---

4   Dr. and Mrs. Howard Taylor, *Hudson Taylor and the China Inland Mission: The Growth of a Work of God*, 2 vols. (London: Morgan & Scott, L.D., 1920), 428-429, 576.

Christ. In the United States, a poor widow gave all that she had, saying, "I can do without meat, but the poor Chinese cannot do without the gospel of Jesus Christ."

Do you also believe that God provides for His children out of His great love? He calls you to trust for His provision. Would you hear Him if He called you to sacrificially give for a need He lays upon your heart, and what would your answer be?

He trusted in a God who never leaves or forsakes us:
When J. Hudson Taylor departed the first time for China and left all behind, he knew God was going with Him. Whenever he traveled to remote places, he faced various challenges and obstacles. He often had no idea where he would rest or find his food, but he did not fear, for he knew his Lord was with him, just as He promised.

Near the end of his life, as his body was failing him and the Lord had taken his dear wife Jennie home to glory, he spoke to a group of young workers who were just setting out for inland stations in China. He said, "The Lord Jesus will never leave us nor forsake us. Count on Him, enjoy Him, abide in Him. Do, dear friends, be true to Him and to His Word . . . You may be tired often and lonely often, but the Lord knows just how much each cup costs. Look to Him; He will never disappoint you."[5]

FOR REFLECTION

What does it mean for you to live your life day by day, knowing and trusting God? How has this lesson blessed you in the past? How can you continue to grow in this regard? Ask God to help you in this, and He surely will.

---

5   Taylor, *Hudson Taylor and the China Inland Mission*, 607.

24

ON BEING TOGETHER FOREVER

February 3, 2019

I took Helen to the airport, and she is now on her way to Texas to spend a few days with our son Jonathan, his wife Jackie, and their two sons Archer and Theo. Helen is especially excited about meeting baby Theo, our newest grandson. I would love to be with her, but travel is unsafe for me now, and I should not miss any treatments. I will miss her while she is away this week, but I know it will not be long until I see her again. I am happy for her that she will be with family whom we both love. This reminds me that one day we will part again for a little while because of death, but there will be victory and joy through faith in the Lord Jesus Christ.

After I received my diagnosis of multiple myeloma, Helen and I have had a number of conversations about our mortality. All of us are mortal, of course, but many people prefer to ignore this truth. We have determined to face it with eyes wide open and see our current situation as a gift of God. This helps us live each day aware of our mortality and the sure hope of eternity. We are encouraged by the promises of God.

When one of us departs this earth for heaven, we anticipate the other will encounter a combination of joy and sorrow, just as we have experienced when other loved ones have died. As the apostle Paul described it, we will grieve, but we will do so with hope (1 Thessalonians 4:13).

Though we will miss each other while apart, we know that this separation will not be for long. Whichever of us remains in this mortal body will thereafter anticipate the fulfillment of God's promise that we will also soon be at home with the Lord (2 Corinthians 5:8).

Though I think it is likely I will precede Helen in death, she rightly points out this is God's call not ours, because He is the one who numbers our days (Psalm 139:16). By faith I know that if it is God's will, I will achieve remission from cancer and regain strength to continue my earthly journey. Otherwise, I will soon be promoted to glory. Peace is found in trusting God, whose will for His beloved children is always good.

How blessed we are in Christ to face our mortality each day with confidence and have an eternal perspective and hope. We who have been so blessed are also responsible before God to speak of this truth to others, for the gift of eternal hope and everlasting life is freely given to all who put their trust in Jesus. I am reminded of this while receiving weekly treatments. Last week for example, I was in the chemotherapy room with a friend whom I see each week, and two new patients joined us. I invited them to share their stories, and I shared mine with them.

I commented that though none of us volunteered for our diagnosis, we were given a gift and an invitation with it. The gift is a reminder of our own mortality, for these bodies are temporary. The invitation is to come in faith to Jesus who gives hope, forgiveness, and life with eternal perspective rather than attempt to walk this journey alone.

It turned out that one of the new patients was a Christian, as was his wife, and they asked if I would please pray with them. I was glad to do that, and the others listened in. When I had finished, a nurse asked me if I was done, and I replied with a smile, "For now yes, but I will never stop praying and leaning on the Lord."

Believing God's promises and trusting in Jesus as Savior and Lord brings us comfort and hope that nothing else brings. We are therefore assured that in God's time, all who are His children through faith in Jesus Christ from every nation and generation will be together with Him in heaven, never to be separated again. What a wonderful day it will be when *We who are alive, who are left, will be caught up together with them in the clouds to meet the Lord in the air, and so we will always be with the Lord* (1 Thessalonians 4:17). This is a promise to hold on to.

FOR REFLECTION

To what degree are you accepting your own mortality? Are you living with joy because of the Lord's promise to you of being together with Him forever? If not, why not? If so, how is this assurance affecting you day by day? What does God want that would help you experience joyful anticipation in His promise of everlasting life? Ask God to help you in this, and He surely will.

25

ON STRENGTH IN LIFE'S UPS AND DOWNS

February 12, 2019

This has been a week of ups and downs for me, which I fully expect you can identify with. But through it all, our Lord's words and His presence has encouraged my heart. God has been speaking to me through a particular Scripture, which leads to a devotional theme.

During a prolonged period of struggle for God's people, much of which was a direct consequence of their rejection of the Lord, the Philistines captured and removed the ark of God, which represented His presence among His people. Then the people were afraid and suffering. Discouragement was common to all. But a remnant prayed and sought the Lord, and by His great grace and mercy, God answered. Then the glorious day came when the ark of God was returned and placed inside the tent that had been prepared for it by King David.

David's call to worship that day included these compelling words: *Oh give thanks to the Lord; call upon His name; make known His deeds among the people. Sing to Him, sing praises to Him; tell of all His wondrous works! Glory in His holy name; let the hearts of those who seek the Lord rejoice! Seek the Lord and His strength; seek His presence continually* (1 Chronicles 16:8-11). Verse 36 adds, *Then all the people said, "Amen!" and praised the Lord.*

David expressed what I have experienced through the years, especially in this difficult season of my life, that God loves us with an everlasting love. But because we live in a broken world and experience the consequences of our sins and those of a sinful culture, our lives include ups and downs, times of struggle and times of joy.

What then can we do, no matter what our circumstances are? We can hold on to our faith. We can *seek the Lord and His strength*. We can *seek His presence continually*. This is what we can do. Is this what you are doing? For me this week included both ups and downs.

My ups were occasions of much joy and blessing, which prompted praise:

1. Helen was in Texas for six days; she enjoyed special times with our son Jonathan and his family and welcomed the arrival of our fourth grandson, Theo Stephen Gammon. What joy I received from the pictures Helen sent and from FaceTime conversations with the family.

2. While Helen was away, various people from our church family visited me and brought food, fellowship, and in one case Communion. Several other friends and family called to encourage me.

3. On Sunday our daughter, Amy Hatcher, MD, took part in three worship services of their local church in Wasilla, Alaska, during which she was interviewed by the pastor. She shared her testimony of how she has witnessed God heal miraculously. As Helen and I watched the live feed, we were blessed by our daughter and God's grace extended to many through Amy's life.

All these ups brought me joy to praise our Lord. I have learned that it is good for us to pause and reflect on the blessings that have occurred in our lives. This requires prayerful reflection, for praising God is not an automatic response. Praise is an intentional offering, and when we choose it, God is honored, and He pours more strength into us.

This does not mean that we should gloss over the downs or struggles of our lives. Though our individual battles are unique to each of us, struggles are common to all. As I look back over my own life, I recall many struggles I experienced along the way, and I rejoice that I have known to turn to my Lord. He has always been faithful to me.

Downs are circumstances that discourage us. This week included those too:

1. I was not able to join Helen on the Texas trip. Though I understood why, it was still a disappointment.

2. The past two weeks I have been fighting another upper respiratory infection. Though at first I was encouraged that my immune system fought back hard, after two weeks, my condition began to worsen. I now have a bacterial bronchial and sinus infection that requires another course of antibiotics. I have been dealing with pain, shortness of breath, and difficulty sleeping, which discourages me.

David's encouragement applies. Rather than allowing difficult circumstances to discourage me or diminish my faith, I can choose to offer it to the Lord and receive His peace in the midst of my struggle. This is what I will do. David reminds us to, *Seek the Lord and His strength; seek His presence continually.* This means every day and in all situations, even in all the ups and downs of our lives.

As you experience struggles, do you let them determine your worldview and limit your faith, or do you follow what the apostle Peter encouraged us to do: *Casting all your anxieties on Him, because He cares for you*? Do you say yes to David's encouragement to *seek the Lord and His strength; seek His presence continually*? This will not be an automatic response. Let it be a choice of faith.

In all your life circumstances, to whom do you turn? When we do what God invites us to do, we receive His peace and strength. By His grace to me, this has been my experience through the years, especially in this season of ups and downs.

FOR REFLECTION

What has been the effect of ups in your life on your relationship with God? What has been the recent effect of downs in your life on your personal relationship with God? What does God want from you so that you may seek His face regardless of circumstances? Ask God to help you in this, and He surely will.

26

ON LESSONS LEARNED WHEN SHORT OF BREATH

February 24, 2019

Being short of breath is scary, especially when it persists. I expect that you have experienced this symptom at some time, perhaps at high elevations, with strenuous exertion, or during a respiratory illness. I have reflected on this recently because I am experiencing shortness of breath.

The intensity of it fluctuates. Sometimes it is merely a nuisance, but at other times it is a hard struggle. I thank God for helpful inhalers, skilled medical care, and reminders that this condition is temporary. Today I give thanks to God for the way He is using even this struggle to speak to me about the depths of my longing for Him.

When we are short of breath, our focus tends to narrow to one primary thing – More air! There have been times this week when I could think of little else. If you have ever held your breath for a while like when swimming underwater, you know what I mean. When our heart and lungs are screaming at us for air, our mind becomes sharply focused on our need to breathe freely again. We know instinctively that we must breathe if we are to keep on living. No one has to explain this to us. We simply know it.

This reminds us that our greatest need and deepest longing is for

God – to receive and enjoy the full and abundant life that is available to us through faith in Jesus Christ who said, *I came that they may have life and have it abundantly* (John 10:10). This means breathing freely and deeply of the life-giving Spirit of God, who satisfies our whole being. From our creation to our restoration to our consecration and our eternal salvation, we need the Lord. We need Him more than we need our next breath or next heartbeat. We need Him more than anything. God's Word illustrates this.

Creation
Then the Lord God formed the man of dust from the ground and breathed into his nostrils the breath of life, and the man became a living creature (Genesis 2:7). We need to remember that none of us chose to be born, nor did we give ourselves the gift of life. God gave it to us when He created us in our mother's womb and gave us the breath of life, for it is *In Him we live, and move and have our being* (Acts 17:28).

Restoration
Thus says the Lord God to these bones: Behold I will cause breath to enter you; and you shall live. And I will lay sinews upon you, and will cause flesh to come upon you, and cover you with skin, and put breath in you, and you shall live, and you shall know that I am the Lord (Ezekiel 37:5-6). God alone offers us the miracle of restoration. We need the Lord in order to live again and live forever as He has made us to live. No matter how broken, lifeless, or despondent we may feel now, God is able to restore.

Consecration
Jesus said to them again, "Peace be with you. As the Father has sent me, even so I am sending you." And when He had said this, he breathed on them and said, "Receive the Holy Spirit" (John 20:21-22). Jesus Christ offers His peace and the compelling privilege of consecration to His purpose and calling to all of His disciples, even to you and me. We need our Lord in order to do whatever He calls us to do.

Salvation
For by grace you have been saved through faith. And this is not your

own doing; it is the gift of God, not a result of works, so that no one may boast (Ephesians 2:8-9). None of us is saved because we have been good enough. We are saved by God's grace and through our faith in the Lord Jesus Christ. We are saved because of who He is and what He has done for us. Through faith in the Lord Jesus Christ, we realize that we are undeserving recipients of His love for today, tomorrow, and forever. None of us earns our salvation, but by His perfect sacrifice, Christ has made us worthy. The more we grasp these truths, the more our love for Him grows in gratitude, devotion, and longing.

In the biblical languages the word for *spirit* is the same as *wind/air/breath*. For example, in His conversation with Nicodemus about being spiritually born, Jesus said, *That which is born of the flesh is flesh, and that which is born of the Spirit is spirit. Do not marvel that I said to you, "You must be born again." The wind blows where it wishes, and you hear its sound, but you do not know where it comes from or where it goes. So it is with everyone who is born of the Spirit* (John 3:6-8). The same Greek word is translated here as "wind" and "spirit," which shows that our spiritual life and breath come entirely from God.

The Spirit of God is the life-giving Breath of God. We need the Breath of God; we need His Spirit and His Life. This need is not only for a religious few. It is for every person, including you and me. Breathing in the Spirit, the Breath of God, is not an occasional need either. We need God's life-giving presence continually, in the same way that our lungs must continually breathe. On this theme I have been prayerfully singing to the Lord a couple songs that express my deep longing for more of God.

One is a hymn by the nineteenth-century Anglican vicar and hymn writer Edwin Hatch, "Breathe on Me, Breath of God." It includes this prayer: "Breathe on me, breath of God. Fill me with life anew. That I may love what thou dost love, and do what thou wouldst do." What a great prayer! Will you join in praying it to our God?

Another song I have been singing to the Lord is by Mercy Me called, "This is the Air I Breathe." It is a prayer that acknowledges Christ living in me as my daily bread and His word spoken to me as my desperate need, just as I need to breathe. This song reflects my need and the longing of my heart.

To realize that our deepest longing is for God and to know that He created us for personal, lifelong relationship with Him is a blessing. If we never experienced shortness of breath, or never longed for more of God, we might foolishly conclude in our self-sufficiency that we need nothing more.

But in His great love, God allows us to lack and long. Our longing draws us to Him, panting for the freshest air we have ever known, which is the breath of life, the breath of heaven. His breath is freely given to all who come to Him. By faith His life is ours as we are in personal relationship with the Son of God, our Savior, the Lord Jesus Christ.

I have thus been thanking God for my recent shortness of breath, for it reminds me that one day I will take my last breath in this mortal body, and then I will enter eternity. Because of Jesus Christ, so can you. I look forward in faith to what God has prepared for me and for all who have trusted in Him. Are you motivated by this promise too?

Are you living each day in light of eternity? Are you breathing deeply of Him, hour by hour and moment by moment? Are you longing for God even more than your next breath? I testify to you that He deeply satisfies, and I am praying that you will long for Him with intensity and find yourself fully satisfied.

I thank you again for praying for Helen and me. This week we return to the Dana Farber Cancer Institute in Boston to discuss potential stem cell transplant. Your prayers are appreciated, as we continue seeking the Lord for His direction, wisdom, and healing.

FOR REFLECTION

How does shortness of breath and longing to breathe freely speak to the depth of your need and longing for more of God? How does this apply to your life? How can you grow so you may long for more of Him and find yourself satisfied in Him? Ask God to help you in this, and He surely will.

27

ON DISAPPOINTMENT TO DELIGHT

March 3, 2019

I admit that I experienced much disappointment when Helen and I went to Boston last Friday to see a multiple myeloma specialist at the Dana Farber Cancer Institute. When I last saw her in late December, I came away with the clear impression that I was responding well to chemotherapy, and the next step in my treatment would be a stem cell transplant (SCT). The oncologist said then that I should be a good candidate for SCT, and I was scheduled to return in early March to evaluate my progress and meet with her and another member of the transplant team.

Over the past two months, I have done significant homework on stem cell transplants for multiple myeloma; I read various studies that compare this process to other treatment options. I arrived at my appointment on Friday with numerous questions that I prepared and bathed in much prayer. I trusted that when a decision was required, my God would confirm what He would have me do.

But I was not expecting what happened. With my most recent lab results in hand, they informed me that at this time I am not considered a good candidate for stem cell transplant, because I still have significant cancer cells in my blood and bone marrow. For the SCT to be effective, the myeloma (cancer) cells must be completely or nearly gone, but my current levels remain too high. Before this conversation, I was unsure if I would agree to an SCT, but I had not considered the possibility that it might not even be an option for me. I was disappointed.

Disappointment is common to us all. You have surely experienced it, and so have I. Whenever this happens, we face a choice. If we allow the disappointment to become our primary focus, we may become depressed and discouraged. I was tempted to respond in this way, but my Lord reminded me that this does not reflect faith in His character.

All who know Jesus Christ are called and enabled to choose to trust Him. He is never distant or powerless or surprised by our circumstances. He is always with us, always able, and always working out His will for our good and for His glory. As I pondered these revelations, His peace flooded my soul. After all, we asked God to lead us. We committed ourselves to Him and invited others to pray with us for His will and glory. Surely these are prayers the Lord answers for all who love and trust Him.

I therefore made a choice to drive past disappointment and to steer toward delight. Disappointment fixes our gaze upon our circumstances, which are often out of our control. But true delight fixes our eyes on the Lord Jesus Christ whose character is compelling, whose love is constant, whose relationship with us is forever, and whose promises triumph over every disappointment.

Regarding my cancer treatment now, the doctor prescribed another chemotherapy drug to be added to the ones I have been taking. This drug will be administered weekly via intravenous infusion. After nine weeks, I will return to the Dana Farber Cancer Institute to assess my progress and consider whether stem cell transplant will then be an option.

I appreciate all who are praying for us. Please join us in praying for a good response to chemotherapy and for God's continued leading in every step along the way. Pray especially that God will be glorified through all of this and that we will continually choose delight in Him over disappointment about our circumstances. We are praying the same for you.

FOR REFLECTION

What disappointments have you faced in life that steered you toward discouragement? When and how has the Lord taught you to drive past disappointment to delight in Him? How does God direct you so you may delight in Him more no matter your disappointments? How does this lesson apply to your circumstances? Ask God to help you in this, and He surely will.

28

ON ADMITTING OUR NERVOUSNESS

March 10, 2019

Last week when I met with my oncologist, we discussed the new chemotherapy drug I am to begin tomorrow, which was prescribed because the current regimen is no longer effectively reducing the myeloma (cancer) cells in my bone marrow and blood. A change is needed now. I will receive the new drug intravenously over several hours.

The first dose will be administered this week over two days and thereafter one day weekly for nine weeks. Though this drug is expected to effectively kill myeloma cells, my oncologist warned that it can also cause harsh side effects. At the conclusion of our conversation, she handed me a printed list of potential side effects and said, "You have good reason to be nervous."

I heard what she said, and I read the literature she gave me. Though I do not want to be nervous, I find that I am. I am nervous about whether this drug is going to work for me, and I am nervous about the unpleasant reactions I may have. Should I be nervous? And what are we to do when we are nervous?

I expect you can relate to this, because we all face uncertainties and challenges in life. You might be nervous about something you are facing now or are going to face in the near future. Inwardly we might wonder how we will endure it, or if we will have the wherewithal to triumph. I have learned and am continuing to learn that it is futile to pretend calm when an inner storm is brewing. In fact, by His grace our God would use our nervousness for His glory and our good, as He draws us closer in our dependence upon Him.

Can you recall from your childhood, or perhaps from raising children, what comforts a little child best when they are nervous or afraid? They want to be held. They want to feel safe in the arms of their parent or caregiver. This is where we all want to be. In the same way our nervousness calls us toward nearness to God, where we can rest safely in His arms in complete trust and reliance.

We instinctively realize that we cannot face this challenge alone, nor should we try. So with deep longing and earnest faith we come near to our heavenly Father and snuggle into His arms, and there we can rest. As we do this, nervousness gives way to peace. He can transform our nervousness into something that is beautiful.

In speaking of transformation, Rick Warren, author of *The Purpose Driven Life,* observed that, "God changes caterpillars into butterflies, sand into pearls and coal into diamonds using time and pressure. He is working on you, too." Oh yes. He surely is. So let's bring our struggles to the Lord and trust Him for something beautiful to come of it.

Many places in Scripture show that God invites us to turn our nervousness and burdens over to Him. Accepting His loving invitation to do this presumes that we admit our struggles and conclude that we need the Lord now. This conclusion is not automatic, for we can all be prone to despondency or to delusion, and think we must fight this battle in our own strength.

Making such a choice may leave us with a burden of anxious nervousness. But when we admit our struggle and confess to the Lord our need, we say yes to His invitation. Then like little children, we can let Him hold us close, and we find peace and rest.

I hope and pray that you too will consider and believe these personal invitations from your heavenly Father, as they are intended for you. If nervous, you can do what He is calling me to do. Trust in the Lord who holds you close and find in Him your rest.

Cast your burden on the Lord, and He will sustain you; He will never permit the righteous to be moved. (Psalm 55:22)

My presence will go with you, and I will give you rest. (Exodus 33:14)

Be strong and courageous. Do not fear or be in dread because of them, for it is the LORD your God who goes with you. He will not leave you or forsake you. (Deuteronomy 31:6)

Come to me, all who labor and are heavy laden, and I will give you rest. (Matthew 11:28)

To my Lord and to you I admit my nervousness. I also admit my utter dependence upon the Lord. In my nervousness, I come to Him now with childlike wonder and trust Him to hold me close. In Christ I find peace and rest, for He reminds me that I have no cause for worry. I pray for such peace for you too. How blessed we are to be part of God's forever family and to uphold each other in prayer.

FOR REFLECTION

What are you most nervous about now? What does the image of a child peacefully nestling in the heavenly Father's arms say to you about your circumstances? How can you leave your nervousness with Him? Do you believe that God's personal invitations to release our burdens to Him and to find rest in Him are intended for you? How readily have you accepted His invitations? Ask God to help you in this, and He surely will.

29

ON PRAYER AND PRAISE

March 11, 2019

I am blessed to share a testimony of praise for how God answered my prayer today. Today was my first day on a new chemotherapy drug, one that I was warned often brings unpleasant side effects. The nursing staff watched me throughout the day, ready to respond to any potential problem. I spent seven and a half hours at the hospital, and I felt great the entire day. My doctor looked relieved and told me so. I sang praises to God the whole way home.

As many of you are warriors in my prayer army, I wanted to share this brief praise report with you, because this was an answer to prayer. As the intravenous infusion started, the nurse who was administering it added her prayers to yours and mine. She prayed, "Lord God Almighty, protect this man from any negative reaction today. Send this treatment to the cancer cells and let them be destroyed. In Jesus's Name. Amen." What a blessing to pray and to be prayed for, and what a joy to give God the praise! May our prayers and praise continue, for our God is forever faithful.

FOR REFLECTION

What prayers has God answered for you lately, for which you are giving Him praise? What does God desire from you so your heart may be filled with prayer and praise? Ask God to help you in this, and He surely will.

30

ON ENDURING GRATITUDE

March 16, 2019

This week I have reflected on enduring gratitude; I've savored a particular Bible verse that is repeated word for word multiple times in the Scriptures, thus implying that the Lord wants to ensure that we get it. It says, *Give thanks to the Lord, for He is good; for His steadfast love endures forever.* (1 Chronicles 16:34; Psalm 106:1; Psalm 118:1; Psalm 136:1). What follows are brief reflections on the three phrases in this verse and the challenge to live it as God is blessing.

Give thanks to the Lord
Scripture tells us to give thanks to God as a way of life. Giving thanks is much more than mere sentiment. It is a decision that leads us to action. After all, what good is unexpressed gratitude? Whom does it encourage or bless? But expressing true gratitude accomplishes considerable good. I know it, for this week I was a recipient of such blessing.

As you may have experienced, or can imagine, feeling weak or sick for a prolonged period is tough. This has been such a week for me, as I endured side effects of my illness and the drugs that I am taking. Though I am making good progress and doing okay overall, the cumulative effect of the battle at times discourages me.

But last evening I was blessed to receive beautiful expressions of love and gratitude from our church family, which has lifted my soul. The Church of the Apostles, the congregation I loved and served, presented me with a bound photo album and a framed collage of church family members with handwritten notes inscribed upon it that expressed love and gratitude. No words can describe how this blessed me.

These expressions of love, encouragement, and appreciation have inspired me to express my enduring gratitude to Helen and others who have blessed me. I thank and bless all who have prayed for me. I especially give thanks to God, the One who gave me life, and who has been and will forever be the source of every blessing.

But does it seem strange that we have to be reminded to be grateful? Shouldn't gratitude be a natural response from those who have been given so much? But thankfulness is not automatic. Rather, enduring gratitude is a decision that we must make and then act upon.

For He is good
We are called to believe this truth, that our God is good. And when we believe it, we must declare it to God and to the world. We are to declare this rock of truth and stand upon it in faith, no matter what troubling circumstances may swirl around us. This is to be an act of faith, hope, and confidence for us.

Though my own circumstances, and undoubtedly yours, have at times been more than a little difficult, this never alters the sublime truth that God is good all the time. I believe and declare this truth, and I will stake my life upon it. The Lord has shown Himself faithful to me, over and over again. He is ever faithful and true *for He is good*.

His love endures forever
God urges us to envision eternity, to look beyond the temporal nature of the here and now and to dream of what is to come. He desires us to long with joyful expectation for the promise of God's never-ending love. This is far more than an ethereal hope of what might yet be. It is a confident expectation of what will be – an absolute assurance that in Jesus Christ we are loved by God and He is going to love us forever.

Is this not reason for enduring gratitude? Oh yes. It surely is. I am forever grateful, for in my soul there is no doubt of it. I know with certainty that when my heart beats its last, God's love endures forever. Though I cannot fathom what forever means, I know that His love for us will never fade, never fail, and never end; never.

So, do we have cause for enduring gratitude? Yes, we surely do. *Give thanks to the Lord, for He is good. His love endures forever.*

FOR REFLECTION

How has enduring gratitude been evident in your heart and in your actions? What are you most grateful for and how can you best express it? What does God tell you about how to live a life of enduring gratitude? Ask God to help you in this, and He surely will.

Cover of the Book of Memories presented to Steve by Church of The Apostles

Signed Collage given to Steve showing many members of Church of The Apostles

31

ON TREASURES TO HOLD ON TO WHEN STRUGGLING

March 24, 2019

If you pulled into your driveway today and saw that your house was burning down, and you had only a moment to grab whatever earthly treasures you hold most dear, what would you retrieve? For me it would be photos of treasured people and precious memories that I do not want to lose. Other things I would let go.

I am glad I have never faced this situation, but lately in the fire of the cancer I am now enduring, I have reflected on the struggles that I have faced and what I may yet lose. The fact is, in time we will all lose most of what is around us now. Is it not wise therefore for us to treasure what matters most, that which endures forever?

My difficulties this week were due to the fire of physical struggles. On Tuesday I experienced an allergic reaction during chemotherapy. The doctors had to pause my treatment for a while and administer other medicine to counter the reaction; then they resumed the infusion at a slower rate. I was at the hospital nine hours that day and have felt weak and exhausted since then, presumably because of reactions to the drug. Today I feel some better, but tomorrow I will receive another dose. So I have been pondering, "What treasures am I clinging to in the face of these current struggles?" Here are three that I am holding tightly:

God's Relationship

Nothing matters more than personal relationships. Helen is my life partner and the dearest person in the world to me. I hold on to her. But far more I hold on to God who created us for relationship with Him forever. How incredible! When sin separated us from Him, with extraordinary and infinite love, God did what was painfully necessary to restore us to right relationship with Him by the perfect atoning sacrifice of Jesus. To the praise of the glory of His grace, all who believe in Jesus and receive this gift are forever adopted as God's own children (Ephesians 1:3-6). This means we are in personal relationship with God and will remain so forever. Nothing is worth more than this. So in the face of present struggles, I cling to God's relationship.

God's Reliability

God has been, is now, and will forever be reliable. He is faithful, even in the face of our struggles. One of my favorite passages on this theme is found in the book of Lamentations, which is a collection of laments on the suffering and pending destruction of Jerusalem. In the midst of such tragedy, these verses remind us of God's faithfulness: *The steadfast love of the LORD never ceases; His mercies never come to an end; they are new every morning; Great is Your faithfulness* (Lamentations 3:22-23). Verse 24 adds a personal faith response in the face of personal difficulty: *"The LORD is my portion," says my soul, "therefore I will hope in Him."* This is a here and now decision. In my present struggles, I am holding on to God's reliability. His faithfulness is forever.

God's Rest

This treasure brings together the two that I have already mentioned, for the rest God offers is found in loving personal relationship with Him through Jesus Christ, because of His great faithfulness. When we trust Him, we are enabled to rest in Him, no matter what our current struggles are.

Jesus's invitation to us presumes that at times we will carry heavy burdens. Yet He says in Matthew 11:28, *Come to me, all who labor and are heavy laden, and I will give you rest.* May we also recognize the words of Augustine: "Thou hast made us for thyself O Lord, and our heart is restless until it rests in thee."

Yesterday as I was FaceTiming with my daughter Amy, my little grandson Luca was feeling sick. How I loved what I saw him doing. Amy held him close, and he laid his head on her shoulder. He rested in his mother's arms. This is what we can do in God's arms. I will therefore hold on to His rest. I will trust Him for today, tomorrow, and forever, with confidence that He will never let me go. And as I hold on to God's relationship, God's reliability, and God's rest, I hope and pray that you will do the same. These treasures are worth far more than anything we could lose.

FOR REFLECTION

In your current season of life, how are you holding on to your relationship with God? How are you holding on to His reliability and faithfulness? How are you holding on to and enjoying His rest? What does God desire from you to enable you to hold on to Him? Ask God to help you in this, and He surely will.

32

ON FINDING CONTENTMENT IN OUR DEEPEST VALLEYS

March 31, 2019

When God puts it on our hearts to pray for someone, we are blessed to do so. We are also blessed to receive fresh measures of God's grace in our own life through the faith-filled prayers of others. Through such mercies the Lord reminded me to intercede often for my family and for others who are now in need of prayer. Several times this week my Lord has also reminded me that someone is praying for me now and that He is right now answering their prayers.

Though we are always in need of prayer, we are more prone to recognize this when we acknowledge that our burdens are too heavy for us to carry alone. This is one of the sweet blessings of being in great need, for we can see afresh the depth of our dependence on God. In faith we can seek and receive contentment not in our circumstances but in sweet personal relationship with God. For this I give God praise.

This week I was pleased to learn that my new chemotherapy drug is reducing the cancer cells in my blood. This news has encouraged me greatly, and for this I give God praise. At the same time I experienced some days of feeling miserable, tired, and weak. Though I know whom to lean on, and though I find Him ever faithful in this season of my life, I still admit that living with this cancer is hard.

One day this week I felt particularly weak and discouraged; I prayed, "Lord, I hate this. This is getting old. Please help me." As I spoke these words out loud, Helen heard them and realized that this was an honest admission. Then she prayed for me. What a treasure she is.

I share this with you to acknowledge that like everyone else, I am still a work in progress. I also want to show that we ought always to be honest with God and with others when we are struggling. In such authentic admissions, we can confess our dependence upon Him for our next heartbeat and breath and for everything that we need.

I am blessed to report on a sweet ministry opportunity the Lord afforded me this week to speak via Skype at a Christian retreat in the state of Washington. My friend Marc Gauthier who is a retired U.S. Army Chaplain was the speaker at a weekend retreat sponsored by Officer's Christian Fellowship for active duty military and spouses. The theme of the retreat was The Slippery Art of Contentment; it focused on biblical teaching on finding contentment in the Lord. A few weeks ago Marc asked if I would be willing to join the retreat from a distance for one session to address "Finding Contentment in Our Deepest Valley." When I asked the Lord if this assignment was from Him, He assured me that it was. Yesterday I was blessed to do this for about an hour.

As every Bible preacher and teacher knows, before we can faithfully speak God's Word, we must first faithfully hear His Word. This assignment was a gift to me, as I was able to hear and then share biblical insights on experiencing true contentment in the Lord, even in the face of cancer or other hard circumstances. The primary insight I shared is that contentment, as God defines it, is not found in situations to our liking, for in this broken world, there will inevitably be circumstances we do not like.

The Bible teaches that lasting and true contentment is found completely through faith and in personal relationship with God through Jesus Christ. If we insist that our circumstances must be to our liking for us to be happy and content, we are effectively choosing to be dissatisfied and depressed, for in this broken world with pain, loss, and struggle, there is much we simply cannot change.

As Jesus realized that struggles were going to come for His disciples, including us, He spoke wonderful words of assurance. He said, *I have said these things to you, that in me you may have peace. In the world you will have tribulation. But take heart; I have overcome the world* (John 16:33). Jesus teaches us that through relationship with Him and by faith, His peace and contentment are known, even in our deepest valleys.

I have been living this truth. I have walked with the Lord since I was a little boy, but in my current struggles, I am learning fresh lessons on being content in any and every circumstance. I can identify much more now with Paul who wrote from his prison cell, where he surely did not want to be. He wrote his own personal testimony of learning the secret of contentment. *I have learned in whatever situation I am to be content. I know how to be brought low, and I know how to abound. In any and every circumstance, I have learned the secret of facing plenty and hunger, abundance and need. I can do all things through Him who strengthens me* (Philippians 4:11-13).

I am learning this too. I am learning that contentment in our deepest valleys is not found in circumstances that are to our liking. Rather, it is found in longing for Jesus Christ, leaning on Him, and loving Him most. This treasure is worth infinitely and eternally more than good health or vigor, or any other situation or material thing. Knowing Christ is worth far more than pleasant circumstances; and so with great love our Lord teaches and invites us to know Him and to love Him most. If hard circumstances are needed for us to learn this lesson, so be it. This is a small price for such great treasure.

FOR REFLECTION

When have you perceived that your burdens are too heavy for you to bear alone, and what have you learned from it about the true source of contentment? How are you learning now that personal relationship with God satisfies, no matter your circumstances? How does God guide you so that you may experience contentment in Him? Ask God to help you in this, and He surely will.

33

ON WHAT TO DO WHEN WE FEEL LIKE WE ARE LOSING IT

April 7, 2019

Sometimes along this earthly journey, we become discouraged. Sometimes we are physically or spiritually weak. Sometimes we are afraid, lonely, grief-stricken, or in physical or emotional pain, and it can feel like we are losing it. You know what I mean, don't you? Living in this broken world is for us a struggle at times.

Like you, I have struggled at various times along my earthly journey, and some days it feels like I am losing the battle. So what do we do when it feels like we are losing it? I have faced this question in various seasons of personal struggle and in times when I came alongside others who faced grief, trials, or pain.

This week I experienced some real personal struggles, in part because of physical difficulties and their cumulative effect on me and in part because of discouragement. I do not seek sympathy but only desire to testify as Paul did: *If we are faithless, He remains faithful – for He cannot deny Himself* (2 Timothy 2:13). Yes, our Lord is ever faithful, even when we are not.

The Lord is inviting and teaching all of His children, including me, to come to Him in childlike faith, no matter what circumstances we are dealing with. We can lean upon Him as a child held in loving arms, and receive from Him all that we need. I have learned and am re-learning five lessons on what to do when it feels like we are losing it.

Be real with God

Pretense is foolishness. When we struggle, we should admit it and tell Him. When we hurt or feel vulnerable, we can offer all of ourselves to God. He helps us, not when we proudly pretend that we are okay and can handle things ourselves, but when we humbly admit our struggle and need for Him.

One passage that calls us to such authenticity says we are to *put off your old self, which belongs to your former manner of life and is corrupt through deceitful desires, and to be renewed in the spirit of your minds, and to put on the new self, created after the likeness of God in true righteousness and holiness* (Ephesians 4:22-24). In other words, we must humbly acknowledge that we need to be renewed by God, and through faith in the Lord Jesus, we must be real with God about it.

A song by the David Crowder band has blessed me greatly. It is called "Come as You Are," and it invites us to authenticity. It says, "Lay down your hurts, lay down your heart, come as you are." We can do this whenever it feels like we are losing it.

Share your heartache with somebody

God does not want any of us to face our struggles alone. The Scriptures urge us to share our burdens with each other: *Bear one another's burdens, and so fulfill the law of Christ* (Galatians 6:2). This speaks of the gift and blessing of being in a Christian family and community, as God has designed us to be.

If you are God's child through faith in Jesus Christ, He would have you rejoice that you are not an only child. God places His children in a forever family with dear brothers and sisters to love, listen, support, and pray; this family will speak truth to us that we need to hear. It helps us to share our heartache with somebody. We can do this whenever it feels like we are losing it.

Cherish the promises of God

God has given many promises that speak life and hope and help to His children. When it feels like we are losing it, we need to remember and hold on to His promises. Two particular promises of God that have blessed me lately are the promises of His faithfulness and of His presence.

The faithfulness of God is the character of God. The Old Testament book of Lamentations is a collection of laments on the suffering and pending destruction of Jerusalem. In the midst of the laments, we find this testimony of God's great faithfulness: *The steadfast love of the Lord never ceases; His mercies never come to an end; they are new every morning; great is your faithfulness* (Lamentations 3:22-23).

The next verse reveals a personal faith response in the face of such difficulty, one that blesses all who will confess it: *"The Lord is my portion," says my soul, "therefore I will hope in him."* Amen. This is what I will do. Whenever it feels like we are losing it, we can cherish the faithfulness of God. He has been faithful to me. Hasn't He also been faithful to you?

It also helps to remember the promise of His presence, for God is ever with us, even in the midst of our struggles. When Moses approached death, he blessed Israel and commissioned Joshua to lead the people across the Jordan River and into the promised land. In Moses's final words recorded in Deuteronomy 31, he reminded them that they would not be going alone, for God would go with them. Though the obstacles might be many and the enemy might be strong, the Lord essentially said to Joshua and the people, "Do not be afraid. You have got this, for I will be with you!"

Jesus made the same promise in His parting words to His disciples. Before ascending to heaven, He said to them and us, *Behold, I am with you always, to the end of the age* (Matthew 28:20). It helps us to cherish again the sweet promises of God, especially His faithfulness and His presence. We can do this whenever it feels like we are losing it.

Give praise to God

God is always worthy of our praise. Praise is not a feel-good emotion that requires us to wait until our situation has improved and we feel happy again. Praise is an act of our will that shifts our focus from ourselves and our circumstances to God whom we adore.

Whenever I look beyond my difficulties and sing songs of praise to the Lord, I can see His glory, which lifts my heart every time. Paul and Silas beautifully modeled this in Acts 16. They had been beaten and were chained in a Roman jail. Though mistreated and in physical pain with much reason to complain, that is not what they did. Rather, they sang songs of praise to God. And as they did so, others listened and marveled at how they could do this in the face of such dire circumstances.

I am humbled that I have been asked similar questions by some who have witnessed my struggles, heard my joyful praise, and wondered how this could be. What a blessing is ours to testify of God's grace in our lives. As Paul and Silas praised God in the midst of their difficulty, He shook off their chains. In their praises God received glory, the Philippian jailer and his family came to faith in Jesus, and we are still being blessed by their witness. Praising God is good for us, and we can do it whenever it feels like we are losing it.

Live with joyful expectancy of heaven
A joyful perspective brings motivation and strength today. Jesus Christ left the glory of heaven to come to us. Forty days after His resurrection, He ascended and returned to heaven. One day soon our Lord will return from heaven. To all His disciples, Jesus said, *Let not your hearts be troubled. Believe in God; believe also in me. In my Father's house are many rooms. If it were not so, would I have told you that I go to prepare a place for you? And if I go and prepare a place for you, I will come again and will take you to myself; that where I am you may be also* (John 14:1-3). This perspective blesses me whenever I feel like I am losing it.

Such expectancy includes looking ahead with joyful anticipation to the fulfillment of God's promises as revealed in Revelation when *He will wipe away every tear from their eyes, and death shall be no more, neither shall there be mourning, nor crying, nor pain anymore, for the former things have passed away. And He who was seated on the throne said, "Behold I am making all things new." And He said, "Write this down, for these words are trustworthy and true"* (Revelation 21:4-5). When we feel like we are losing it, we can hold on to this promise, and as we do, joy and eternal perspective will flood our souls.

The closer I get to arriving in heaven, the more my excitement builds. Lately I have been dreaming about it with joy. We who know the Lord

Jesus Christ are blessed to be living with joyful expectancy of heaven. We can do this whenever it feels like we are losing it.

What do we do when it feels like we are losing it? These lessons are helping me, and I commend them to you in the Lord:

1. Be real with God

2. Share your heartache with somebody

3. Cherish the promises of God, especially His faithfulness and His presence

4. Give praise to God

5. Live with joyful expectancy of heaven

FOR REFLECTION

When struggling, have you been more prone to pretense or to being real with God? When your heart has ached, have you tended to bear it alone, or have you attempted to share it with somebody else? How do the promises of God's faithfulness and of His presence with you apply in your current situation? When and how has God taught you to give Him praise, no matter what your circumstances are? How is joyful expectancy of heaven affecting your strength and motivation now? Ask God to help you with this and He surely will.

34

ON HOW GOD BLESSES US IN THE MIDST OF OUR STRUGGLES

April 14, 2019

Living with cancer has not been easy for me. In fact, it has been one of the harder challenges I have ever faced. Fatigue and physical weakness, social limitations, and bouts of discouragement have made it a hard road to walk. Several days this week I struggled because of physical weakness, largely because of the cumulative effects of chemotherapy. Yet through it all, I have seen my God bringing good to me and others, and much glory to Himself. For this I rejoice.

One day this week I visited a friend who also has multiple myeloma, and whose battle is nearing an end. I was blessed to be an instrument of God's love, comfort, and eternal hope for him and his wife. This blessing flowed through my own struggles, as I recalled four reflections on how God blesses us in the midst of our struggles:

God continues to provide divine appointments

Ephesians 2:10 says, *For we are His workmanship, created in Christ Jesus for good works, which God prepared beforehand, that we should walk in them.* In other words, God has prepared good works for each of us in His service. This includes you and me, and this promise surely applies even when we are struggling.

My desire is to recognize and faithfully respond to every divine appointment that God has prepared for me. We are all responsible for each good work He has for us to do. Though I have lived this principle through the years, when my cancer diagnosis came and I was sidelined, I wrongly presumed that I would have fewer significant assignments in God's plan. But I was wrong. God has continued to lead and guide me to divine appointments. He intends the same for all His children until He calls us home.

A few years ago I was blessed to read a wonderful book written by Billy Graham when he was ninety-three years old, titled *Nearing Home – Life, Faith, and Finishing Well*. One point he made that has remained with me is that God intends fruitful service for His children until He calls us home to heaven. Dealing with the limitations of his own failing body, he said that though we cannot do all that we did in previous days, we can still be available to our Lord and so respond to the opportunities He gives us. I fully agree. It is a great joy to offer ourselves to the Lord each day and thus live this principle.

God's presence with us is real
Isaiah 43:2-3 says, *When you pass through the waters, I will be with you; and through the rivers, they shall not overwhelm you; when you walk through fire you shall not be burned, and the flame shall not consume you. For I am the Lord your God, the Holy One of Israel, your Savior.* And verse 5 adds, *Fear not, for I am with you!*

Though God is always with us, it is in the midst of our struggles that we may most powerfully know it. One of my favorite Bible stories when I was a boy remains a favorite today, as it provides a vivid picture of God's faithfulness to His children in our times of greatest need. It is the story told in Daniel 3 of Shadrach, Meshach, and Abednego. When these young men of faith were cast into a fiery furnace, the Lord joined them in that furnace. God was with them, loving them, sustaining them, and guarding them (Daniel 3:19-25).

Few desire or volunteer to suffer. While receiving my chemotherapy treatments, I have often said to other patients that none of us volunteered for this, but God is able to bring good from it. I want them to know that God comes to meet us in our struggles.

Though Shadrach, Meshach, and Abednego did not choose or desire their fiery furnace, it became an instrument of blessing for them, as they experienced firsthand the tangible presence of God. Even Nebuchadnezzar, the King of Babylon, marveled when he saw them and told others what God had done for them. These servants of God came through the fire unharmed and gave praise and testimony of the faithfulness of God. They never regretted the struggle they faced, which brought them to the furnace and through it by God's tangible presence with them in the fire.

Looking at my own life, I am thankful for the struggles I faced, for God strengthened and blessed me every time; He held me, taught me, and blessed me in countless ways. I have learned this treasured lesson throughout my life, and I am still learning it – that God is always present with me. He does not exempt us from trials, but for all who love and trust Him, He does something far better. When we call upon Him in faith, He meets us in our trials, and His presence is very real.

The burden is lightened through intercessory prayer
It humbles me when someone says they are praying for me. This means more to me than my words can express, for I know it is a major reason for the strength I am receiving. When we intercede for someone, we join them in the struggle and help carry the load.

The apostle Paul was vividly aware of his own need, for his life was often hard. He urged people to pray for him. He knew he needed prayer support. He believed, as do I and as I hope you do, that intercessory prayer is a powerful and essential gift. None of us have sufficient strength on our own, nor can we consistently escape what would destroy us. Knowing this, Paul urged the church to pray for him and wrote, *I know that through your prayers and the help of the Spirit of Jesus Christ this will turn out for my deliverance* (Philippians 1:19). Amen. I too know that this is true.

Paul also knew that his prayers and the prayers offered on his behalf should always be only for God's will. Paul invited prayers from the church of Rome that *by God's will*, he would soon be with them (Romans 15:32). He understood that our prayer requests must follow the pattern of Christ, who taught us to desire and pray, *Your will be done* (Matthew 6:10). Jesus showed us how to pray, when he prayed to

His Father and surrendered to His will, *yet not as I will, but as you will* (Matthew 26:39).

Can we admit that it would not be good for us if our prayers were always answered the way we think is best when we prayed? After all, our perspective is limited and our wisdom is finite. But as we pray, we look to the One whose perspective is perfect, whose love is proven, and whose wisdom is infinite. We can therefore determine to trust God, desiring and believing that His perfect will for us is for our good and for His glory.

This confidence blesses me. In the midst of my struggles, the burden is often lightened through intercessory prayer. The assurance that others are praying with me and for me is a sweet gift worth more to me than perfect health or any transient blessing.

God carries our worries for those whom we love
I marvel at my dear wife Helen, for she manifests such strength through all of this, a sure testimony of her faith and of God's sustaining her so well. My Lord has often reminded me that He has her tenderly and protectively in His loving hands, and He will never let her go. Helen has been a true and faithful witness to me and to so many, and I am reminded that God's plan for her is good.

God reminds me of this truth regarding everyone whom I love, for He loves them too with an everlasting love, and He promises to always care for them. As this truth seeps into my soul, my worries for those whom I love melts away like snow in the spring sunshine.

In His Sermon on the Mount, Jesus taught that those who trust and follow Him have no reason for worry. This is a great blessing to all who believe and belong to Jesus. He taught in Matthew 6:25-34 that because God provides for us as we seek Him first, we have no reason to worry about anything.

I have seen this promise fulfilled in my life, and lately I have heard these promises applied to the church family that I have loved, and to Helen, our children, grandchildren and our extended family and friends. I will not worry for those whom I love, for my God holds them close, and He promises that He always will.

God says He does not want us to worry about those whom we love.

In the midst of our struggles, God lifts our worries and assures us that He carries them, and He always will. God has promised and He is and will be forever faithful to be with those we love and to care for them, just as He has always cared for you and me. I rest in this assurance.

How does God bless us in the midst of our struggles? In these ways and more:

1. God continues to provide divine appointments.
2. His presence with us is real.
3. Our burden is lightened through intercessory prayer.
4. God carries our worries for those whom we love.

FOR REFLECTION

What divine appointments have you experienced in the midst of your struggles? How have you experienced His real presence in a time of personal struggle? When has your burden been lightened through intercessory prayer? How has God's promise to care for all whom you love affected your worry about them? If you struggle with worry because of your struggles, ask God to help you with this and He surely will.

35

ON THE WONDERFUL GRACE OF JESUS

April 20, 2019

Oh *the wonderful grace of Jesus!* By God's grace we are offered sweet opportunity to remember the incredible events of the cross and the empty tomb of the Lord Jesus Christ by which we may be forever changed. I know this story well, and perhaps you do also, for it is the essence of our Christian faith. For all who believe it, everything changes.

In every year of my life journey, I have either attended or led Holy Week services to remember and commemorate the greatest events of human history through which salvation and eternal life have been freely offered to all who believe and receive the good news of Jesus. But this year's observance has been different for me, because my illness keeps me from corporate worship, as I deal with ongoing fatigue and other symptoms, and immune deficiency that requires me to avoid crowds.

As I grieve this loss, the Holy Spirit reminds me that nothing can deter true worship, as I remember and believe the following truths about the wonderful grace of Jesus.

Remember and believe WHO by grace broke into human history
God did. *He was in the world, and the world was made through him, yet the world did not know him . . . The Word became flesh and dwelt*

among us, and we have seen His glory, glory as of the only Son from the Father, full of grace and truth (John 1:10, 14).

Almighty God came to us! How amazing and how wonderful!

Remember and believe WHAT by grace Christ accomplished
Jesus suffered and died for sinful humanity; He bore the judgment that we all deserve. By His perfect sacrifice, He offers the priceless gifts of salvation and everlasting life to all who believe in Him. His Word declares it clearly.

> *Behold, the Lamb of God, who takes away the sin of the world.* (John 1:29)
>
> *For God so loved the world, that He gave His only Son, that whoever believes in Him should not perish but have eternal life.* (John 3:16)
>
> *I am the Good Shepherd. I know my own and my own know me, just as the Father knows me and I know the Father, and I lay down my life for the sheep . . . My sheep hear my voice and I know them, and they follow me. I give them eternal life, and they shall never perish, and no one will snatch them out of my hand.* (John 10:14-15, 27-28).

Jesus Christ willingly gave His life for my salvation and yours – how remarkable and life-changing.

Remember and believe WHY by grace He accomplished it
God's love prompted His sacrifice.

> *By this we know love, that He laid down His life for us.* (1 John 3:16)
>
> *God shows His love for us in that while we were still sinners, Christ died for us.* (Romans 5:8)

The Lord's great love led Him to lay down His life for me and for you – how sacrificial and very personal.

Remember and believe HOW by grace He has transformed us
We who believe and receive Jesus Christ are accepted and forgiven; we can therefore live our lives with newfound purpose as we serve our Lord and enjoy enduring personal relationship with Him.

> *Therefore since we have been justified by faith, we have peace with God through our Lord Jesus Christ. Through Him we have also obtained access by faith into this grace in which we stand, and we rejoice in the hope of the glory of God.* (Romans 5:1-2)

We are therefore forgiven and restored – how freeing and joy-giving.

Remember and believe WHERE by grace we will forever be
We who are in Christ Jesus now are destined to be forever in His holy presence.

> *He who raised the Lord Jesus will raise us also with Jesus and bring us with you into His presence . . . So we do not lose heart. Though our outer self is wasting away, our inner self is being renewed day by day. For this light momentary affliction is preparing for us an eternal weight of glory beyond all comparison, as we look not to the things that are seen but to the things that are unseen. For the things that are seen are transient, but the things that are unseen are eternal.* (2 Corinthians 4:14, 16-18)

I therefore know that all of my present struggles are temporary. I also know that I will be forever at home in His holy presence – how reassuring and motivating.

This week my Easter memories took me back to many wonderful observances. As a little boy, I stood on a hilltop in the snow and watched the sunrise on Easter morning. I sang with my family and congregation "Up From the Grave He Arose" and listened as my dad proclaimed the good news that Jesus Christ is risen.

I recall an Easter Sunrise service in 1994; I stood with Marines on

Mount Fuji in Japan, as the bright red sun arose below us, and we celebrated the triumphant resurrection of our Savior. Twenty years later, in 2014, I led a sunrise service on the beach at Guantanamo Bay, Cuba, and rejoiced in the victory of our Lord over sin and death.

In 2016, I preached the Easter message to two to three thousand Marine recruits at Parris Island. How God moved among us that day. I recall many precious times through the years as a pastor, when I declared the glorious news of Jesus's resurrection.

All of these memories and many more point me now toward a glorious future through the wonderful grace of Jesus. If you also remember and believe, if you have received by faith the gospel of the Lord Jesus Christ, then you too know by faith that when time is no more and we are forever together in His holy presence, we will remember and celebrate His grace. But let us not wait until then to rejoice in the Lord. Let us worship Him now. Let us worship Him today in this moment and in this season, remembering and believing:

1. WHO by grace broke into human history – God did.

2. WHAT by grace Christ accomplished – Our salvation.

3. WHY by grace He accomplished it – His great love.

4. HOW by grace He transformed us – We are accepted, forgiven, and restored.

5. WHERE by grace we will forever be – Forever in His holy presence.

Oh, the wonderful grace of Jesus.

FOR REFLECTION

What memories do you treasure of the Easter messages that especially impacted you? Reflecting on the Who, What, Why, How, and Where of the grace of Jesus, how is this blessing you now in your current circumstances? How might God be guiding you so you may realize the wonderful grace of Jesus? Ask God to help you in this, and He surely will.

36

ON HARD STRUGGLES AND TRUE FAITH

April 28, 2019

Hard struggles and true faith are not foreign to each other. Faith in God does not exempt us from hard struggles. Rather, faith in the true and living God allows us to face and endure trials, even to rejoice in the midst of them. Faith allows us to experience firsthand God's presence with us, as He works good in our lives and brings glory and honor to His name. I have learned and relearned this lesson, and am learning it anew at this time.

I am struggling right now, and you probably are too. The ultimate reason we all struggle while on this earthly journey is rooted in the repercussions of humanity's rebellion against the Lord our Maker, as described in the first three chapters of Genesis. God warned our first ancestor, Adam, that sin would bring consequences. Sin is the reason creation is broken and why we now have cancer, disease, hatred, spiritual darkness, broken hearts, broken relationships, devastations, calamities, sorrows, sighing, and death. None of us are exempt from such struggles. We share this story, which explains why creation groans and suffers.

But with infinite, matchless love and amazing grace, Almighty God promised to do something about it. And in the fullness of time, He did. God fulfilled His promise by sending His only begotten Son to be our Messiah and Redeemer. All who by grace and through faith believe in the Lord Jesus Christ, receiving and loving Him, are forgiven (Ephesians 2:8-9). Having been set free from sin, we enter into restored relationship with God as His own beloved children (John 1:12).

Our amazing personal relationship with the Lord of all is not merely for a little while. It is forever, thus transcending all of our current and temporary struggles (John 3:16). Because of who Jesus Christ is, and because of what He has accomplished for us by His substitutionary death and victorious resurrection, our faith in Him triumphs over all of our struggles. We can look ahead with hope as we eagerly and expectantly long to *obtain the freedom of the glory of the children of God* (Romans 8:21). I will therefore give thanks to God for my struggles, for by His grace they are strengthening my faith.

I do not mean to suggest that dealing with this illness is easy. In fact, it is hard. The cancer I am fighting and the cumulative effects of many months of chemotherapy have produced some difficult symptoms, including decreased strength, increased fatigue, peripheral neuropathy, and sore and swollen feet and ankles. I experience reduced mobility and am using a cane. These realities are part of my struggle.

Because my oncologists concur that stem cell transplant (SCT) offers me the best hope for any durable remission, I have agreed to pursue it. I am therefore undergoing a number of medical exams and evaluations to determine if I am a good candidate. It is still possible I will not be accepted for an SCT. Then the next treatment steps would be determined. Though such uncertainties are part of the struggle now, I can state with confidence that I know I am not in this alone, nor will I ever be, for my Lord is with me. He sustains and holds me; He reminds me of His faithfulness and love. I am therefore not afraid but am at peace in the struggle. Do I like it? No. But can I see the hand of God in it? Yes, I certainly can.

I have gratefully witnessed God's provision and care for Helen. In sincere faith she leans upon her Lord, who is with her now and will surely be with her whatever may come. We can both tell you firsthand that having faith in the Lord makes all the difference in this world when dealing with present struggles. We pray that in any struggles you face or will face, you will know beyond all doubt that you are not in this alone and that faith in the Lord will be your strength too.

Some suggest that if we have sufficient faith, we should be having no struggles but only victories. But this is not biblical or true. In the Old Testament, a man named Job and many other faithful servants of God had great faith, yet they suffered loss. In the New Testament, the apostles and many early Christians trusted the Lord, and yet they suffered much.

Christians throughout history and even today throughout the world have faced imprisonment, torture, or even martyrdom for following Jesus. No one is exempt from sorrow and death. Jesus reminded us that God has a greater purpose than to exempt His children from suffering. Our Lord pointed to a cross, a vivid symbol of suffering and death, and He said, *If anyone would come after me, let him deny himself and take up his cross daily and follow me* (Luke 9:23).

Living by faith in the Lord Jesus is not about escaping all the struggles of this life. Rather, having faith in Jesus means welcoming Him into our struggles where we can experience His presence, His peace, and the delightful assurance of His promises. Faith in the Lord Jesus Christ brings real hope and help and heavenly perspective. Such treasures far exceed the painful costs of our temporary struggles.

Having faith in Jesus enables us to experience firsthand the perspective that was expressed by the apostle Paul when he wrote, *For this light momentary affliction is preparing for us an eternal weight of glory beyond all comparison, as we look not to the things that are seen but to the things that are unseen. For the things that are seen are transient, but the things that are unseen are eternal* (2 Corinthians 4:17-18). Yes! I agree!

FOR REFLECTION

When have you wrestled with the tension between hard struggles and true faith? How has your faith made a difference in dealing with your struggles? How does 2 Corinthians 4:17-18 apply to your current situation? How may God help you experience His grace whenever you face hard times? Ask God to help you in this, and He surely will.

37

ON HELPING SOMEBODY BY PRAYING

May 5, 2019

Along this multiple myeloma journey, God has connected me with many friends who have blessed me. One such friend is Bud, who also fights this disease. He loves the Lord, so we are blessed to lean on Him together. One way Bud has blessed me is by sharing DVD movies from his collection. Several of these are based on real events that demonstrate and proclaim the good news of Jesus Christ.

One such movie, *Miracles from Heaven*, is based on the true story of the Beam family whose ten-year-old daughter Anna had a rare and incurable disease. At one point in the story, Anna had fallen thirty feet into the center of a hollowed-out tree. She was unconscious and unresponsive; it took emergency responders more than three hours to extricate her from the tree.

While responders worked feverishly to rescue Anna, her mom knelt by the tree and cried out to God. Her husband joined her, as did Anna's sisters. Other friends and relatives soon joined them in prayer; they knelt around that tree and interceded for Anna. Don't you know, God heard and answered their prayers for that little girl? Miracles happened. No spoiler here, but be assured that we know and serve a personal, loving, miracle-working God. There is nothing our God cannot do!

Through the years I have been reminded that it is our privilege to participate in God's miracle-working grace by praying. When we pray prayers of faith for each other, in agreement with one another, and with our Lord, we are like the believers gathered around that tree, desperate for God, pleading for His mercies and trusting for His grace. With infinite love our God hears and answers the prayers of His children.

The apostle Paul understood his own great need. He faced tremendous challenges and difficulties, as many followers of Jesus Christ in his time did. He wrote to Christians in Corinth and urged them to help him by praying: *You also must help us by prayer, so that many will give thanks on our behalf for the blessing granted us through the prayers of many* (2 Corinthians 1:11).

Amen. Whenever God lays upon our heart to pray for someone in need, it is not to prompt us to worry about them. It is instead so we will pray for them. And when we answer His call to pray for that person or situation, we are helping in the work of God. It is quite amazing that God blesses us in this way, as a part of what He is doing for His glory. With this in mind, I have told God how grateful I am for every person who has prayed for me. Thank you!

Regarding the cancer I am now fighting, my deep longing is not that my way is made easy. Rather, I pray that God will be glorified. Will you join me in this prayer? I believe in miracles, for believing in God requires it. I have seen the mighty power of God demonstrated in amazing ways. God could be glorified through my miraculous healing; He could restore strength and health to me for more years of fruitful service. If this is His glorious purpose, it is what I ask for and pray, "Yes Lord, let it be!"

He could also be glorified by my continuous struggle, as I lean upon Him and testify of His grace through it all. If this is His will, it is what I desire and pray, "Yes Lord, let it be!" My deepest longing is that God is glorified, and toward that end I am praying, and I ask you to please pray.

Your prayers are requested this week, as on Friday I will return to the Dana Farber Cancer Institute in Boston for a consultation and to continue to be evaluated for a potential stem cell transplant. I do not yet know what the outcome will be, as my response to chemotherapy has been atypical. Please pray with me for God's wisdom and healing and ultimately that God will receive the glory. Thank you for joining me around this tree. Your prayers are a great help to Helen and me, and we are grateful.

FOR REFLECTION

How and when have you recognized that you have been helped by the prayers of others? How have you seen your prayers making a difference in helping others? Why was Paul asking for help through the prayers of the church? When have you requested such help, and what help are you asking for now? How seriously have you regarded the blessing of intercessory prayer, and what is your desire going forward? Ask God to help you in this, and He surely will.

38

ON WAITING WELL

May 13, 2019

Waiting is part of life for all of us. We wait for something to happen or for someone to act. We apply to a school or for a job or for a place to live, or we wait for news; sometimes the waiting seems to take forever. We arrive for an appointment; they tell us to wait. We look at the calendar or clock and wonder what is taking so long. We endure a test; then we wait for results. We arrive at the bedside of someone we dearly love, and we wait.

And as we wait, we pray. We ask God and wonder, when will change come? When will healing come? When will I see returns on my investment? When will I receive what I am longing for? When will my direction be made clear? When will joy return? And we wait.

Along my journey with multiple myeloma, I have experienced a lot of waiting. This has prompted prayerful reflections on what it means to wait well. Sometimes we can wait with anxiety, fear, or despondency. How much better it is to wait with hope, trust, and joy. Recently, in my waiting, I prayerfully focused on three biblical lessons on waiting for positive change.

Haven't we all longed for positive change? I have been longing for more strength. I am waiting to get better. It was ten weeks ago, with much hopeful anticipation, that I went to the Dana Farber Cancer

Institute (DFCI) in Boston to discuss a potential stem cell transplant (SCT), as this was the recommended means of my getting better. They told me that I was not yet a candidate for an SCT, as some of my blood work was going in the wrong direction, and the cancer cell count was too high for an SCT to be successful.

I faced a choice that day between anxiety and hope. The doctor prescribed another chemotherapy drug to be added to my drug regimen. I was to take it intravenously for nine weeks and then return for reassessment. Last Monday was my ninth treatment, and I was anxious to learn if there was measurable improvement. I have been waiting for positive change.

The side effects of the various drugs I have been on have left me feeling weaker, but that is okay with me if it is for a positive purpose. Though I prefer for positive change to come quickly, I have had to wait. This week when I returned to DFCI for reassessment, they affirmed that positive change has occurred. The myeloma (cancer) cells in my blood have decreased by 60% over the last nine weeks. They then said that more waiting is still needed, so that chemotherapy can reduce the myeloma cells even further. The Lord has been teaching me three lessons about waiting well for positive change:

Lesson 1: Waiting well means choosing hope over anxiety.
Biblical hope is not wishful thinking. Rather, it is confident expectation in the Lord Himself, and thus in the certainty of His promises. The psalmist affirmed that such hope is well placed, for as we wait for the Lord who is able, we are effectually choosing hope over anxiety.

> *I believe that I shall look upon the goodness of the LORD in the land of the living! Wait for the LORD; be strong, and let your heart take courage; wait for the LORD!* (Psalm 27:13-14)

Waiting for clear direction: Aren't we all longing and waiting for clear direction? I am. As I have mentioned, for some time now an SCT has been described by my oncologists as the preferred course of treatment for me, offering me the best hope of a potential durable remission. Because medical opinions can vary on whether an SCT is the best course with the significant risks involved, and because this treatment would be very hard on me physically, I have asked my Lord for clear direction, and I have waited.

Because all of my oncologists are now recommending the SCT, I have prayerfully agreed to pursue this course of treatment if and when I am medically cleared for it. So last week my VA oncologist wrote a referral to formally recommend me for a stem cell transplant. A package with various evaluations and test results will go to a VA Transplant Review Team for their review and decision. If they give a favorable decision, they will want Helen and me to go to Nashville as soon as possible and probably stay for a couple months. I continue to pray, and I am waiting for clear directions. I thank you for praying with me and for me.

Lesson 2: Waiting well is choosing trust over fear.
We can make this choice when we know and love the Lord, for we know that He loves us and He will surely lead us well. Can you imagine loving parents leading their children to play in traffic or in a field filled with landmines? Of course not! Children who know their parents love them will trust their parents to lead them well. Waiting well therefore means choosing trust over fear.

> *Trust in the LORD with all your heart, and do not lean on your own understanding. In all your ways acknowledge him, and he will make straight your paths.* (Proverbs 3:5-6)

Waiting for longed-for reunions: Aren't we all waiting and longing for a reunion with somebody? I certainly am. With a diagnosis of multiple myeloma and immune deficiencies, I have had to take careful precautions to evade illness. I have therefore avoided crowds, especially public transportation. This deprivation has increased my longing for reunions with people I love.

Since our fourth grandson, Theo Stephen Gammon, was born in January, I have longed to see and hold him. I long for all of our children, grandchildren, and extended family. I also long to reunite with church family and Christian brothers and sisters who are family to me. While waiting for precious reunions, I am sometimes tempted with despondency, for being apart is hard. But God reminds me to wait with joyful anticipation of longed-for reunions that will still come.

Because the stem cell transplant is likely to be soon, which will necessitate reducing my social contacts even more, Helen and I intend to risk a flight to Minnesota this Friday, taking precautions on the way. We hope to see our sons Jonathan and Carl, our daughter-in-law Jackie, our grandson Archer, and our newest grandson Theo. We appreciate your prayers for a blessed time together and for God's strength and protection through it all.

I have been awaiting for this reunion and soon it will happen. This will be a foretaste of the longing and joy of reunions that will occur when we arrive in heaven. We will then see the Lord in the fullness of His glory and know that we will forever be with Him and all the saints who have gone before us. Such reunions are so worth waiting for.

Lesson 3: Waiting well is choosing joy over despondency.
While we wait, we can choose joy over despondency. This happens as we believe the promises of God and anticipate the fulfillment of His promises. When Jesus told His beloved disciples that He would soon leave them physically, they were confused and sad. But after His resurrection and prior to His ascension to heaven, Jesus instructed them to purposefully wait for the coming Holy Spirit. So they did. They waited, but not with despondency. They waited with joy in the promise of the Lord.

> *And while staying with them He ordered them not to depart from Jerusalem, but to wait for the promise of the Father.*
> (Acts 1:4)

So, our waiting continues. By God's grace, let us be waiting well, which includes:
1. Waiting for Positive Change – Not with Anxiety, but with Hope.
2. Waiting for Clear Direction – Not with Fear, but with Trust.
3. Waiting for Longed-for Reunions – Not with Despondency, but with Joy in what will soon come.

FOR REFLECTION

What are you waiting for now, and what has it been like for you to wait? What does it mean for you to wait for positive change with hope not anxiety? How can you wait for clear direction from the Lord and maintain trust not fear? What will it mean for you to wait for longed-for reunions with joy not despondency? Ask God to help you in this, and He surely will.

39

ON PROMISED REWARDS EXCEEDING TEMPORARY RISKS

May 26, 2019

Risk-taking is part of life for all of us. I have taken many risks in life, and so have you. When I contemplated joining the military, I wrestled with that decision in part because I knew there were significant risks. I did not know where it would lead me, how often or how long I would be away from my family, or if I would be called into harm's way. In the years that followed, I recall several times when I knew I was taking a risk, but I did it anyway.

I remember fast-roping out of a hovering helicopter, presiding at a reenlistment ceremony on the deck of a sunken ship ninety feet below the surface, and participating in SPIE Rigging extraction (Special Patrol Insertion/Extraction). That involved swinging on a rope with seven Marines beneath a helicopter flying 1200 feet above the ground. I remember rappelling over a ninety-foot-high cliff, and more. In all these cases, I judged that the rewards exceeded the temporary risks.

When I think of the risks I have taken in life, my mind inevitably goes back to the day when I was twenty years old, and I asked Helen if she would marry me. How my heart raced. I knew I was taking a risk, for we could not possibly foresee our future. But I am forever glad I took that risk, and I am so glad she said yes, for the promised rewards have infinitely exceeded all temporary risks.

Last week I took another risk – this time to board a plane for Minnesota. This was the first time I had boarded a plane since I was diagnosed with active multiple myeloma. Because of my compromised immune system, doctors and nurses cautioned me to avoid public places where I might be exposed to illness. This precluded air travel, so medically speaking, boarding a plane is risky for me.

But in Minnesota I have two sons, a daughter-in-law, and two grandsons, one of whom I had not yet met. I have missed them all greatly. Because I may soon undergo a stem cell transplant, which will prevent me from traveling thereafter for as long as a year, I weighed the risks. And because promised rewards were so great, I decided to go.

The trip was hard for me. On the flight I felt weak and sick. By the time we arrived in Minnesota early on Saturday, I had a bad cough, and by Saturday evening I had a rising fever. While there I spent much of the time resting in bed. We returned home late Wednesday, and on Thursday I visited a physician who confirmed that I now have a bronchial infection. An X-ray revealed a partially deflated left lung.

Despite these difficulties, the trip was worth it to me. The promised rewards have far exceeded the struggle. The time spent with family was priceless. I laughed and played with my grandson Archer, who is now almost four years old. I met and held my newest grandson, Theo, for the first time. I loved the time together and conversations with our son Carl, and our son Jonathan and his wife Jackie. I loved the time on the entire journey with Helen. The trip was not easy, and yes, it was risky. But the rewards were greater.

This is a picture of life, which has prompted three reflections on risk-taking as we live for Jesus:

Growing in Christ necessitates risk-taking.
In his excellent book *Experiencing God*, Henry Blackaby said, "You cannot stay where you are and go with God."[6] In other words, we must all risk change if we want to grow with God. Leaving our spiritual comfort

---

6   Henry Blackaby and Claude V. King, *Experiencing God: Knowing and Doing the Will of God* (Nashville: B&H Publishing, 2014), 247.

zone can feel scary to us, but it is necessary if we want to grow and realize our God-given potential. And let us remember that our God has promised to always be with us, protect us, and provide everything we need along the way.

Still, some of us may be nervous about trusting Christ; we might be fearful of what it means or of what He might require of us. We can be reluctant to risk. But in a relationship with Jesus Christ, there is room for only one Lord. He is Lord, and we are not.

When we realize how wonderful our Lord is and how amazing and true His promises, we will gladly say, "Yes Lord, I am wholly yours. I will go wherever you send me. I will say whatever you give me to say, and I will be whatever you want me to be." The promised rewards of personal relationship with Jesus Christ far transcend all temporary risks.

Jesus often warned His disciples against risk avoidance. He said to those who would follow Him, *You will be delivered up even by parents . . . and some of you they will put to death* (Luke 21:16). He did not say this so we would run away from Him. He wants us to run to Him.

He also said, *If anyone would come after me, let him deny himself and take up his cross and follow me. For whoever would save his life will lose it, but whoever loses his life for my sake will find it. For what will it profit a man if he gains the whole world and forfeits his soul? Or what shall a man give in return for his soul?* (Matthew 16:24-26).

It does sound risky, doesn't it? Well, it is risky. Notice again that Jesus had said, *some of you they will put to death*. Reflect on that for a moment. He wants us to know that this could very well be you or me. We just don't know. But such is the nature of risk. Following Jesus Christ means laying it all down for Him, for He has come to mean more to us than anything else in life. Growing in Christ requires risk-taking.

Christ calls His followers to take risks for Him and His kingdom.
Avoidance of risks and difficulties cannot become our goal. The philosophy of this world invites us to secure and maximize our own comfort. But Jesus Christ never taught this. Rather, to His timid disciples who wavered on the margin of risky obedience, Jesus said: *I tell you, my friends, do not fear those who kill the body, and after that have nothing more that they can do* (Luke 12:4). In other words, our Lord calls us to

count the cost and then take bold risks for Him and His kingdom, for great will be our eternal reward.

Paul's words to Timothy remain true today: *All who desire to live a godly life in Christ Jesus will be persecuted* (2 Timothy 3:12). *All* means all, doesn't it? So this includes you and me. Does Jesus intend for us to allow these realities and warnings to become an excuse for inaction? Surely not. Rather, He calls us to step out in faith and take risks for His sake.

The eternal rewards of obeying Christ exceed all temporary troubles.

Rooted in deep faith in the Lord Jesus, the apostle Paul testified of this truth from his own personal struggles when he wrote, *For this light momentary affliction is preparing for us an eternal weight of glory beyond all comparison* (2 Corinthians 4:17).

Paul learned what we are now blessed to learn, that there is a qualitative and quantitative difference between our *temporary troubles* and *eternal glory*. Though he had been repeatedly beaten and jailed, and once left for dead, he often took bold risks for the kingdom of God. Though he suffered much because of it, Paul still referred to all such trials as *light and momentary afflictions*.

Paul could describe his struggles in this way because through eyes of faith he saw something far greater. He glimpsed the eternal rewards waiting for him and for every Christian. The transcendent glory of heaven was and is *beyond all comparison*.

Have you and I learned this too? Are we learning it now? Do we believe it? If so, we will do what Paul did. We will take risks for the kingdom of God. We will risk sharing our faith. We will risk going beyond our own comfort zone. We will take risks for our Lord, because we have come to know and believe these enduring truths:

1. Growing in Christ necessitates risk-taking.

2. Christ calls His followers to boldly take risks for Him and His kingdom.

3. Eternal rewards of obeying Christ far exceed all temporary troubles.

FOR REFLECTION

How risk averse have you been in your walk with God? Why does growing in Christ necessitate risk-taking? How does Christ's call for His followers to take risks for Him and for His kingdom apply to your life now? Looking ahead, what are some implications for your life of living the truth that eternal rewards from obeying Christ will far exceed all temporary troubles? Ask God to help you in this, and He surely will.

Meeting Theo   With grandsons Archer and Theo

Helen and me with sons Carl and Jonathan and grandson Archer

Helen and me with son Jonathan, daughter-in-law Jackie, and grandsons Archer and Theo

40

ON FINDING CALM IN A LINGERING STORM

June 2, 2019

Lately I feel like I am in a lingering storm. But storms come to all of us in life, don't they? The weather is not always sunny, nor are the winds always fair. Strong gales of illness and weakness can come and raging waves of grief and loss can pound the shores of our hearts. The driving rains of pain and disappointment can raise flood waters of despair. All of these are hard for us to endure.

In my own experience, I find it easier to endure a storm today if I know the forecast for tomorrow is for fairer skies. But what happens when a storm lingers? How do we endure it, and how can we then find calm?

Eight months ago I was diagnosed with active multiple myeloma. This might not sound like extensive time to you, but to me it has felt like a lingering storm. The inclement weather has not cleared, and the wind and waves and rain have persisted. After these many months, I am weaker. It seems like it has been a long time since I have felt well. And recent blood labs have shown that my response to chemotherapy is not as good as we had hoped. This is discouraging. Though I have longed for this storm to lift, it has not – at least not in the way I would choose.

But throughout this lingering storm, I have heard the voice of my

Lord, and I have experienced His presence very near. I can attest to you that it is far better to be in a lingering storm with the awareness of the Lord's nearness than to be in calm winds and fair skies but separate from the Lord.

So what are we to do when a storm lingers? Where are we to find calm? Peace can be found by faith and in personal relationship with the One who made us and who knows and loves us. Those who have come to know the Lord Jesus Christ and who therefore trust and rest in Him find firsthand that this treasure supersedes all that is going on around them. Though the storm may rage, in the center, in the eye of the storm, our Lord is powerfully and personally present. This is where calm is found.

Through the years I have been blessed to learn and sing worship hymns that express profound truths and a response of faith to the Almighty. Because many such hymns are planted in my heart, the Lord sometimes brings them to my memory to remind me of His timeless truths. One hymn that has been ringing in my heart lately that I have been praying and singing to my Lord is "Be Still My Soul" by Jean Sibelius and Veikko Antero Koskenniemi. Two stanzas in particular invite me to calm in the lingering storm. I share it here, along with His invitation to believe and live as the hymn suggests.

> Be still, my soul: thy God doth undertake
>   To guide the future, as He has the past.
> Thy hope, thy confidence let nothing shake,
>   All now mysterious shall be bright at last.
> Be still, my soul: the waves and winds still know,
>   His voice who ruled them while He dwelt below.
>
> Be still, my soul: begin the song of praise,
>   On earth, be leaving, to Thy Lord on high;
> Acknowledge Him in all thy words and ways,
>   So shall He view thee with a well pleased eye.
> Be still my soul: the Sun of life divine,
>   Through passing clouds shall but more brightly shine

A passage of Scripture that has blessed me on this theme is Psalm 107. This Psalm does not present an unreachable portrait of life the way it ought to be. Rather, it offers a picture of what life is and what it can be. For all of us life includes failures, struggles, and storms. But here we see what people of faith are able and blessed to do.

> *Then they cried to the Lord in their trouble, and He delivered them from their distress. He made the storm be still, and the waves of the sea were hushed. Then they were glad that the waters were quiet, and He brought them to their desired haven. Let them thank the Lord for His steadfast love, for His wondrous works to the children of man! Let them extol Him in the congregation of the people, and praise Him in the assembly of the elders.* (Psalm 107:28-32)

Four lessons from this passage speak to my heart on what to do in a lingering storm:

Know Whom to call on – and do it:
Then they cried to the Lord in their trouble. That's the thing about being in a lingering storm; we come to the realization that we are in trouble and need help. God wants us to know that we can always call upon Him, but knowing this is not sufficient alone. We must *do* it. We must personally exercise faith by crying to God, "I need you Lord and I turn to you now."

Believe and see what God can do:
And He delivered them from their distress. He made the storm be still, and the waves of the sea were hushed. Then they were glad that the waters were quiet, and He brought them to their desired haven. This prayer of faith asks God to see us through. To *see* what God can do we must *believe* what God can do. In my own lingering storm, my Lord has often reminded me that He will bring me safely to my desired haven. What is my longed for destination? I am longing for God to receive the glory in and through my life until my last breath. I long for the fulfillment of

His promise of everlasting life with Him in heaven. Because I believe God will do this in the midst of this storm, I can experience calm.

Thank God for His steadfast love:
Let them thank the Lord for His steadfast love, for His wondrous works to the children of man! No matter what storms we are in now, or what storms we have come through, or what storms lie ahead, we who know the Lord Jesus Christ and the triumphs of His grace have cause for much thankfulness, especially for His steadfast love as expressed in wondrous ways. As I look back over the years of my life, including in this lingering storm, I am reminded that I have always experienced His love. For this I am forever thankful. Thankfulness brings His calm into the midst of any storm.

Praise God for Who He is:
Lift your focus from the storm to the All-Powerful God, *Let them extol Him in the congregation of the people, and praise Him in the assembly of the elders.* Praising God is our great privilege, for He alone is worthy. Praise lifts our focus from the storms that rage around us to the Eternal and Almighty God who is infinite in majesty, everlasting in glory, perfect in holiness, and praiseworthy in all His creation. Praise is making a faith decision to look beyond the raging winds of the lingering storms to give to the Lord something that only I can give – my praise. No one else can offer praise for me. I can choose to give it to God right here and right now in the midst of this lingering storm.

The experience of lingering storms can be hard for us, but we can thank God for bringing good in the midst of it. I thank God for these lessons on what to do in a lingering storm:

1. Know Whom to call on and do it.

2. Believe and see what God can do.

3. Thank God for His steadfast love.

4. Praise God for Who He is.

FOR REFLECTION

What lingering storms have you been in? If you know whom to call on, to what extent are you doing it? When have you experienced that to see what God can do, we must believe what God can do? When has thankfulness brought calm into your lingering storm? How does praise lift your focus from the storm to the Almighty? Ask God to help you in this, and He surely will.

41

ON NOT JOURNEYING TO DIFFICULT PLACES ALONE

June 9, 2019

Sometimes we find ourselves heading somewhere we do not want to go. In such times, it helps to know that we are not traveling this road alone, for we have family with us.

This week I recalled a particular Saturday evening in early June 1969, exactly fifty years ago. My parents and my older brother David had gone out for the evening, and I was home with my younger siblings. When the phone rang and I answered it, the caller asked to speak to my father. I reported that he was not at home, and I asked if I could give him a message. The answer was yes.

The caller asked for the scheduled time of the worship service the next morning at the Warren Baptist Church, in Warren, Maine, where my Dad served as pastor. After I answered the question, he asked me to inform my father that the pastoral search committee from yoked congregations in Fair Haven and Hydeville, Vermont, would be in attendance the next morning.

Because I had recently graduated from eighth grade and was excited about beginning high school with my friends, I was unhappy with this news. When my parents returned later that evening, I gave the message to my dad, and I let him know that I did not want to move to Vermont.

He reminded me that God directs us, and if He should lead us to move, He would go with us, and we would go together as a family. Though this assurance helped, I still did not want to move. But at the end of that summer, only three days before I started high school, we moved as a family to Fair Haven, Vermont. Though this was not what I wanted, it was precisely what God intended for us.

This sort of thing has occurred several times in my life. In the years that I served in the military, for example, I experienced several deployments that required me to be away from Helen and our children. Though this was always hard for me and for our family, and though inwardly I often resisted the absence, I learned that our heavenly Father always knows what His children need, and He faithfully provides.

When I was away on deployment, our extended family and local church loved and supported Helen and our children. Friendship and fellowship with other service members and dear Christian brothers and sisters were a blessing to me. No matter where we are going, or what we may feel about it, to know that we are not alone in this earthly journey helps us.

I have experienced this truth recently, for it appears I am headed to a place I am not sure I want to go – stem cell transplant. I have completed the last pre-test, and with no identified issues to preclude me from going forward, a referral has been made to a VA Transplant Review Board in Nashville for a decision that is expected soon.

If this is God's will for me, I will proceed, though I wish I did not have to. I understand this experience will be very hard, and some effects will be prolonged, so I wish it were unnecessary. I wish that God had killed every cancer cell, restored my immune system, and miraculously healed me. But I am reminded of my dad's words to me fifty years ago. I know I can trust God to lead, for He always goes with us. I also trust that wherever God leads me, I will have family. This truth comforts me.

Yesterday our daughter Amy and her six-year-old son Levi arrived at our home. They traveled from Wasilla, Alaska, to be with us for a few days, and Helen and I are loving it. Our grandson is full of energy, and we love having him here. We play games; he reads to me; and we enjoy great conversation. Helen and Amy enjoy time together, and Amy went with me as I received my chemotherapy treatment. We are family now and forever. My family knows that what I am going through now is hard, and they remind me that I am not in this alone.

The church does this, for we who are in Jesus Christ are family now and forever. Church is not *like* family; it *is* family. God is our Father, and by faith we have become brothers and sisters in Jesus Christ. Family is the primary way members of the early church identified themselves. In the New Testament letters, the term *brother* was the predominant descriptive word used among Christians to refer to other followers of the Lord. The church was referred to collectively as the *children of God* (2 Corinthians 6:18; John 1:12) or as the *family of God* (Ephesians 1:5; Hebrews 2:11).

Sharing life as family is therefore integral to experiencing church as the Lord intends. As God's family we are to always love, care, pray, forgive, support, weep, rejoice, uphold, and walk with one another through whatever struggles and challenges may come in this life, all for the praise and glory of our God.

This is how God lovingly cares for His children. We truly are not on this journey alone. He gives us family with whom we can share life, even in hard transitions. He reminds us that we do have family and that we are loved. But experiencing such blessing requires on our part willingness, vulnerability, and trust. We must choose to participate, and we must be real with each other; we must tell someone when life for us is hard or when we are experiencing painful consequences of our sin. We must risk loving, trusting, and sharing that we may know the blessing of being together as His family.

Again, I thank all who are praying for Helen and me and all who have reminded us that we are loved and not alone on this hard journey. Thank you! Let me remind you that in Jesus Christ you are not alone either, nor will you ever be. This is God's promise (Matthew 28:20; Hebrews 13:6), and I testify that it is wholly true.

FOR REFLECTION

When and how have you realized and experienced that you do not journey to difficult places alone? As the fullness of these blessings requires our willingness, vulnerability, and trust, how have you risked offering these, and what has been the effect in your life? How does this lesson apply to your circumstances? Ask God to help you in this, and He surely will.

42

ON WHAT TO DO WHEN FACING A DAUNTING TASK

June 16, 2019

This week I received a call from a nurse at the Providence VA Medical Center informing me that I have now been invited to Nashville to undergo a bone marrow (stem cell) transplant. She said that specific dates are not yet scheduled, but it should happen soon. I was glad for this call, as I have been asking for the Lord's direction. It now appears that this is His will for me.

Still, this feels to me like a very daunting task, for it promises to be hard physically. It may also be hard emotionally because of the prolonged isolation that will be required. I know that I will need to be extremely cautious and careful because of the risks of infection, which could be life threatening. Though at this point a stem cell transplant appears to be the right thing for me to do, it feels like a daunting task.

When Helen and I discussed this, she observed that in every transition of life I have felt this way. She reminded me that every time I accepted a new responsibility, I felt like I was in over my head. When I accepted the pastorate of one of the three local congregations I served, when I answered the call to a new military assignment, or when I accepted responsibility as Conference Minister (Executive Director) for the CCCC, my denomination of ministers and churches, I felt incapable of doing it in my own strength. She is right. I have always been and I remain today entirely dependent on the Lord. This realization is His grace to me.

I have prayed about what to do when facing a daunting task. The many biblical examples of God's people when they faced challenges far bigger than they were show us how the great love and grace of the Lord saw them through. God is the same today. He is ever faithful and true, and He teaches us what to do when we face a daunting task.

The biblical account through which God has been speaking to me this week is found in the book of Nehemiah. They were facing a grueling task. The city of Jerusalem was in rubble, and it needed to be rebuilt from the ground up. At first the people were highly motivated for this work of rebuilding, but the task was so great, and their strength was so limited, they soon became tired and discouraged.

Then strong opposition came, which often happens when we are doing what pleases God. Then, when they received threats of imminent attack and death, they were afraid. So what did they do? Nehemiah tells us: *We prayed to our God and set a guard as a protection against them day and night* (Nehemiah 4:9). Together they prayed to the Lord, and each of them did their part in defense against attack.

One verse in this story illustrates what I have experienced and what it can be like for anyone who is facing a formidable task: *The strength of those who bear the burdens is failing. There is too much rubble. By ourselves we will not be able to rebuild the wall* (Nehemiah 4:10).

The people were afraid, for they faced real dangers and threats. I can relate to this. Can you? They were tired and weak, for their own strength was failing them. I relate to this too. Can you? They felt overwhelmed by the magnitude of the situation, and they concluded that they were not up to this task. I relate to this too. Can you?

In the face of their fears, fatigue, and discouragement, Nehemiah spoke God's Word that still speaks today to me and you and to all who hear it. He said, *Do not be afraid of them. Remember the Lord, who is great and awesome, and fight for your brothers, your sons, your daughters, your wives, and your homes* (Nehemiah 4:14).

What then are we to do when we face a daunting task? The Lord reminds us to do these things:

Remember the Lord
Change your focus now. Do not ruminate on the obstacles and challenges that are before you. Rather, remember your God, who is great and awesome. Remember who He is, what He has done, and what He can do. And remember that He is with you now.

Release the fear
Let it go. When we remember the Lord, and choose to trust Him, our fears melt like ice in the spring sunshine.

Resume the work
Do your part. Faithfully fight for what is right, and willingly do whatever you have been called to do.

Nehemiah tells us of the astonishing miracle that took place in his day. Despite all the challenges and struggles encountered by the people who faced this task, as they remembered the Lord, released their fears, and resumed their work, *the wall was finished . . . in fifty-two days* (Nehemiah 6:15). This surprised everyone but God. And God received praise.

As I reflect on these things, excitement grows within me. I am remembering the Lord now and looking forward to God receiving praise for what He has done. I am releasing the fear now and looking forward with expectation to the peace He gives me. I am resuming the work now, determined to face whatever challenges may come. By His grace and in faith I am willing to do my part throughout this process.

In the face of their formidable task, Nehemiah led the people of his day to pray and remain diligent and on guard. He said, *We prayed to our God and set a guard as a protection against them day and night* (Nehemiah 4:9). With this in mind, Helen and I humbly request and appreciate your prayers as we prepare for a likely stem cell transplant. We will share scheduling details as they develop.

When on your life journey, you face a daunting task, please let other Christians know. This affords them the privilege of being part of a prayer team that expresses faith and utter dependence on God. It allows the great blessing of participation in giving God the praise He is due for all that He has done.

FOR REFLECTION

What daunting tasks have you faced or are you now facing that have reminded you that you cannot possibly do this alone? How have you learned in such times to remember the Lord? To release the fear? And to resume the work? How does this apply in your situation? Ask God to help you in this, and He surely will.

43

ON BELIEVING IN GOD AND ETERNITY

June 23, 2019

Believing in God includes believing in eternity. Some say that such faith is illusory, no more than wishful thinking, but I assure you that this is not so. I believe in God, for I have lived my life in personal relationship with Him, the One who created everything, including you and me. God has demonstrated His power, grace, and love. I believe in everlasting life because God whom I know and love is eternal, and He has made us in His image for everlasting life in Him.

As a young boy I was given the gift of faith. In my heart I believed in Jesus Christ, God's only begotten Son. He was very real to me then. I loved Him with childlike faith, and I understood even then that with much love the Lord gave His life on the cross for me and for all who will believe in Him. Throughout my adult life, He has been my dearest and ever-present friend. And because God is eternal, I know that my relationship with Him is eternal too.

This week I have been rejoicing in this truth, because in my flesh I am facing reminders of my physical mortality. These reminders do not scare me. Rather, I see them as a gift, for they point me to the eternal One whom I love and in whom I have put my trust.

As the time for my expected bone marrow (stem cell) transplant approaches, I have been reminded of the risks that are involved. The printed materials that were sent to me with information and guidance for making preparations encouraged me to have my will prepared and to discuss my wishes with my family if I die. Helen and I have applied this counsel, and we have been blessed by our conversations, for we both believe the promises of God.

Yesterday brought another reminder, as I visited the emergency room; I have developed yet another infection. Though I feel physically unwell, and though I have longed to be well again, by God's grace to me, I am not depressed by these struggles. Why not? Because I believe in God and in the sweet promise of eternal life with Him.

The apostle John summarized the good news of Jesus when he wrote, *And this is the testimony, that God gave us eternal life, and this life is in His Son. Whoever has the Son has life; whoever does not have the Son of God does not have life* (1 John 5:11-12). He also quoted the Lord Jesus who declared, *My sheep hear my voice, and I know them, and they follow me. I give them eternal life, and they will never perish, and no one will ever snatch them out of my hand* (John 10:27-28).

These Scriptures remind us that when God gives a gift to His children, He does not take it back. His gift to me and you and all who believe in Him is *not* life and relationship with Him only for a little while. His gift to us is everlasting life in personal relationship with Him forever. Surely this is cause for very great joy in our hearts.

I have been reflecting on three implications of this truth this week; may we all prayerfully accept by faith:

The brevity of this life:

James addressed the common propensity that is present even in the church for ignoring this truth when he wrote, *Come now, you who say, "Today or tomorrow we will go into such and such a town and spend a year there and trade and make a profit" – yet you do not know what tomorrow will bring. What is your life? For you are a mist that appears for a little time and then vanishes* (James 4:13-14).

No matter the number of years we are granted to live in our mortal body, in light of eternity our remaining days here are very few. This is true whether we acknowledge it now or not. But when we acknowledge it and profess our faith in the Lord Jesus Christ, He enables us to live each day thereafter with His eternal perspective. He blesses us with priorities that matter, with hope that endures beyond our last heartbeat, and with life and peace that carry us through our remaining days and into life everlasting.

The infinity of everlasting life:
This can be hard for us to grasp, because so far we have lived our lives within the finite limitations of this world. All of us are going to have a finite number of minutes, hours, days, and years to live in our mortal body, and we have a limited supply of strength and endurance. But heaven is not like that. Like God, eternal life is infinite. Moses said this as he prayed: *Lord, you have been our dwelling place in all generations. Before the mountains were brought forth, or ever you had formed the earth and the world, from everlasting to everlasting you are God* (Psalm 90:1-2).

In John's glorious vision of heaven as portrayed in Revelation, he saw and heard this majestic scene: *And I heard every creature in heaven and on earth and under the earth and in the sea, and all that is in them, saying, "To Him who sits on the throne and to the Lamb be blessing and honor and glory and might forever and ever!"* (Revelation 5:13).

Everlasting life is infinite in scope and duration, like God who lives *forever and ever*. Though we cannot fully grasp this, we can believe it. I do, and I pray you do too.

The certainty of God's promise:
The apostle John, who had often heard the Lord Jesus teach on this promise and believed it, encouraged believers in the Lord on the veracity of this promise when he wrote, *I write these things to you who believe in the name of the Son of God, that you may know that you have eternal life* (1 John 5:13).

Paul also wrote of this promise in the introduction of his letter to Titus: *Paul, a servant of God and an apostle of Jesus Christ, for the sake of the faith of God's elect and their knowledge of the truth, which accords with godliness, in hope of eternal life, which God, who never lies, promised before the ages began* (Titus 1:1-2).

God wants all who believe in Jesus to know in the depths of our souls that His promise of eternal life is true. Because I know this, I am now blessed beyond measure. Though none of us can know all that the future holds, we do know who holds the future. And because we believe in God, we also believe in eternity. By faith therefore, I accept the brevity of my life, the infinity of eternal life, and the certainty of God's promises. I believe in God and in eternity, and I pray that you do too.

FOR REFLECTION

Why does believing in God also mean believing in eternity? How does the evident truth of the brevity of life affect the way you are living each day? What does God's promise of everlasting life mean to you? How will God's promise of eternal life affect the way you will live in the days and years that ahead? Ask God to help you in this, and He surely will.

44

ON ALWAYS BEING READY TO PREACH, PRAY, OR DIE

June 30, 2019

My grandfather, Pastor Morley Durost, was a devoted follower of the Lord Jesus Christ and a minister of the gospel. When I was young, I learned much from his words and example. One lesson he taught me that has come to my mind countless times through the years is "Always be ready to preach, pray, or die."

Though we could be inclined to presume that such counsel applies to clergy, in fact it reflects biblical principles for all followers of Jesus. The essence of my grandfather's encouragement was to always be ready. The reason for our perpetual readiness is that we never know when our Lord may call upon us to do any one of these actions for Him.

Always be ready to preach
Several times over the years I have been called upon to preach with little or no notice. One such memorable occasion happened about five years ago. At that time I was stationed at Guantanamo Bay (GTMO) in Cuba, where I had been deployed for about six months. Our son Jonathan was graduating from Law School, and I did not want to miss it, so I flew to Virginia for a few days to join Helen and attend Jonathan's graduation.

The graduation was on Saturday morning. On Sunday morning we attended worship services together at a nearby church pastored by a friend. I had corresponded with my friend about the strong possibility of our attendance that day. Upon our arrival at the church that Sunday morning, it became evident that my earlier communications with the pastor had not been clear.

Helen, Jonathan, and I would be going our separate ways after the worship service, with Helen returning to Colorado, Jonathan remaining in Virginia, and me returning to GTMO. Because I was going to be traveling that day, I dressed in casual, comfortable clothes; my Bible was stowed away in my luggage.

After being ushered to our seats, and as the service was about to begin, Jonathan handed me the worship bulletin and pointed to the name of the person listed as today's guest preacher. The name was mine. Jonathan then asked me what I would do. I replied, "Hand me the Bible in the pew, as it appears I am preaching today!" I then bowed in prayer and asked the Holy Spirit to lead me.

Because I had walked with God for so long and His presence and His Word were changing me every day, I had plenty of good content to declare. I only needed God to anoint and lead me for this opportunity, which He did. With the Holy Spirit's leading, and with the Word of God as our guide, followers of Jesus Christ can always be ready to speak of His good news.

The apostle Peter urged Christians: *In your hearts honor Christ the Lord as holy, always being prepared to make a defense to anyone who asks you for a reason for the hope that is in you; yet do it with gentleness and respect.* (1 Peter 3:15). Did you notice the prerequisite Peter gave us for being prepared to share the truth of the gospel? It was and is *in your hearts honor Christ the Lord as holy* (ESV), or *in your hearts revere Christ as Lord* (NIV). In other words, we must first settle our own devotion to Christ and put Him first in our hearts. Then we will be ready to declare His gospel and make a defense of our faith. This is true for me and for you.

Peter's exhortation to *always be prepared to make a defense* of our faith was not directed only to church leaders. He addressed every person who belongs to Christ by faith. I rejoice that I am included in this number. How about you? We are all to be ready to share the reason for the hope that is in us.

The apostle Paul also urged Timothy to be always faithful to God's Word, no matter what opposition he faced. Paul said, *Preach the word, be ready in season and out of season, reprove, rebuke, and exhort, with complete patience and teaching* (2 Timothy 4:2). We are to be always ready to declare the good news of Jesus.

One of the hard consequences of my illness is that I have missed regular opportunities to preach the Word of God. The last time I preached God's Word in a Sunday service was nine months ago. That day was October 7, 2018, only a few days after I learned that I have active multiple myeloma and must begin chemotherapy. Two weeks later, I resigned from my pastoral office. Since then I have had to avoid crowds, including at church, in order to prevent potential exposure to illness. Not preaching has been a loss for this preacher.

But next Sunday, God willing, I will preach again at Church of The Apostles. I long to do this because Helen and I expect to depart soon for Nashville where we will stay for a couple months as I undergo my stem cell transplant. Then, after we return home, it will be many months before I am again able to attempt church attendance.

With this in mind, my desire was to be with my church family one more time before heading for Nashville. So next Sunday, I will once more worship and fellowship with our church family, and I will preach the good news of Jesus. For this your prayers are appreciated. Please pray that my health and stamina will allow this. Pray that God will anoint this time; may He be glorified through it all. May we always be ready to preach the good news of Jesus.

Always be ready to pray
Many thousands of times through the years I have been suddenly called upon to pray right here and right now. I hope this has also been true of you, for it is a privilege available to us all through our Lord Jesus Christ. Readiness to pray seems obvious and natural, as this is based on a key ingredient for all healthy personal relationships, which is clear communication.

Early in the life of the church, Paul encouraged Christians in

Thessalonica to *rejoice always, pray without ceasing, give thanks in all circumstances; for this is the will of God in Christ Jesus for you* (1 Thessalonians 5:16-18). The apostle's exhortation to *pray without ceasing* is directed to everyone in the Lord's church then and now, even you and me.

Prayer was a common theme in the New Testament. Paul urged the church in Colossae to *Continue steadfastly in prayer, being watchful in it with thanksgiving* (Colossians 4:2). And the writer of Hebrews urged, *Let us then with confidence draw near to the throne of grace, that we may receive mercy and find grace to help in time of need* (Hebrews 4:16).

Our Father in heaven wants every one of us to know that through faith in His Son, the Lord Jesus Christ, we have become His dearly loved children, so we are free to approach His heavenly throne. He invites us to come near. Knowing we can do this does not bring blessing by itself. The blessing comes when we actually do it, when we approach God's throne in a lifestyle of prayer and enjoy the sweet fellowship of personal relationship with Him.

Though I have been blessed through the years to live a life of prayer, lately I have heard God's invitation to come even closer, to enjoy even more of the blessing of daily communion with Him. But this does not automatically happen. We must intentionally accept and say yes to His invitation to us. Then we must actually do it; often and regularly, as a way of life, we must pray. We are to always be ready to pray.

As you may imagine, I have lately had much on my mind and heart. I have even been tempted to worry as I wonder how things will work out. But as I pray, I have heard my Lord inviting me to leave it all at His feet and to rest in Him. I know He loves me. And you know He loves you. We know He is with us. So as I pray, I experience His peace, for I know He hears me. Let us all be always ready to pray.

Always be ready to die

The Bible says, *It is appointed for man to die once, and after that comes judgment* (Hebrews 9:27). I hope this doesn't shock you. I think we have all lived long enough to grasp the solemn truth that everyone will die. We have stood at the graves of loved ones and been stunned at the tragedy of sudden loss.

But coming to grips with our own mortality is another thing entirely. We prefer to think that our life as we know it will go on indefinitely, so we may foolishly incorporate this perception into our world view. We can do this until circumstances preclude us from doing it anymore.

Job certainly came face to face with his own mortality. He lost children, property, and his own health. He expected to die soon, and at times he longed to do so. But in faith, Job could pen these powerful words of faith: *For I know that my Redeemer lives, and at the last he will stand upon the earth. And after my skin has been thus destroyed, yet in my flesh I shall see God, whom I shall see for myself, and my eyes shall behold, and not another* (Job 19:26-27).

Paul also came face to face with his own mortality. From death row in a Roman prison, as he expected to be put to death, Paul longed for the fulfillment of God's promise. In faith he wrote these words to Timothy: *For I am already being poured out as a drink offering, and the time of my departure has come. I have fought the good fight, I have finished the race, I have kept the faith. Henceforth there is laid up for me the crown of righteousness, which the Lord, the righteous judge, will award to me on that day, and not only to me but also to all who have loved his appearing* (2 Timothy 4:6-8).

Both Job and Paul were ready to die. They expected that very soon they would breathe their last in this mortal body, and they would then see the Lord and experience the fulfillment of His promises. Such certainty and confidence can only be fully accepted by those who have come to terms with their own mortality. For Job this came about through his afflictions. For Paul it was through his imprisonment. For me it has been through cancer. I have come to terms with my mortality, and by God's grace in Jesus Christ, I am ready to die.

Like all of us, I have no idea when I will die. I know that in the sovereignty of God it could be within the next month, or next year, or twenty years from now, or at any point in between. The Scriptures tell us that all of our days were numbered by God *before one of them came to be* (Psalm 139:16 NIV). Surely we can trust Him in this.

I know that in Jesus Christ, because of His perfect sacrifice for me, I am forgiven, accepted, and loved by God. Do you know the same? I also know that in light of eternity, I, and everyone who belongs by faith to Jesus, will soon be with Him in the glory of heaven. In this let us greatly rejoice.

As I am always ready to preach and pray, I am also ready to die. I hope and pray that you are too. Through faith in the risen Lord, God has made the way for us to approach our death not with dread but with longing, not with despair but with hope, not with regret but with great joy. This is possible through faith in the Lord Jesus Christ. I know it is so, for I am living it now.

I have been thinking much about my grandfather's exhortation to "always be ready to preach, pray, or die!" As I live it, I pray that you too will know such blessing.

FOR REFLECTION

How have you approached each day prepared and ready to share the reason for the hope that is within you? As God has also called you to always pray, how are you doing at this, and to what effect? Do you feel prepared to die? If not, what must you do to become ready? Ask God to help you in this, and He surely will.

45

ON TRUSTING GOD WHEN WE CANNOT SEE

July 2, 2019

Yesterday I was reminded of what it feels like when dense fog unexpectedly settles upon us, and we cannot see our way out. Imagine riding a bicycle on a twisting bike trail through the woods, guiding a kayak on a winding river with occasional rough rapids, or walking along a narrow pathway that borders a deep precipice. Suddenly you cannot see your hand in front of your eyes. In the dense fog, you do not know which way to go, but you know if you go the wrong way, danger and harm will come.

So what do you do? As you cannot safely continue the way you were going, you might conclude that the best thing to do is to stop and stay where you are for a while. This is a good time to wait, listen, pray, and trust until the thick fog has lifted, and you can see clearly again.

Has anything like this ever happened to you? It has felt like this to me since yesterday regarding the treatment plans for my cancer. A thick fog rolled in, and I am waiting for it to lift so I can know which way the Lord would have us go. I need your prayers.

Yesterday afternoon I had a scheduled phone appointment with a member of the stem cell transplant team at the VA Hospital in Nashville. I had been told that today we would settle on my scheduled arrival date in Nashville for later this month, but this did not happen. Instead, they told me the disappointing news that I am not yet a good candidate for an SCT. Even after eight months of chemotherapy treatments, the cancer levels in my blood and bone marrow remain too high to proceed.

When I heard this news, I felt a thick cloud settle over me. I had no idea which way I should go. I had been told that an SCT was the right course for me, but now it seems that this might not be an option at all. I felt disoriented, like I was on that winding bike trail or river or narrow path, encompassed by a thick fog.

I do not know what the way ahead will be for me. I do not know how God will lead out of this fog. But today I did not ask my Lord for such answers, though I trust that in His time answers will come. Rather, I have determined to remain where I am in His presence – waiting, listening, and praying until the fog lifts and I can see clearly again.

I hear my Lord calling me to trust Him. Helen has heard the same. God calls all of us to trust Him when we cannot see the way ahead, for we know that He knows the way. When Helen and I determined today that we will trust God in the midst of our uncertainty, peace rolled in like a gentle breeze. We sensed the clouds lifting, and by faith we knew that God is near. He has a good plan for all of His children.

Stem cell transplant could still happen for me in God's good time. Or perhaps the Lord will heal me in an instant and bring testimony of His great power and fame. Or perhaps He will soon promote me to His glorious presence in heaven and bring glory and praise to His holy name.

I do not know how my Lord is going to direct me, but I do know that He will lead. Though I cannot see what my future will hold, I know without any doubt that His plan for me is good. All of God's children can know this. Real peace is found in trusting God who loves us, is with us now, and who will steer us through every cloud.

FOR REFLECTION

When were you unable to see the way ahead, and you heard God calling you to trust Him? How strong is your confidence that God is with you now and that He is going to lead you? In what ways lately have you experienced a "fog" of uncertainty, and how is your faith making a difference? Ask God to help you in this, and He surely will.

46

ON THE BLESSING OF BEING WITH FAMILY

July 8, 2019

Sometimes we just want to be with family. Nothing else can substitute. God created us this way for His glory and our good. On Sunday morning I experienced this blessing with our local church family, and it was wonderful.

Nine months ago was the last time I had preached from God's Word to my local church family. I will not forget that Sunday because all of our adult children were with us. Carl, Amy, and Jonathan had traveled to be with us from their homes in Minnesota, Alaska, and Texas.

The previous Monday I had been informed of my diagnosis of active multiple myeloma and told that I must immediately begin chemotherapy treatments. I had been warned that because of my compromised immune system, I should avoid crowds and public transportation and other places where I could be exposed to sickness. Church services were included on the list of places that I should avoid. This was painful to hear. The following weekend I was sick at home, and the week after that, with sadness yet confidence that this was God's leading, I had resigned from my position as overseer of the flock.

My lifestyle changed, as my focus shifted from pastoral ministry to battling cancer. The hardest loss for me these last nine months has been missing fellowship with my church family and the complete absence of time with children, grandchildren, and extended family. The adage is proving true for me that "absence makes the heart grow fonder."

Helen and I had been preparing to travel to Nashville for my stem cell transplant; we expected to be there about two months. Then we expected to return home for many months of relative isolation and recuperation. Because I knew that it would likely be a long while before I could visit our church family again, I was determined to take necessary precautions but to attend church services last Sunday morning – one more time before we departed.

When this decision was made, I was also invited to preach that day if I was able. I gladly agreed. Being with our church family Sunday morning was a great blessing to me, and I pray to others also. It was wonderful to worship, to hear and proclaim God's Word, and to have Presbyters of the church anoint me with oil and pray over Helen and me. We enjoyed the sweet fellowship with brothers and sisters in Christ. This is a foretaste of heaven.

One of the Scripture texts that was read on Sunday was from Galatians 6, which focused on what it means to be united to one another with pure affection. This theme is carried through the text and includes our responsibility in Christ to come alongside one another to lovingly correct and help whenever sin has become evident, and to *bear one another's burdens* (Galatians 6:2). This instruction presumes that we have entered into relationships with each other and grown to know and trust each other well enough to speak into each other's lives. Then we can share our burdens with each other, pray for one another, and do whatever we can to help one another.

This is God's will for His church. Healthy family life reflects our Lord's character. But it does not just happen. It requires intentional vulnerability and risk within God's family. This is why the apostle Paul introduced this chapter by referring to other members of the church as brothers. This is the most frequent word in the New Testament in reference to God's family, the church. It reminds us of the familial connection that is ours in Jesus Christ because we are God's own children.

When this word is used in this way in the New Testament, it is a gender inclusive term, referring to all followers of Jesus Christ, both brothers and sisters. We who believe in the Lord are God's forever family together. Because of this, whenever we gather as His family, whether in large groups or small, we are expressing our love to God and His love to our brothers and sisters. In such family reunions, we experience a wonderful foretaste of heaven.

This week Helen and I will travel to our family's lake cottage in Maine for a few days where we will enjoy a reunion with my siblings and their spouses. This reunion has been planned for months. Because I had expected to be in Nashville now, I had presumed that Helen and I could not attend. But because the SCT is halted for now, we are able to join my siblings. In this I rejoice.

I cannot wait to see my brother Gary and my sisters Cheryl, Marcia, and Marilee, and their spouses. It will not be the same for us as in previous family reunions because within the past two and a half years our older brother David and both of our parents have been promoted to glory. Of the five of us who remain, I am now the oldest.

Because we are geographically scattered, living in Rhode Island, North Carolina, Georgia, and Maine, it requires considerable effort and planning for us to come together. I am glad that we are making this effort, and I look forward to being with them. Please pray that I may have sufficient physical stamina and protection from illness to enjoy our time together. This too will be a foretaste of heaven.

I also received an update on the likely way ahead in my cancer treatment. On Monday I received a phone call from a transplant physician at the Nashville VA Medical Center who oversees my case. He told me that their program is in partnership with the Vanderbilt University Medical Center and the success rates of their bone marrow transplant program is in the top ten such programs in the USA. This was encouraging to me.

All of my recent and pending tests will be sent to this transplant physician for review, including blood labs, bone marrow biopsy results, and PET/CT scan. He explained the targets that we must reach in order for the SCT to proceed with success. He said a stronger chemotherapy regimen should now be given for two or three cycles to help me reach the targets sooner. When the stated targets are reached in my bone marrow and blood, we will proceed with the SCT. We agreed that if the stated targets are not be reached, the SCT will not happen, because durable remission would be unlikely. If we can proceed with the stem cell transplant, it will most likely be done in the fall.

Helen and I remain determined to trust our Lord concerning how this unfolds. Please continue to pray with us for God's will only and that His glory will be revealed to many. Day by day I see evidence of God's grace in what I am going through, and for this I rejoice. Today, for example, as I sat in my chemotherapy chair receiving intravenous immunoglobulin (IVIG) treatment, God's presence was very real to me.

Four other patients were with me, and we had a lively discussion about our mortality and what follows death. Two of these men professed that they do not believe in God or in any after life, but they asked questions that allowed me to testify to the truth and evidence of the gospel of Jesus Christ. Not only were other patients listening attentively, so were several staff, particularly one who stood at the door for a long time. It is such a privilege to serve the Lord wherever and however He leads us.

How wonderful to know that God is holding us in His hands. How blessed Helen and I are to have family who love and pray for us, including so many of you. I pray that by His grace you also experience or will experience the great joy and blessing of being part of His eternal family.

FOR REFLECTION

What are some ways that you have been blessed from your adoption into God's eternal family? How have you experienced or are you now experiencing the family blessing of *bearing one another's burdens*? What does the Lord desire from you so you may more fully experience this blessing? Ask God to help you in this, and He surely will.

47

ON FINISHING OUR COURSE WELL

July 17, 2019

This morning my Bible reading included the apostle Paul's meeting with the elders of the church in Ephesus as described by Luke in Acts 20. Paul was in a hurry on his way to Jerusalem and hoped to arrive before Pentecost. To save time, from Miletus he sent a message to the Ephesian elders and asked them to come to him, which they did.

As Paul had spent two years in Ephesus, pouring his life into the church, these men were like family to him. He knew that on this side of heaven he would not see them again, so on that memorable evening he poured out his heart to them and reminded them of various things he had taught them, the life he had lived among them, and the responsibility that was entrusted to them by God.

I can relate to the apostle Paul's heart as revealed in this passage, for I too perceive that I will not be going back to life and ministry as I once knew it. And I too rejoice in those whom God has called and equipped to continue in faithful service. With prayer and much gladness I commend to the Lord the local churches where I have served, the CCCC (the Conference of ministers and churches with whom I have partnered), and the faithful chaplains serving in various branches of our military.

I wish that I could be more involved in the lives of my grandchildren, and perhaps in God's plan and timing I will still have that opportunity.

But I rejoice now in the love and faithfulness of my daughter Amy, and of her husband Joey, and my son Jonathan and his wife Jackie, as they are committed to teach their children and raise them in the faith and love of the Lord Jesus Christ. As Paul committed the elders of Ephesus to the Lord for the work to which He called them, so I am blessed to do the same for those who follow me.

The apostle Paul testified in Acts 20:22-23 that the Holy Spirit had confirmed that many hardships were ahead for him. But no fear was evident in Paul, for he knew that God would be with him through it all. Paul's love and trust for His Lord was evident. His declaration in verse 24 is also true in my heart today: *But I do not account my life of any value nor as precious to myself, if only I may finish my course and the ministry that I received from the Lord Jesus, to testify to the gospel of the grace of God* (Acts 20:24).

I long to finish well the course and ministry I have received from the Lord Jesus. Whatever this may mean in God's will, whatever it looks like in His eyes, this is what I desire, and by faith I know it will be. If hardships are to be included, so be it. If difficulties are to be many for me, it is okay. If I must suffer in order to fulfill His good plan for me and testify to the gospel of the grace of God, then I bless and welcome His plan.

This past week has included a few memorable events for me. On Wednesday I met with a Christian friend who is a funeral director in order to do advance preparations for my funeral. Of course, I have no idea when it might be. I trust the Lord who numbers my days and yours (Psalm 139:16). I did this as a gift for Helen. In doing so, I was reminded again of the gift of life though I am determined to live every remaining day that the Lord gives me to honor Him and fulfill His purpose for me.

On Saturday I received my latest blood lab results, and I was encouraged to see that in the last three weeks, the cancer cells in my blood were reduced by 18%. In the previous three-week period, these levels had decreased by less than 1%, so an 18% reduction in so short a time is remarkable. Your continued prayers for me are appreciated, and I join you in giving God the praise! In order to proceed with the stem cell transplant, a further reduction of about 50% from current levels is required. Thank you for praying with me towards this end.

This week Helen and I enjoyed a few special days of fun and fellowship with siblings and their spouses in Maine at our family's lake cottages. It was wonderful. Sunday morning we had a family worship service to praise the Lord and rejoice in our faith. I was blessed to share from God's Word. Together we looked at Psalm 23, a psalm so often read at funerals. But David did not write it as a funeral dirge. He wrote it as a testimony of his life. These were lessons he learned as a young boy while caring for his father's flock of sheep.

In verses 1-3, he told of experiencing the Lord as his shepherd, who was always with him in personal relationship, who guarded him, guided him, and always provided everything he needed. In verses 4-5, he testified of God's grace in hard times, even when he walked through the valley of the shadow of death, for in such times the Lord was with him; He comforted him and dispelled his fears. The psalm concludes in verse 6 with David's testimony of future confidence in the Lord his Shepherd, who gave him hope for this life and the next: *Surely goodness and mercy shall follow me all the days of my life, and I shall dwell in the house of the LORD forever* (Psalm 23:6). These sure promises are ours through faith in the promised Messiah, the Son of David, the Lord Jesus Christ.

In light of all this, I remain confident in the promises of God, determined and sure that I too will *finish my course and the ministry that I received from the Lord Jesus, to testify to the gospel of the grace of God* (Acts 20:24). I pray that you already know or will soon come to know the joy of prayerful commitment to do the same. God is forever faithful, and He calls and equips us for faithfulness to finish our course well.

FOR REFLECTION

What would it mean for you to finish well the course and ministry that you have received from the Lord Jesus? How have you testified, how are you testifying now, and how will you testify to the gospel of the grace of God? Ask God to help you in this, and He surely will.

With siblings, Gary, Cheryl, Marcia, and Marilee

Helen and me at the lake

48

ON WHAT TO DO WHEN FEAR PURSUES US

July 20, 2019

As much as we might wish it were not so, all of us experience fear at times. Even when we can identify no rational reason for our fear, and we comprehend that God is with us, we can still find ourselves nervous and afraid because of circumstances or the uncertainty of the future. Wishing fears away or pretending that our fear is not real is certainly not the answer. So what are we to do?

I raise this issue because I have confronted fear at various times along my life journey, including this week. On Friday Helen and I drove to the Jamaica Plains VA Medical Center in Boston where I was scheduled for a PET/CT Scan (Positron Emission Tomography and Computed Tomography) to check for potential bone lesions and for abnormal metabolic activity and tumors.

I was not nervous about what the scan might find, for I trust the Lord for the outcome. I was however nervous about the procedure itself. Because this was to be the third time since my diagnosis that I underwent a PET/CT scan, I knew what to expect. I knew that I would be strapped into a tubular machine unable to move for the duration of the scan, which would take about forty-five minutes because of my height.

If you read this and think "no problem," you clearly have no issues with claustrophobia. But closed-in spaces and the inability to move are hard for me, which causes fear. Though such a reaction might seem irrational and unreasonable, it is still real. Prior to the scan, as I lay on a bed for an hour and waited for the nuclear contrast to work its way through my body, I contemplated getting up and walking out. But as I prayed, the Lord met me and assured me of His presence and His promise. He reminded me again of what I am blessed to do. As I listened and followed His lead, by God's grace, my fears melted away.

In my Bible reading this week, I was reminded that confronting fear with faith is a privilege that is available to all who believe in the Lord. In Psalm 27, as he faced his fears by exercising his faith, David revealed four insights on what to do when fear comes. When fears pursue us, we are called and blessed to:

Have confidence in God

David had walked with God long enough to know that He could be trusted in the face of every challenge. In light of this, David drew a contrast between his fears and the ever-present protection of God. With confidence in God, he made a faith-based decision to trust God for protection against the source of his fears. He thus declared, *The Lord is my light and my salvation; whom shall I fear? The Lord is the stronghold of my life; of whom shall I be afraid?* (Psalm 27:1). We are called and blessed to make a faith decision to have confidence in God.

Desire God most

David had known countless pleasures in life, especially being chosen and anointed as King of Israel, winning victories in battle, acquiring much wealth, and receiving earthly acclaim. But these things were not his greatest treasure. His ultimate and most prized treasure was God Himself, whom he desired above all else.

David wrote, *One thing have I asked of the Lord, that I will seek after: that I may dwell in the house of the Lord all the days of my life, to gaze upon the beauty of the Lord and to inquire in His temple* (Psalm 27:4). When we fix our attention upon God as our greatest desire, our focus shifts from whatever it is that we fear to the One who conquers our every fear. We are called and blessed by faith to choose to desire God most.

Take shelter in God
We are invited to enter into God's sanctuary and enjoy His protection. When dangers approach us and we volitionally enter God's secure fortress, we feel protected and safe, no matter what dangers are outside. David expressed his own experience when he wrote, *For He will hide me in His shelter in the day of trouble; He will conceal me under the cover of His tent; He will lift me high upon a rock* (Psalm 27:5). We too have been called, and we are blessed to make a faith decision to enter into God's holy sanctuary and trust and enjoy His protection.

Choose joy because of God
This is a choice God enables us to make, a choice that transcends our circumstances. As David put confidence in God, desired Him most, and took shelter in Him, he released his fears and was able to sing and choose joy. He testified, *And now my head shall be lifted up above my enemies all around me, and I will offer in His tent sacrifices with shouts of joy. I will sing and make melody to the Lord* (Psalm 27:6). You and I have also been called and enabled by God to choose joy because of Him.

I wish that I no longer had to confront fears. Perhaps you have wished the same, or maybe you are confronting fears now and wondering what to do about it? David's example and my experience have reminded me that God has a good purpose in our fears. For all who know the Lord Jesus, our fears need not defeat us. God has shown us what to do. Whenever we are afraid, like David we can have confidence in God, desire Him most, take shelter in Him, and choose joy because of Him.

As I have prayerfully reflected on these things and applied them to my life this week, my fears have melted away like ice in the sun. On Friday I experienced joy at how fast the PET/CT scan seemed to go, how tangible God's presence was, and how relaxed I felt through it all. Like David, I even found myself singing. We know what to do when fears follow us. May God help us do what we know to do whenever we are afraid.

FOR REFLECTION

What fears have you confronted recently, and what have you done with those fears? What would it mean for you to have full confidence in God? What would it be like for you to make a faith decision to desire God most? What does it mean to enter God's sanctuary to trust and enjoy His protection? In the face of your fears, how can you choose joy because of God? Ask God to help you in this, and He surely will.

49

ON OUR PROMISED UPGRADES: A NEW RESURRECTION BODY

July 28, 2019

Last weekend in Rhode Island where we live and across much of the USA, we experienced a heatwave. Temperatures approached 100 degrees Fahrenheit, and with high humidity it felt even hotter. Enduring such heat requires drinking lots of fluids and doing whatever we can to keep cool. This included frequent trips to our refrigerator for cold drinks and ice. But on Sunday afternoon, I discovered that our refrigerator had quit. Everything in the freezer had melted, and the food in the refrigerator was ruined. Our refrigerator was dead and we needed a new one.

Have you had life experiences like this through which you have heard God speaking important lessons for life? This was such a week for me, as our broken refrigerator and need for a new one became a parable through which I heard my Lord speaking scriptural life lessons to my heart.

While I have been dealing with cancer and the natural processes of aging, I have become aware that my body is wearing out. These bodies are temporary after all, and we all know it. We might choose to live as though it was not so; we might pretend our bodies will keep going indefinitely.

Before last Sunday I had given no thought whatsoever to our refrigerator dying. I had presumed it would just keep going indefinitely. I was wrong, but Helen found the original owner's manual that was passed to us when we purchased our home, where she read that our refrigerator had been purchased in 1990. This meant it had been working for twenty-nine years, which is a long time for a refrigerator. In light of its relative longevity, its demise should not have surprised us, nor should our physical mortality.

So we went shopping for a new refrigerator, and we now have a significant upgrade. When we ordered the new one, we were excited about its features. Delivery was promised in a few days, so we would have to wait, which we were willing to do. The new refrigerator was delivered Friday, and we are not missing our old one at all.

In Christ we have been promised a sweet upgrade in the new resurrection body. We must wait a little while for delivery, until the day of our Lord's promised return, but the wait will be worth it. We will receive a body that is far better than we have thus far known or imagined, and the warranty is the best ever. It is guaranteed for eternity by the Lord God Almighty.

In 1 Corinthians 15 the apostle Paul provides wonderful teaching on the promised resurrection of the dead when we will receive our new bodies. This promise is guaranteed to all who belong to Jesus Christ by faith, because of His victory over sin and death. Paul describes what our resurrection body will be like.

Using imagery of planting seeds and harvesting produce, the apostle declares, *What is sown is perishable, what is raised is imperishable. It is sown in dishonor; it is raised in glory. It is sown in weakness; it is raised in power. It is sown a natural body; it is raised a spiritual body. If there is a natural body, there is also a spiritual body* (1 Corinthians 15:42-44).

Four Fantastic Features of Our Promised Upgrade:

Imperishable

Our new resurrection body will be imperishable (v. 42). Unlike our current body, it will never wear out. Our new body will never be subject to physical decay or aging. The Bible says there will never again be pain, suffering, sickness, sin, or the ultimate consequence of sin, which is death. It will be imperishable. How does this feature sound to you?

Glorious
Our new resurrection body will be glorious (v. 42). It will be physically perfect, reflecting the glory of God. It will be beautiful beyond what we can now imagine. It will be glorious. How does this feature sound to you?

Powerful
Our new resurrection body will be powerful and strong (v. 43). It will have more capability and stamina than we have ever known in our current body. Jesus's promise will be realized by all who are in heaven. Those who were once blind will see with eagle eyes; those who were once deaf will hear quiet whispers; those who were once paralyzed or lame will dance and run like the wind. It will be powerful. How does this feature sound to you?

Spiritual
Our new resurrection body will be spiritual, like Christ's resurrected body (v. 44). Our new body will be alive forever in the presence of Almighty God. Our physical body will be spiritual. How does this feature sound to you? Living in this broken world and in this failing body, God's promised upgrade sounds wonderful to me.

In 1 Corinthians 15 Paul contrasts the natural body that we have known and which is only temporarily alive with the new spiritual body that we will have – forever alive with God. He illustrates this contrast by going back to the creation story and comparing the two Adams. Through the first Adam who is our natural parent, all humanity inherited physical life, for we were all created by God. After God formed man from the dust, He breathed life into him.

Through the last Adam, who is the promised and long anticipated Messiah and Savior, all who believe in Him and receive Him by faith inherit His treasured gift of everlasting life. This gift is available only through faith in the Lord Jesus Christ who declared, *I am the way, and the truth, and the life. No one comes to the Father except through me*

(John 14:6). There is no middle ground concerning who Jesus is or what He declared or accomplished. His identity, victory, and message have been confirmed by His resurrection from the dead.

After He died on the cross, Jesus physically arose from the dead on the third day as He promised. His body was no longer decaying in the tomb. Jesus was alive again. His resurrected body was tangible, for he ate food and people touched him. His resurrected body was recognizable, as Thomas recognized his voice and appearance and replied in faith, *My Lord and my God!* And Jesus's resurrected body was also spiritual, for He was no longer bound by the former limitations of his mortal body, thus appearing to His disciples behind closed doors.

When Jesus Christ returns as He has promised to do, all who loved and trusted in Him in this life are going to receive a new body like His resurrected body. Like the Lord Jesus, our resurrected body is going to be tangible, recognizable, powerful, spiritually alive, and empowered by God Himself.

So how are we to respond to this hope? What effect does this promise have on us today? This week I have been prayerfully reflecting on two personal responses to the Lord's promise of a new resurrection body:

Devotion and Motivation

Devotion

To be wholly devoted to Christ, for He is worthy of nothing less from me.

Having only a little devotion to Christ is not rational. Only full devotion to Christ is reasonable. *I appeal to you therefore, brothers, by the mercies of God, to present your bodies as a living sacrifice, holy and acceptable to God, which is your spiritual worship* (Romans 12:1). The Greek words used by Paul translated here in the ESV as *which is your spiritual worship* are "τὴν λογικὴν λατρείαν ὑμῶν/ten logiken latreian hymon," which translates more literally, "which is the divinely reasonable service of you." In other words, no other response makes sense.

Only a little desire for holiness is not reasonable. Complete holiness is. So, *since we have these promises, beloved, let us cleanse ourselves from every defilement of body and spirit, bringing holiness to completion in the fear of God* (2 Corinthians 7:1).

I again heard my Lord's invitation and am determined to be wholly devoted to Christ for as long as I live in this mortal body, and then by His grace forever. He invites us and all who know Him to such wholehearted devotion.

Motivation
To be wholly motivated to serve the Lord, for He is worthy of my best.

Decreased motivation in His service depresses us, but increased motivation inspires us. *Therefore, my beloved brothers, be steadfast, immovable, always abounding in the work of the Lord, knowing that in the Lord your labor is not in vain* (1 Corinthians 15:58).

I acknowledge that it is a challenge to stay motivated when things are not going as we desire. I have experienced discouragement. When this happens to us, we may be tempted to move from the playing field to the sidelines. We may focus primarily on our own struggles and become depressed. But God reminds us of His deep, deep love for us, His unending faithfulness to us, and His guaranteed promises to us for today and for eternity. He calls us deeper.

May God's sure promise of a resurrection upgrade motivate us now. May the surety of it inspire us. May God's love for us and our love for Him energize us, for He is ever with us and He is ever faithful. We know that we owe Him everything. And so I want to serve my Lord as long as I can and however I can. His promised upgrade motivates me now. How about you?

FOR REFLECTION

How has God's promise of a new resurrection body affected you? Reflecting on the four features of the resurrection upgrade listed by the apostle Paul in 1 Corinthians 15:42-44, how do these features encourage you now? Concerning the responses of devotion and motivation, what will be your personal response to the promise God has made to you of a new resurrection body? Ask God to help you in this, and He surely will.

50

ON SHEDDING DISCOURAGEMENT WITH GOD'S HELP

August 4, 2019

Sometimes we find ourselves wearing garments of discouragement. It might be because of difficult circumstances, which may include feeling physically poor, or spiritually weak, or emotionally fragile; maybe anticipation of an unpleasant future for ourselves or those we care about weighs on us.

Whenever a garment of discouragement covers us, we might simply suffer under it and think we have no other option. Or we might do our best to peel it off, only to discover that we cannot shed discouragement in this way. When we are discouraged, God would have us realize that we need His help and that we can call upon Him. And when we do, He answers.

This truth flooded my awareness one hot day this week when, for the life of me, I could not shed the shirt I was wearing. I had been outside in the heat of the day, and I was hot and sweaty. The pullover shirt I was wearing had plastic sports team logos on the front and on the back, and the logos stuck to my skin. I was uncomfortable so I attempted to remove the shirt, but I struggled and struggled to pull it off. The shirt was firmly stuck to me. When at last I concluded that I could not remove this garment by myself, I called out to Helen who came to my rescue. The shirt that had been stuck on me was removed.

Later that same day I called upon my Lord to peel off my discouragement. I had tried unsuccessfully to shed it on my own, but I could not do it. I needed His help, so I called out to Him and asked for His help. And He gave it to me.

Several reasons caused the discouragement I was wearing that day. The greatest source of it is the cumulative effects of dealing with active multiple myeloma for ten months now, which brought many hard changes to me. The lingering and unpleasant effects of chemotherapy discourage me. And though a potential stem cell transplant has been suggested as the best hope of remission, thus far nothing has happened, for I am still not medically ready.

To be deemed eligible for a SCT, the cancerous myeloma cells in my blood must fall below a certain threshold, and this week the lab results showed only a minuscule decrease. These results discouraged me more than I expected. I calculated in my mind that at this rate of decline, it could be nine months or more before I might be able to proceed, which would then be followed by a full year of recuperation with isolation. As I pondered all of this, discouragement covered me like a heavy, uncomfortable garment.

I wore that garment for a while that day, and I hated it. Like a flashing light on the dashboard of my heart, discouragement warned me that something was wrong and attention was needed now. I had no ability to correct this alone.

So that day I did what I have learned to do when my soul is heavy. I went to the Lord to pray and asked Him to examine my heart and motives that I might see what I cannot see. I prayed the prayer of Psalm 139, which is so effective when we are discouraged and cannot shake it off: *Search me, O God, and know my heart! Try me and know my thoughts! And see if there be any grievous way in me, and lead me in the way everlasting* Psalm 139:23-24). Whenever we pray this way, wanting God to show us what we cannot see and trusting Him to unfold His good purpose for us, then His help surely comes.

The Psalms include honest expressions of discouragement and remind us that we do not have to pretend with God that everything is fine when it is not. Rather, we can bring our discouragement to Him and ask for His help, for He is forever faithful and can be trusted. The psalmist's prayer in Psalm 42 reflects the perspective God is calling forth from me and you as we deal with our discouragement: *Why are you cast down, O my soul, and why are you in turmoil within me? Hope in God, for I shall again praise Him, my salvation and my God. My soul is cast down within me; therefore I remember you* (Psalm 42:5-6).

The psalmist made a proactive faith decision to do something with his discouragement. He knew that holding on to it was not right for him, so he determined to put his hope in God. His ultimate hope was not found in circumstances working out as he wanted. His hope was in God alone. Is the Lord your ultimate hope too, no matter what discouragement may be going on in your life and in the world around you?

In my own heart this week, I reaffirmed that God is my hope and that He will be so forever, and I praised Him. The Lord is my salvation and my God. I remember who He is and all that He has done for me. I am holding on in faith to His sure promise that He is with me now; ready to help me as I call upon Him. I asked my Lord to help me, and He came to my rescue.

I also ask God to help you, knowing that as you seek Him, He surely will. Though God may not immediately change our circumstances as we wish He would, He does come to our rescue. He removes our garment of discouragement and replaces it with a garment of praise.

Have you been wearing a garment of discouragement? Do you wish to keep wearing it, or do you wish to shed it? In faith can you decide with me that you will put your hope in God? Will you prayerfully determine to trust Him no matter what your disappointments or circumstances are? Whenever we ask the Lord to help us with this, He comes to our rescue.

Now, as the garment of discouragement is peeled away, let us in faith put on the garment of praise, which fits us far better. I so appreciate your prayers for me, as I also pray for you. May God bless you with encouragement in the Lord Jesus Christ.

FOR REFLECTION

When have you struggled with shedding a garment of discouragement and discovering that you could not remove it yourself? What sources of discouragement do you struggle with now? What will it mean for you to put on a garment of praise, and how will this help in dealing with discouragement? How does this lesson on proactively choosing to ask God to help with discouragement apply in your life? Ask God to help you with this, and He surely will.

51

ON TRUSTING GOD FOR DISCERNMENT TO DO HIS WILL

August 19, 2019

On several occasions I have been asked how I am able to have such peace in the face of cancer, the various losses I have experienced, and the reminders of my mortality. My answer is that it is because of Jesus. I belong to Him. I love Him. I trust Him. I have His presence with me. And I believe His promises. I know what He has done for me and that He loves me. Jesus Christ is the source of my peace.

We who have been blessed to walk with God for any length of time carry the grace of experience with His presence and direction, His faithfulness and peace. I have known this blessing, and it strengthens me now. The treasures of His comfort, confidence, and hope are given by our loving heavenly Father to all who believe in Jesus Christ and who therefore love, trust, and follow Him.

This requires that we have personally acknowledged and confessed that Jesus Christ is the Son of God and Savior and that we have invited Him to sit on the throne of our lives forever. When we do this, He becomes far more than merely a great historic or religious figure that we might choose to worship from time to time. He becomes our first love and the very center of our being; He sits on the throne of our hearts today, so that our supreme desire is to love and please Him in all that we do. When we trust and love the Lord Jesus Christ, we long to discern and do His will.

From this perspective the apostle Paul urged all who know the Lord: *Whatever you do, in word or deed, do everything in the name of the Lord Jesus, giving thanks to God the Father through him* (Colossians 3:17).

Do everything in the name of the Lord Jesus. Everything! If you cannot do whatever you are doing in the name of the Lord Jesus, then stop. Do not do it. If you can do whatever you are doing in the name of the Lord Jesus, thus to honor and glorify Him, then proceed. This has long been the desire of my heart and of Helen's too. Throughout the forty-three years of our married life, we have shared a prayerful desire to trust God, to discern, and then do His will.

We can testify that our Lord has always guided us, granted us His peace, and confirmed His purpose through every transition. Of course He has, for He is forever faithful in every situation, in every season, and in every generation. Though our futures might seem uncertain now, God's presence, promises, and peace are certain.

At this point I am very uncertain about my future cancer treatments. The chemotherapy regimen I have been on for multiple myeloma has failed to sufficiently reduce the cancer cells in my bone marrow and blood for an SCT to be a viable option for me. Medically speaking, an SCT remains my best hope for achieving a durable remission, so for now it is still the treatment goal. But because it is taking so long for me to be able to proceed, I have felt like I am running a long race in which the finish line keeps moving. This has been hard.

One of the intravenous drugs I have been receiving for many months was initially administered weekly. Then because of toxicity, it was reduced to every two weeks. And now it can only be safely given to me every four weeks. This means another chemotherapy change is needed. For this reason I have scheduled a consult appointment next week with a specialist at the Dana Farber Cancer Institute in Boston to see what is recommended. Please pray with us for the Lord's clear leading in this too.

As the apostle Paul taught, we who follow the Lord Jesus are called to trust Him and to seek His leading in everything we do. And then we are to do it. We are called to *do everything in the name of the Lord Jesus*. This includes where we will live.

Last week Helen and I spent a few days in Minnesota, where we were blessed to be with our son Carl, our son Jonathan and his wife Jackie, and our grandsons Archer and Theo. While there, Helen and I agreed to take steps toward moving there. We are asking and trusting God to guide us in this. We want to discern and do His will.

Twice before we have lived in Minnesota: when I attended Seminary from 1977 to 1980 and when I served as Conference Minister of the CCCC from 2003 to 2011. The prospect of living there again and being near children and grandchildren attracts us. I would also have access to the superb care available at the VA Medical Center in Minneapolis. Furthermore, my oncologist recently told me that she believed the Mayo Clinic in Minnesota offers the very best care available anywhere for fighting multiple myeloma. Because I have been an atypical patient, such expertise could benefit me in the future.

For these reasons, moving to Minnesota soon makes some sense to us. But there is grief in it also, because we love and hate to leave our dear friends and family in New England, especially our local church family. Still, we are agreed that the only way to discern if God is leading us in this way is to take some initial steps to see what God will do.

I have been reminded of some words that a wise friend said to me when I was unsure if God would have me consider a potential move. He said, "Well, even God doesn't steer a parked car." In other words, divine direction can often be discerned only as we get moving, desire His will, and go the way He steers us. In light of this, Helen and I have now listed our home for sale; we took this step prayerfully with James 4:15 in mind: *If the Lord wills, we will live and do this*.

We need God's guidance, provision, and leading, for we are dependent upon Him. We will need a buyer for our current home and His leading to a new home. I will need to be physically well enough to proceed with the transplant.

Following the transplant, which may happen soon, I must remain at our home for at least a year to receive follow-up medical care while I recover. For this reason, we are asking the Lord if He would have us move before the SCT is done. Our prayerful aim is to discern and then do His will.

Would you pray with us toward this end? As you pray for Helen and me, please know that we are also praying for you. I pray that you might know in the very core of your being that God has always loved you, He loves you now, and He always will. His love for all His children is everlasting. His plan and purpose for you is always for His glory and for your good.

No matter what our current circumstances are or what uncertainties we may be facing, we can trust Him. May our desire and prayer always be to discern and then do His will, for this is a prayer He will surely answer.

FOR REFLECTION

How are Christians able to have peace, whatever may happen? What is the connection between loving and trusting God and wanting to discern and then do only His will? What decisions are you facing or will you soon be facing for which this lesson applies? What does the Lord desire of you so you may experience more of the blessing of His peace, and the confidence of His leading in every decision? Ask God to help you in this, and He surely will.

52

ON RECEIVING ALL THAT WE NEED

August 26, 2019

On Friday I went to the Dana Farber Cancer Institute in Boston to check in with my multiple myeloma specialist. I was prescribed another chemotherapy drug. Though the amount of cancer cells in my blood continues to fall, it is doing so very slowly. I was told that I am getting closer to becoming eligible to proceed with the SCT, and this new drug should get me there sooner.

Our home in Rhode Island is on the market now, as we prepare to move to Minnesota where we will be near our two sons and daughter-in-law and two of our grandsons. We will also be near the Mayo Clinic, which offers the best available care for treating multiple myeloma.

Because the SCT could be offered soon, and we will be required to remain wherever we are for at least a year while I receive follow-up care post-SCT, we are asking for God's clear leading soon. We are also asking that if it is His will, our home may sell soon. In this too we will trust Him. As God's wisdom is perfect and ours is limited, we have learned to ask and trust Him to lead according to His will. How comforting to know that He will do just that. Such confidence dispels our worries and sets our hearts at ease.

While approaching this transition, which in itself can be stressful, I have had some days lately of feeling quite weak and yucky with various unpleasant symptoms. I expect the primary reason for this is the cumulative effects of chemotherapy, which I have now been receiving for over ten months. This is hard physically, and I expect it may continue until the SCT happens and beyond.

But God knows all of this, doesn't He? He reminds me that He knows what I need and what everyone of His children needs. He knows and loves us, and He is able to meet every need. How reassuring is that!

How then are we to pray? Are we to simply present Him with our shopping list of all the things we think we need, listing them one by one, with our best argument for why we think we need it? If we take this approach, and our list is focused on temporal and material things rather than on what is eternal, relational, and spiritual, then we need a fresh reminder that God is not finished with us yet. He is growing us up spiritually; He calls us and invites us to trust Him and find in Him all that we really need.

So What Do We Really Need?

What we really need, or better, *Who* we really need is the Lord Himself, for in our relationship with Him, we find every need supplied.

I reflected this week on Psalm 119, the longest chapter in the Bible. The theme of this psalm is the Word of God and how God supplies our needs. David gave many illustrations of how God is the One who meets our needs. I have reflected on four particular needs that we all share:

We all need guidance which leads to clarity.
God meets this need; He leads us. *Your Word is a lamp to my feet and a light to my path* (v. 105). I am therefore not worried about the way I am to go, for I know He will lead me. He is all I need.

We all need safety which leads to hope.
God meets this need: He protects us. *You are my hiding place and my shield; I hope in Your Word* (v. 114). I am therefore not afraid of what the future might bring or of how hard things may be, for I know He protects me. I feel safe and hopeful in His arms. He is all I need.

We all need Presence which leads to peace.
God meets this need: He is with us. *They draw near who persecute me with evil purpose . . . but You are near me* (v. 150-151). I am therefore not troubled by uncertainties, for I sense His presence and enjoy His peace. He is all I need.

We all need salvation which leads to Life.
God meets this need: He saves us. *I long for Your salvation, O Lord, and your law is my delight. Let my soul live and praise You, and let your rules help me. I have gone astray like a lost sheep; seek your servant, for I do not forget your commandments* (v. 174-176). I am therefore not afraid of death or of whatever hardships that may be ahead, for I trust my Savior, and I know by faith that I am His, and I will live forever with Him. He is all I need.

Ultimately, we all need the greatest gift that has ever been given to humanity, even the Lord Jesus Christ. In the first chapter of the book of Hebrews, the writer describes the supremacy of God's Son, the Lord Jesus Christ: *Long ago, at many times and in many ways, God spoke to our fathers by the prophets, but in these last days He has spoken to us by His Son, whom He appointed heir of all things, through whom also He created the world* (Hebrews 1:1-2). Jesus is therefore the highest expression of God's Word, for He was and is the living incarnation of the eternal Son of God.

How I thank God for the lifelong joy I have had of living in personal relationship with the Lord Jesus. He has guided me through life as I have sought Him first, and I know He will continue to do so for the remainder of my days and then forever. Jesus Christ protects me from every evil threat because of His triumphal victory over sin, evil, temptation, and death. He gives me a sure hope for today, tomorrow, and forever.

Jesus Christ is with me continually, and He is with you if you know Him by faith. He is with us forever, as He promised. So why should we be worried about tomorrow? Jesus Christ is our Savior, the Way, the Truth, and the Life. He assures us of His presence and of everlasting life with Him. He is all that we need.

Alvin Slaughter wrote a gospel song that has been ringing in my heart lately, drawing me closer in dependence upon my Lord. It is called

"He's All I Need." The lyrics speak of the fact that Jesus is all I need; He satisfies and supplies; He is my life and my breath.

This song affirms that Jesus represents the Triune God with whom He is One and in whom we have all we need. I believe the testimony of Jesus Christ, the Son of God, who confessed in John that *I and the Father are One* (John 10:30). I also believe the testimony of the apostle Paul who affirmed the divinity of Jesus as the true doctrine of the church when he said *for in Him the whole fullness of deity dwells bodily* (Colossians 2:19).

We all need our heavenly Father to adopt us as His own and to father us forever. We also need the Holy Spirit to teach us, fill us, and empower us. And we all need the Lord Jesus, the Son of God, to save us from our sins and be our shepherd, friend, and Lord always and forever. Because Jesus Christ embodies the fullness of God in human flesh, Paul declared, *And my God will supply every need of yours according to His riches in glory in Christ Jesus* (Philippians 4:19). *Every need* means just what it says, "every need." There are no exceptions to this.

I am determined to look to the Lord from whom I have received, am now receiving, and will forever receive all that I need. I pray you are doing the same and are thus receiving:

- *Guidance* that leads to clarity - Praise God, for He leads us.
- *Safety* that leads to hope - Praise God, for He protects us.
- *His Presence* that leads to peace - Praise God, for He is always with us.
- *Salvation* that leads to life - Praise God, for He saves us, today and for eternity.

He is all I need! What about you?

FOR REFLECTION

What is your testimony of receiving from the Lord all you have ever needed? In what areas of your life are you currently in need of: Guidance that leads to clarity? Safety that leads to hope? His Presence that leads to peace? Salvation that leads to life? Will you trust God for all that you need? Ask God to help you in this, and He surely will.

53

ON WAITING WHEN WE WOULD RATHER NOT

September 1, 2019

Do you like waiting? Me neither. Sometimes I am rather tired of it, as I wait for so many things:

1. I am waiting to feel better.
2. I am waiting for the end of chemotherapy.
3. I am waiting to be medically cleared to proceed with the SCT.
4. I am waiting for remission.
5. I am waiting for increased energy.
6. I am waiting for a buyer for our home and direction on our move to Minnesota.
7. I am waiting with increasing anticipation for heaven, in God's appointed time.
8. I am waiting for my Lord's return, as He has promised.
9. I am waiting for so many things.

How about you? What are you waiting and longing for? It isn't always easy to wait.

Little children especially do not like waiting. When we tell them, "Not now," they sometimes respond in childish anger or emotional outbursts. As adults we might not respond in such childish ways, but we can still feel the frustration. It can be hard for us to wait for what we want. Our modern society reinforces this struggle. When we want something, we expect immediate answers. We hate waiting, and the more the world caters to our immediate desires, the less we are willing to wait.

This is my predicament and yours. While we want our lives to be easier and according to our preferred timetable, God is working within us on His timetable and for His lasting purposes. He aims to make us more like the Lord Jesus, and our waiting is a necessary part of that process. God wants us to learn that following Him with complete love and trust requires that we wait upon Him. God desires to calm the screaming child that is within us; He want to hold us close and allow us the privilege of leaning into Him to find that we can trust Him for His love, comfort, and peace.

I confess that I do not always want to hear it when my Lord tells me to wait. I have argued as I learn that I must wait longer. Sometimes I have pleaded for a different answer. Can you relate to this? If so, I invite you to join me in giving thanks to God for His great mercy, grace, and patience toward you and me.

As parents grasp the childish ways of their children, how much more does our heavenly Father understand our struggle as we wait on Him. But as we mature in Christ, He enables us to appreciate that He always intends for us what is for His glory and our good. This is a great blessing indeed.

My Lord has also reminded me that our struggle with waiting is not in itself sinful, though it may lead to sin if we allow it to persist. If we convince ourselves and then try to convince God that our wisdom in this particular matter is greater than His, this is sin. And if our insistence on immediate gratification causes us to take matters into our own hands and get ahead of the Lord, this too is sin. Or if we make an idol for ourselves out of whatever we are waiting for, this too is sin because we value a particular outcome above what God wills.

But thankfully, God is loving and merciful to all who repent and come to Him in faith. Jesus Christ is ready to forgive and restore. I have experienced such grace over and over again. My Lord has done amazing things for me through the cancer I now endure. Through it all, He has strengthened my faith and helped me grow up in Christian maturity; He has taught me to trust Him, even as I wait upon Him. These are invaluable lessons to learn, and He teaches them to all who will learn.

In an article called "Waiting When God Seems Silent," published on John Piper's *Desiring God* website, Randy Alcorn wrote of the time his wife, Nanci, was going through chemotherapy. She shared this insightful quote from Andrew Murray's *Waiting on God*: "It is God's Spirit who has begun the work in you of waiting upon God. He will enable you to wait . . . Waiting continually will be met and rewarded by God Himself working continually."[7]

This is true. Whenever God calls us to wait, He also enables us to wait. And while we wait, God is working. He enables me day by day to wait upon Him, and He rewards me as I do. I pray that you are blessed to learn the same.

Waiting on God is a choice we can make by faith. It flows out of a relationship of love and trust in Him. In Psalm 62, the psalmist declared that He was making this choice when he declared, *For God alone, O my soul, wait in silence, for my hope is from Him. He only is my rock and my salvation, my fortress; I shall not be shaken. On God rests my salvation and my glory; my mighty rock, my refuge is God. Trust in Him at all times, O people; pour out your heart before Him; God is a refuge for us* (Psalm 62:5-8).

Amen. This is my testimony too. When I lean upon God while waiting on Him, He gives the grace I need to pray, to listen carefully, and to trust Him fully. I am choosing again today to take a deep breath, release my clenched hands, and let God be God in me and for me. Because I love Him and trust Him, I will wait upon the Lord.

FOR REFLECTION

What is your testimony of waiting upon the Lord? What must happen within you for you to wait upon Him with complete trust and love? In what areas of life are you being called to wait upon Him? Ask God to help you in this, and He surely will.

---

[7] Randy Alcorn, "Waiting When God Seems Silent," www.desiringgod.org.

54

ON DREAMING OF HEAVEN

September 8, 2019

Do you ever dream of heaven? I do. As my life progresses and I continue to struggle physically, the promises of heaven become more and more real to me. I know that God's Word is true, and in it He has spoken clearly and prophetically of the future, when we who are His own sons and daughters through faith in Jesus Christ will forever be with Him in His heavenly glory. I am excited about that.

From time to time I have been given glimpses of heaven through dreams and visions. By such grace God has mysteriously allowed me to anticipate His promise with increasing joy. I perceive that He has shown me these things so I might live every day with eternity in mind, and I might aim to pass along to others our Lord's eternal perspective with full trust in His precious promises.

This week I had another dream of arriving in heaven, which is inspiring me with grateful anticipation of what God has in store for me and for all who know and love Jesus as Savior and Lord. When the dream had ended, I awoke to the exuberant sound of my own joyful laughter. I laughed with great joy because of what I had experienced in my dream. As I write this, I am still overflowing with joy and praise.

I share this with you humbly, certainly not to elevate myself in anyone's esteem or to add anything to the revelation of Holy Scripture concerning the promises of God. God's grace is our only hope, and His Word is the ultimate, infallible standard of God's truth, for it is divinely inspired and thus without error.

Because heaven is infinite in wonder and grandeur, and because our finite minds are limited in knowledge and understanding, we should know that we have grasped only the surface of what will be. The apostle Paul referred to such mysteries when he wrote, *What no eye has seen, nor ear heard, nor the heart of man imagined, what God has prepared for those who love him* (1 Corinthians 2:9).

I have been blessed as the Lord has shown these things to me so vividly. I humbly share some of my dream with you, not seeing or saying anything that is in clear contradiction to the revelation of Scripture. It is my prayerful hope that you too might be pointed toward the Lord and His Word and toward praise and worship, with joyful anticipation of what is yet to come.

In my dream, as I arrived in heaven I immediately knew great joy. I was more excited and happy than I can describe. I knew this is where I belonged – in God's holy presence in the very place He has prepared for me and all of His children. This is where I have longed to be. It is where I want to be. In heaven there is great joy.

There is also great love. His love permeated me and everything around me. Because God is love, His love was tangible and everywhere. I saw it on every face, heard it in every voice, and sensed it in everything. I felt His amazing and infinite love in every pore of my being. In heaven everyone loves and is loved, for God is love.

There is sweet fellowship with God, for humanity is restored to God's created intention, no longer cursed with the consequences of our sin. I intuitively knew with much satisfaction that by God's mercy and grace, I was blessed to live in sweet fellowship with God. Such fellowship begins while on our earthly journey by knowing and following Jesus Christ; it continues forever in heaven, for relationship with God is life everlasting. In heaven is sweet fellowship with God.

There is also sweet fellowship with brothers and sisters in Christ. I was overjoyed to see, greet, and hug some whom I have known and loved. These too are filled with great joy in His presence. This reminds me that all who are in Christ Jesus are forever God's children. We who are His sons and daughters now are forever family with each other. In heaven there is sweet fellowship with forever family.

And in heaven we are known and called by name. Though there are multitudes, I heard my own name. Others were arriving too, from all nations and peoples, but I was not lost in the crowd. I sensed that my arrival was desired and expected, as someone approached me, called me by name, and welcomed me home. In heaven we are all known and called by name.

Sweet personal reunions occur in heaven. I was led to a personal and remarkable reunion that my heavenly Father knows I have longed for. In this reunion my heart overflowed with God's love and joy. I was introduced to a boy named Matthew and a girl named Joy. These were the first two children born to Helen and me, Matthew in 1979 and Joy in 1980.

Because these precious children were born early, and neither survived, our hearts were then broken with grief. Loving each of them dearly, we prayerfully committed them to the love and care of God. In heaven I could see that God has tenderly loved and cared for them, and in heaven we were reunited. With much joy I loved and held and blessed them, and they loved and held and blessed me. Oh, the grace and love of our God! Sweet personal reunions happen in heaven.

Though I could say more, this is enough for now. Of course I have no idea when I will be "promoted to glory," nor can any of us know such things. But we can know with certainty that when our moment comes, because of God's great love for us, we will be with the Lord forever. By His grace through the perfect sacrifice of Jesus Christ for our eternal salvation and His faithfulness in keeping every promise, we have the assurance of being in His glorious presence. This is our blessed assurance, and it is more wonderful than we have ever imagined.

With much joy I look forward to the fulfillment of God's promise of heaven. I am now even more determined to live every day for Him, until I am at last welcomed home and I see Him in the fullness of His heavenly glory. What a glorious day that will be! By God's grace I long to see you there.

FOR REFLECTION

How assured are you of God's promises of heaven, and how does such faith impact your life now? What must happen within your heart for you to live joyfully claiming the sweet promises of God? Ask God to help you in this, and He surely will.

55

ON ADMITTING OUR STRUGGLES AND SHARING HIS SUFFERING

September 15, 2019

God's blessings in my life have been incredible and innumerable, for which I am and will remain forever grateful. Still, I sometimes struggle with discouragement. It is normal for us to struggle when life is hard.

I have lately been discouraged because of the cumulative effects of eleven months of cancer and chemotherapy with no end in sight. Like carrying a heavy load on a long trek, the longer I carry this, the heavier it feels.

My latest blood labs have revealed that the cancer cells in my blood are no longer decreasing, but are in fact increasing again. Because of this, another chemotherapy drug has been prescribed by the multiple myeloma specialist at the Dana Farber Cancer Institute in Boston. This is my third chemo regimen since receiving my cancer diagnosis last October.

I started this new treatment last Monday at the Providence VA Medical Center. The elusive treatment goal is still a bone marrow transplant using my own stem cells. But for this possibility, cancer cells in my bone marrow and blood must be reduced further. I ask for your prayers toward this end.

This latest change has discouraged me. I can also say that it has not defeated me, nor can it, because by God's grace I know Whom to turn to. I know how to pray, and I know He has been faithful to me; He is faithful now and will be faithful forever. Helen and I lean on our Lord, and He sustains us day by day. Living in personal relationship with the Lord of all and having faith in Him makes all the difference when the struggles of this life become hard. I pray that you also experience this truth.

My study of God's Word this week included readings from 2 Corinthians that have been like cool refreshing spring water for my thirsty soul. I love the passage in chapter 4 that reminds us that though the treasure we have from God is carried in fragile *jars of clay* and though *death is at work in us*, we have the resurrection life of Jesus Christ within us (2 Corinthians 4:7, 12).

The apostle Paul then wrote these moving words of encouragement that are as healing medicine for me and for all discouraged followers of Jesus who will receive it by faith: *So we do not lose heart. Though our outer self is wasting away, our inner self is being renewed day by day. For this light momentary affliction is preparing for us an eternal weight of glory beyond all comparison, as we look not to the things that are seen, but to the things that are unseen. For the things that are seen are transient, but the things that are unseen are eternal* (2 Corinthians 4:16-18). Amen! May we all believe and receive this truth.

This promise of God reminds us that He has a redemptive purpose for us even in and through our struggles. The Lord has lovingly reminded me again that He is with me in my struggle, and that He has a good plan for Helen and me. He is working all of this for our good and for His glory.

These timeless truths are for all who believe, love, and trust the Lord Jesus Christ. He never promised that our lives would be exempt from suffering. Those who preach such a message are preaching a falsehood. Rather, God promises something much better. He promises to be with us through it all, up close and personal through every moment and in every difficulty. Our Lord promises to bless us and make us a blessing to others. He promises His children that He has a redemptive purpose for us, even in our struggles.

Every day in this broken world, we witness and experience struggle and suffering. The cumulative effect of the suffering can be the self-protection of indifference or denial. We may attempt to keep our distance from it, neither seeing nor caring.

The causes of human struggle are plentiful: weather, accidents, disease, war, abandonment, loneliness, death, poverty, prejudice, persecution, and the pure evil of humanity's cruelty toward one another. This week, while observing another anniversary of the 2001 attack against America on 9/11, I recalled several divine-appointment conversations I had with people who lost loved ones on that horrific day. I still pray for their comfort and healing, for the hurt and loss remain. In this broken world, struggle and suffering are common to us all.

While experiencing his own struggles in prison, the apostle Paul turned his attention from himself to Jesus and reflected on the suffering of the Lord who lovingly and willingly endured it all for him and for us. Jesus Christ was violently rejected. He was horribly beaten and then nailed to a cruel cross; He bled and suffered until he died. Our Lord willingly did this for me and for you.

As Paul reflected on these things while he suffered imprisonment, he may have recalled with tears how he had once personally rejected and hated Jesus and all who followed Him; he contributed to the suffering of many Christians. As we recall the suffering of our Lord, we also acknowledge and confess our own sins and our need for the Savior.

The Holy Spirit gives us such reflections of Christ's love and mercy to lead us to true confession of our sin, adoration of the Lord, and celebration of His grace. The Spirit endeavors to bring us to grateful devotion and worshipful determination to live for Him. Whatever our present struggles are, may God help us respond to Him in this way.

From his prison cell, the apostle Paul described his worshipful determination to offer his struggles and suffering to the Lord. He wrote, *I count everything as loss because of the surpassing worth of knowing Christ Jesus my Lord. For His sake I have suffered the loss of all things and count them as rubbish, in order that I may gain Christ and be found in Him, not having a righteousness of my own that comes from the law, but that which comes through faith in Christ, the righteousness from God that depends on faith – that I may know Him and the power of His resurrection, and may share His sufferings, becoming like Him in his death, that by any means possible I may attain the resurrection from the dead* (Philippians 3:8-11).

These words have often inspired, challenged, and mystified me. Who in their right mind asks God for suffering? Who wants it? I have been far more prone to ask God to remove my suffering. But here is Paul in the face of discomfort, loneliness, and hardship, expressing his longing to share in the sufferings of Jesus. Bible scholars have reflected on what this means, and differing interpretations have been offered.

While I cannot pretend to comprehend what Paul meant, I can identify at least in part with what he prayed. Longing to share in the sufferings of Christ, even becoming like Him in His death, speaks of sharing in our hearts the redemptive purpose of Christ in His sufferings. It is being willing to endure whatever pain or struggle is required of us, while sharing God's love and longing for the salvation of others. This is the heart of Jesus, and it became Paul's heart too, motivating him in life and ministry.

While he personally endured many difficulties, Paul longed to participate in the purpose of Christ's suffering by extending Christ's love, grace, and life to others. The longing that Paul expressed here was fulfilled for him. His inspired letters, written from prison, his personal example of enduring suffering for Christ's sake, and his faithful proclamation of the good news of salvation through faith in Jesus Christ accomplished God's purpose. This example is speaking to me now in the midst of my own struggles.

Though I have experienced some discouragement lately, and though I have longed for an easier path, by God's grace I can identify with Paul's heart, for I too love the Lord. I too long to participate in the redemptive purpose of Christ's sufferings, so He will be glorified, and by His love, grace, and mercy, others will be drawn to Him too.

It is good to admit to the Lord and others when our struggles are hard for us, for He already knows, and He will stir others to encourage and pray for us. Thankfully, God does not intend for any of us to carry our heavy burdens alone. It is good for us to pray, as did the apostle Paul, that through our struggles Christ's life and love and salvation might be seen and extended to others. It is good for us to offer to the

Lord Jesus our broken lives, especially our suffering, for His redemptive purposes to be fulfilled in and through us. As we do this, we can know His joy and peace.

FOR REFLECTION

What struggles with discouragement have you had lately, and to what extent have you admitted it to God and to others? Do you believe that God has a redemptive purpose for you, even in your struggles? What might that purpose be? What does it mean for you to *share in His sufferings, becoming like Him in His death*? What needs to happen in your heart for you to know His peace in your struggles? Ask God to help you in this, and He surely will.

56

ON TRUSTING GOD THROUGH OUR TRANSITIONS

September 24, 2019

Helen and I have returned home after a few days in Minnesota; we found a townhome for which we are now under contract. We expect to close the last week of October. The home is in Northfield, Minnesota, just 2.5 miles from where our son Jonathan lives with his family. We will own two homes for a while until our home in Rhode Island sells. We continue to trust God to direct in this matter in His time and for His glory.

Before our latest trip to Minnesota, I received a call from the Transplant Center in Nashville, Tennessee, who reported that they have been watching my lab results from a distance. They believe I will soon be ready to proceed with the SCT. Presuming that the new chemotherapy regimen will work as expected, I am penciled in for the SCT in early January. In light of this, Helen and I agreed that we should make our move to Minnesota as soon as possible, while I am still able.

This schedule will allow us time to settle in and for me to transfer my medical care to the VA Medical Center in Minneapolis, so they will be prepared to care for me upon my return from Nashville. Various medical appointments have been scheduled for me as soon as we arrive in Minnesota. We will enjoy celebrating upcoming holidays with our children and grandchildren in Minnesota and Alaska, as I will live in a proverbial bubble for some time following the SCT.

We counted the number of places we have lived together since we were married forty-three years ago, and this move will be our seventeenth. Transitions for us are nothing new. We have found that transitions can be stressful even when they are right, because they involve change from the familiar to the unfamiliar, from people we love and to whom we must say goodbye to places where we must now make new friends.

But at the same time, transitions can be exciting, for a sense of adventure transpires. Though the territory is new to us, we can know with certainty that God's plan for us is good, and we can expect to see new and specific ways the Lord will lead us for His glory.

We have always found joy and peace in our transitions, because each time we have known God's presence and been confident of His leading. We have claimed His promises and have found Him faithful to go before us to lead our way. Many Scriptures promise this, especially Deuteronomy 31:8, which says, *It is the Lord who goes before you. He will be with you; He will not leave you nor forsake you. Do not fear or be dismayed.* This sure promise is comfort with guidance for all who will trust Him.

As I consider the challenges that are ahead for me in fighting cancer, including the expected hardships of going through the SCT, I cling to the Lord's promise from Deuteronomy 1:30, *The Lord your God who goes before you will Himself fight for you.* What a comfort this is! Though I am often weary in this battle, I know with confidence that my Lord is fighting for me, and ultimately victory is certain.

Jesus's Great Commission given to all His disciples moments before His ascension to heavenly glory included this promise: *And behold, I am with you always, to the end of the age* (Matthew 28:20). I testify that this is true, for He has been with me always, He is with me now, and He will surely be with me through every transition; He will be with all of His children through every change. There are no exceptions to *always*.

So what is our part in all of this? It is not to worry or grumble under the stress. Rather, it is to trust the Lord and to ask and allow Him to lead us; it is to give Him our praise and thanks as He leads us.

Your prayers for Helen and me through the transition that is now before us will be appreciated. A few specific prayer requests for us now are:

1. For God to keep me well enough that I can do my part through this move.
2. For the new chemotherapy regimen to effectively reduce the cancer cells in my bone marrow and blood so I will be deemed ready to proceed with the SCT and then for durable remission to be the result.
3. For a buyer for our Rhode Island home, and for God to receive glory in this matter.
4. For God's continued grace and peace for Helen and me as we proceed and for our faithfulness in every divine appointment along the way.

Your ongoing love and prayers for Helen and me are appreciated more than I can express. Thank you, and thanks be to God! I also pray for God's grace in your lives. I pray that in whatever transitions you are in or may soon be in that you will experience firsthand the peace and joy that He freely gives to all who trust Him.

FOR REFLECTION

What promises of God have especially blessed you in and through the transitions of your life? Do you trust that God has a redemptive purpose for you, even in the hard transitions of your life? How have you experienced this? Have you given Him praise and thanks as He has led you? What must happen within your heart for you to know His peace in your transitions? Ask God to help you in this, and He surely will.

57

ON GOING HOME SOON

October 1, 2019

Where do we live now? Where is our permanent home? And where do we want to live? For various reasons I have been reflecting on these questions. Helen and I will soon be moving again; my body is reminding me every day that it is temporary, and my Lord has been speaking to me about what is coming, which motivates me greatly. Allow me to share a few personal reflections on these questions:

Where do I live now?

I can answer this question in two ways. I have a physical address, which will soon change. Because of my faith in Jesus Christ and by His grace, I can also know where I now live spiritually. For the past three years, We have made our physical home in Coventry, Rhode Island, and before this month is over, our new address will be in Northfield, Minnesota. This will be the seventeenth address we will have shared since we were married forty-three years ago.

And where do we now live spiritually?

We live in the same place you live if you belong to Jesus Christ. We live in personal relationship with the Lord. Because of His loving and sacrificial death for us on the cross of suffering and because of His triumphant victory for us over sin and death, we have assurance of eternity with Him. By His great grace and through our faith in Him, we continually live, move, and have our being in Jesus Christ. This means that wherever we may be on this earth, whatever the circumstances are around us, or the struggles that rage within us, we live now in Jesus Christ. There is no greater place to be.

The apostle Paul probably wrote his letter to the Christians in the small city of Colossae from a prison in Rome about AD 62 (Acts 27-28). Severe trials and struggles were common among followers of the Lord Jesus Christ, so Paul sought to encourage these disciples of the Lord to be heavenly minded and to realize that every day and moment they were in Jesus Christ.

To them and to us Paul wrote *If then you have been raised with Christ, seek the things that are above, where Christ is, seated at the right hand of God. Set your minds on things that are above, not on things that are on earth. For you have died, and your life is hidden with Christ in God. When Christ who is your life appears, then you also will appear with Him in glory* (Colossians 3:1-4).

So where do we live now? Physically we live at our home address or wherever He may send us, and spiritually we live in Jesus Christ. All who belong to Him by faith are living continuously *with Christ in God*, which means we never leave this home. We will forever be at home in Jesus Christ.

Where is my permanent home?

Through the years Helen and I have lived in various places, but we have always known that each location was temporary. In addition to the places we lived together, during the years of my military service when forward deployed, I also lived apart from her in other places, including Japan, Australia, South Korea, Cuba, and sometimes out to sea. But every place we have lived, whether together or apart, was temporary. Isn't that true of us all?

Home of Record is a term used in the military that refers to our permanent home. This is typically where we lived when we entered the military, and ostensibly where we will return when our service and journeys are over. This is where we vote and pay taxes and hold drivers' licenses, while we serve on active duty. Though we might be physically living elsewhere, we remain citizens of our permanent home.

The apostle Paul reminds Christians that our "Home of Record" is in heaven. Though for now we reside in various locations while serving the Lord wherever He may lead us, Paul tells us to never forget where we come from and where we are going. He knew that our ultimate loyalties are to be there. Paul taught that *our citizenship is in heaven, and from it we await a Savior, the Lord Jesus Christ, who will transform our lowly body to be like His glorious body, by the power that enables Him even to subject all things to Himself* (Philippians 3:20-21).

So where is my permanent home and yours now? *Our citizenship is in heaven.* We are called and blessed to faithfully love and serve Him wherever and however He leads us, until He calls us to come home.

Where do I want to live?

One year ago today, on October 1, 2018, I received a call from the Dana Farber Cancer Institute in Boston that informed me I had active multiple myeloma; I had to immediately begin chemotherapy treatments. This past year has challenged me and Helen. I struggled physically, and much has changed for us. We have been reminded of our mortality, but how we thank God that we know whom to lean on, for He has wonderfully sustained us. We have received and believed the sure promises of God.

Several times in this past year, the Lord blessed me with vivid dreams of heaven. Each time I have been left with a deep and lingering longing for our heavenly home. The Scriptures have much to say about heaven, and I encourage you to prayerfully reflect on these things. Some passages I commend for your prayerful reflection include Matthew 7:13-14; John 14:2-6; Revelation 7:13-17; and Revelation 21:4-8.

Our Lord wants us to live each day with heaven in mind, so our priorities, attitudes, words, and actions will reflect an eternal perspective and deep confidence in the promises of God. By His grace, my Lord has blessed me with such joyful hope. Though I have not typically shared details of my heavenly dreams, allow me to share a portion of one I had last week, as it addresses a precious reality for all who are in Christ Jesus.

In my dream of heaven, I saw, felt, and experienced the Lord's embrace. His arms were around me. His love flowed into me. His grace covered me. His joy washed over me. I was utterly overwhelmed by His presence and His glory. I remain overwhelmed by it.

How I praise God today that often along my earthly journey I have experienced His love, grace, and joy. I have known and rejoiced in His glorious presence. In heaven it will be like this to an infinite degree. God has declared that by His mercy and through our repentance and faith in the Lord Jesus Christ, He offers us all His amazing grace.

Then in my dream I heard His voice, as He spoke to me. My Lord asked me if I wished to come home now, or to remain in my body for a while longer. I hesitated in my reply. How would you answer this question? I knew in the core of my being that in the arms of Jesus, there is no other place I would rather be. Yet I longed to do His will.

I long to be in heaven, and I know with grateful anticipation that by His grace I soon will be. I really wanted to say to the Lord, "I want to stay here," but instead I replied, "I trust you in this Jesus. I desire only your will. I want only to be where you are, doing only your will, and bringing you praise!" This is the promise of God to all who belong to Him through faith in the Lord Jesus Christ.

In 2 Corinthians the apostle Paul referred to our physical bodies as being like tents that will be destroyed. I can identify with what Paul declared. He wrote, *In this tent we groan, longing to put on our heavenly dwelling* (2 Corinthians 5:2). Having experienced this truth personally, Paul sought to encourage other Christians, especially us, by this beautiful reminder of our Lord's heavenly promise to us.

So Paul wrote, *So we are always of good courage. We know that while we are at home in the body we are away from the Lord, for we walk by faith, not by sight. Yes, we are of good courage, and we would rather be away from the body and at home with the Lord. So whether we are at home or away, we make it our aim to please Him. For we must all appear before the judgment seat of Christ, so that each one may receive what is due for what he has done in the body, whether good or evil* (2 Corinthians 5:6-10).

Where then do we want to live now? Paul declared that his own longing was to be *at home with the Lord*, by which he meant heaven. But until then, he said we *walk by faith, not by sight*, and therefore *we are of good courage*, and *we make it our aim to please Him*. This is how we are to live now while longing for our eternal home.

Where do we live now? – Physically we live at our earthly address or wherever He may lead us, and spiritually we live now *hidden with Christ in God*.

Where is our permanent home? – Our citizenship is in heaven.

Where do we want to live now? – Where He is.

So we long to be *at home with the Lord*, but until then we long to be wherever He will lead us, doing His will and bringing Him praise. How blessed we are to know that by faith we are already home in Christ, and in His time we will be going home to be with Him in the fullness of His glory forever and ever! Amen.

FOR REFLECTION

Where do you live now and why? Where is your permanent home and how does this assurance affect you now? Where do you really want to live and why? Do you believe with certainty that the Lord's promise of heaven is in your future, and on what basis do you believe it? How can you love and treasure His promise more fully that one day soon you will be going home? Ask God to help you in this, and He surely will.

58

ON SAYING GOODBYE

October 9, 2019

Saying goodbye is not easy. It can bring many tears, much sorrow, and a profound sense of loss. Acts 20 describes the occasion when the apostle Paul said farewell to the elders of the church in Ephesus. He had previously lived and loved and served the Lord for over two unforgettable years with these precious friends, as is recounted in Acts 19:1-10. The gospel writer Luke was with Paul when Acts 20 occurred. Luke recounted the tears that flowed that day, including his own, as he described the touching farewell between Paul and the elders of the church in Ephesus.

Luke wrote, *And when he had said these things, he knelt down and prayed with them all. And there was much weeping on the part of all; they embraced Paul and kissed him, being sorrowful most of all because of the word he had spoken, that they would not see his face again. And they accompanied him to the ship* (Acts 20:36-38). These are sad words, and we can relate to them.

Transitions and moves can prompt much emotion. I have lived in thirteen different states in the United States. I have served three congregations and many places of ministry as directed by the Lord. I have loved many people. And on every occasion when it came time to move, even though it was right, it was hard.

When Helen and I raised our three children, we understood that in time each of them would leave our home to pursue their own course. Still, whenever it happened and one of them left our home, I grieved with tears. It is hard to say goodbye. Over the years, each time we visited each other, as great as it was to be together for a while, it has been hard to say goodbye. But this kind of pain is part of loving and living.

And when loved ones have died, and we gathered as family and friends to grieve, remember, and celebrate their lives, sorrow remains – even with the love and joy we share and the memories and thankfulness to God for their precious lives. Saying goodbye is hard.

This reality is upon me again, as we prepare for another departure; this time we move from Rhode Island to Minnesota. We agree in the Lord that this move is right, for we will be near our two sons. We will also be near a major airport in Minneapolis, which offers direct flights to Anchorage, Alaska, where our daughter and her family live. I will have superb medical care at the Minneapolis VA Medical Center, and if needed, I will be able to access the Mayo Clinic in Rochester, Minnesota, which offers the best care available for treating multiple myeloma.

But the sting of it is saying goodbye to family and friends who remain in Rhode Island and New England. I understand the tears that were shed that day at the beach as described in Acts 20. The Lord Jesus is comforting me now with the reminder that because of His glorious promises and His triumphant victory over sin and death, all who belong to Him through faith never really have to say goodbye to each other. We are His forever family, eternally united by our relationship with God in Jesus Christ. We will share eternity with our Lord and with each other.

This truth comforts me now. When the time comes to depart from the people we love, because we are in Christ, we do not really say goodbye. Rather, with sweet assurance in the promises of God, we say, "See you later." How wonderful is that?

Last Sunday we attended the Sunday Worship at Church of The Apostles in Coventry, Rhode Island, where I previously served as overseer. I participated in the laying on of hands upon the one who has been appointed to serve now in that role. The new bishop, Pastor Todd Murphy, has invited Helen and me to express our farewells to the congregation this coming Sunday. I will gladly do so with heartfelt gratitude and praise to God for the blessing we have known from living and serving together. Though I will do this with joy, I also know there will be sorrow in it, but the sorrow is tempered by the sweetness of God's promises.

On the twenty-second of this month, movers are scheduled to arrive. They will pack everything up, load the truck, and depart. As the week progresses, I will have more medical appointments, painters will paint the interior walls, and the home will be cleaned. Then our home will be shown to prospective buyers. On the twenty-fourth, our son Jonathan will fly from Minnesota to Rhode Island to help us with driving about 1400 miles to our new home. On the morning of the twenty-fifth, our journey westward begins. On the twenty-ninth, the moving truck should arrive, and we will move into our new home.

Helen and I thank everyone who has been praying for us through this transition. Please continue to pray that the cancer cells in my blood and marrow will continue to decrease, so that by God's grace a successful SCT can soon be accomplished. Pray too for a buyer for our home in Coventry in God's timing, all for His praise and glory. Pray that we may continue to live each day aware of His presence that we may recognize and respond to every divine appointment that He prepares for us (Ephesians 2:10).

Though there can be sorrow along our earthly journey, let us pray that the peace, love. and joy of the Lord will be our continual experience and that our faithful witness for Christ will glorify Him and be a blessing to others.

FOR REFLECTION

When has saying goodbye to people you love been very hard for you? How has your faith in the Lord helped you through such times, and what promises of God meant the most to you then? How can you better experience and demonstrate the peace, love, and joy of the Lord when you must say goodbye to people you love? Ask God to help you in this, and He surely will.

59

ON RECEIVING STRENGTH THROUGH FAITH AND PERSISTENT PRAYER

October 16, 2019

The Bible teaches, and I have experienced and observed, that someone who receives their strength from God cannot and will not be destroyed when trials come. Though it can be very hard and painful for us, through persistent prayer and dependence upon the Lord, we will not be irreparably broken or destroyed, for we are strengthened by God Himself. By His grace we can endure.

Isaiah makes this promise to all who believe by calling us to fix our focus in faith, not upon our own weakness and struggle, but upon the Lord Himself: *Have you not known? Have you not heard? The LORD is the everlasting God, the Creator of the ends of the earth. He does not faint or grow weary; His understanding is unsearchable. He gives power to the faint, and to him who has no might He increases strength. Even youths shall faint and be weary, and young men shall fall exhausted; but they who wait for the LORD shall renew their strength; they shall mount up with wings like eagles; they shall run and not be weary; they shall walk and not faint* (Isaiah 40:28-31). What a beautiful promise! I will tell you that I have so often experienced the truth of it, and I am claiming it again for today.

The prerequisite that is prescribed by the prophet for us to experience the fulfillment of this promise can be hard to envision and apply. These truths become reality for *they who wait for the Lord*. This requires patience, faith in God, and persistence in prayer. I have been learning this truth again.

For a year I have asked God and waited for Him to remove the cancer cells from my bone marrow and blood. Many of you have prayed with me toward this end. We tried two combinations of chemotherapy drugs; each reduced the cancer cells some, but only for a while. Progress slowed, and eventually each of these regimens stopped reducing cancer cells. So last month I started a third chemo regimen.

Month by month and day by day, I have prayed and waited upon my Lord, all the while dealing with unpleasant side effects of the drug. Listening carefully, I have often heard Him remind me of His presence. I have heard Him calling me to trust Him and depend on Him completely. I have heard His clear call to persist in prayer and to wait expectantly for His answer that is coming in His time for His glory and my good.

Though the waiting has been hard, I have not doubted His faithfulness, for through the years He has shown me that He is faithful, and He can be trusted. I have known His love for me. I know He is able; He hears and answers prayer, and He is being glorified and will be glorified through all of this. I pray and hope that you know the same, for He loves you much.

My oncologists all agree that a bone marrow transplant using my own stem cells is the most promising course of treatment for me, as it offers the hope of prolonged remission. But to be deemed eligible for this with the potential of success, the cancer levels in my blood must be measured below 0.5 milligrams per deciliter. For months now our prayers and the prayers of others have been that this threshold will be reached to warrant a transplant and provide a durable remission. Thank you again to all who have prayed toward this end.

I wonder if you have ever, like me, wondered why the Lord taught us to pray and to continue praying with persistence. After all, He knows what we need even before we ask Him, and He is entirely able to immediately say yes when we pray with a quick and miraculous answer. I have seen God do this many times. Yet for His purposes and for our good, He often wants us to pray and keep on praying with persistence.

Have you experienced this? Are there things for which you have been praying for a long time, faithfully and persistently asking God for His grace and intervention? If so, you are doing what the Lord has taught us to do. He still calls all of His disciples to trust Him and to persist in prayer until we have received His answer.

In Luke we read a parable taught by Jesus of a widow who has been mistreated. Day after day she brings her case before a judge who is indifferent to her request, but then he is compelled to reconsider because she refuses to take no for an answer. He finally relents and says, *Though I neither fear God nor respect man, yet because this widow keeps bothering me, I will give her justice, so that she will not beat me down by her continual coming* (Luke 18:4-5).

Jesus is certainly not teaching that God is like an insensitive judge who must be badgered to respond to our requests. Rather, he is saying that compared to the insensitive judge, God who is our good judge and loving Father will hear and answer His beloved disciples who persist in praying to Him. Luke understood this parable in this way, for he prefaced it with the words, *And he told them a parable to the effect that they ought always to pray and not lose heart* (Luke 18:1).

Luke's choice of the words *lose heart* suggests what can sometimes be our experience when we wait. I can relate to this. When God delays in answering our requests, we may become disappointed or even tempted to give up or lose heart. For this reason Jesus concluded the parable with a rhetorical question for each of us to consider: *Nevertheless, when the Son of Man comes, will he find faith on earth?* (Luke 18:8).

We must all answer our Lord's question personally by examining our own heart. He has asked us to persist in prayer and faith when we face trials and the waiting is hard. He promises that if we do so, He will give us His strength. We will not go through the trial alone, but with Him. He promises to hear and answer our prayers for His glory and our good, and He will do it in His time as we persist in faith and in prayer.

For all who have prayed for cancer cells in my blood to fall below the required threshold so I can safely proceed with the SCT, I offer my deep and profound gratitude. Thank you for persisting in prayer with me. Now I invite you to join me in giving praise to God who has graciously answered our prayers.

For the glory of God and for your blessing, I share this praise report. When I entered this battle last year, the measured amount of cancer (myeloma) cells in my blood was 4.54 milligrams/deciliter. For an SCT to proceed with good potential for successful and durable remission, the amount of myeloma cells in my blood had to be reduced via chemotherapy to below 0.5 milligrams/deciliter. Four weeks ago, after nearly a year of chemotherapy, this level was measured at 0.92 milligrams/deciliter. But this week, after just one four-week cycle on the new chemotherapy regimen, the labs showed a measurement of just 0.27 milligrams/deciliter – well below the required target! Hallelujah! God be praised!

This means my SCT is now scheduled. As Helen and I will be moving next week, I have requested a two-month delay to allow time for getting settled in our new home and connected to my new medical team in Minnesota. Then we can spend the holidays with our children and grandchildren.

The SCT is now scheduled for early January in Nashville, Tennessee, at the VA Medical Center, which is in partnership with the Vanderbilt University Medical Center. Until then I will continue my current chemotherapy regimen to reduce the cancer in my marrow and blood even further, thus improving the potential duration of any remission.

I will continue to put my faith in God and to persist in believing prayer. I hope you will join me in this, for He invites all of us to bring to Him our every burden, concern, and trial, whereby we may receive His strength. We continue praying, for our God is forever faithful.

FOR REFLECTION

Read again Isaiah 40:28-31. When have you had to *wait for the Lord*, and then with faith and persistent prayer, you received His strength? Why did Jesus teach (Luke 18:1) that we *ought always to pray and not lose heart*, and what does this exhortation mean for you? What needs to happen for you to receive even more of God's strength through faith and persistent prayer? Ask God to help you in this, and He surely will.

60

ON COPING WITH PAIN WITH GOD'S HELP

October 22, 2019

Pain is common to all of us, though we may experience it in different ways and intensities. Sometimes our pain is bearable, and at other times it is debilitating. Some types of pain we can face include mental injury or emotional pain, grief and sorrow, spiritual pain and confusion, and physical pain. If we look around, we can all see someone who lives with pain on a constant basis. On any given day or season of life, we might experience pain ourselves, perhaps significant pain.

On Sunday morning Helen and I visited Darlington Congregational Church in Pawtucket, Rhode Island, the church we served from 1980-1989. That congregation called us right after I graduated from seminary, and we concluded our time there when I accepted the Lord's call to serve as a chaplain in the United States Navy. On Sunday I wanted to share with this congregation my testimony of God's faithfulness, even in my recent struggles. I wanted to point them one more time to our precious Lord Jesus. In preparing to do this, I reminisced about how God has led us through the years as we sought Him first and how He has been faithful in every circumstance of our lives.

Reflecting on these truths, I recalled a few of the painful times of life that we experienced, including prolonged times of geographical separation, seasons of grief, and loss. In all of our lives at various times and ways, pain comes to us. But in the midst of the pain, when we choose to lean upon the Lord, we are blessed to know and receive His comfort, strength, and peace.

I was reminded of this yesterday when I experienced intense physical pain. As this is Helen's and my final week in Rhode Island before we depart for Minnesota, I had several medical appointments scheduled. Yesterday was my weekly appointment to receive a chemotherapy infusion. While there, my oncologist also performed a bone marrow biopsy, this time from the sternum.

I am often asked by nurses to describe the level of my pain on a scale of 1 to 10. Generally, my answers have varied from 2 to 5. But this time I would have answered that the pain was a 15. It was off-the-charts excruciating, taking my breath away. But thankfully, it did not last long. After the procedure, I lay in a bed recuperating for thirty to forty-five minutes; then I was moved to a chemotherapy room to prepare for my infusion.

A few minutes later, I had severe chest pains. The pain was intense, and I wondered if I was having a heart attack. I called out to the Lord, and in the midst of the pain, I immediately felt His peace. I asked a friend who was also receiving chemotherapy to call for help. Suddenly the room was filled with people. Nitroglycerin tablets were administered, and I was put on oxygen and hooked up for an EKG. After three nitro tablets the pain was gone. All of this prompted a consult with cardiology and a trip to the emergency room for several hours of evaluation.

Initial tests did not show elevated enzymes that would suggest I had a heart attack, but the ER doctor discussed admitting me for further tests over the next couple of days. Because I was exhausted and knew I needed to rest, which is hard to do in the hospital, I declined. Besides, the movers had just arrived at our home, and we were to be moving later in the week. I promised to immediately return if chest pain returns, and I also promised to follow up on this matter in Minneapolis. The ER doctor blessed this plan.

I rejoice that the intense pain I experienced yesterday from the bone marrow biopsy and later from chest pain is gone now. But through these experiences, the Lord has given me a few vivid biblical reminders about coping with pain with His help. Having reflected on these truths, allow me to share them for your prayerful reflection:

1. The pain is a vivid reminder of what is soon coming, when pain will be no more.

> *For I consider that the sufferings of this present time are not worth comparing with the glory that is to be revealed to us.* (Romans 8:18)

> *He will wipe away every tear from their eyes, and death shall be no more, neither shall there be mourning, nor crying, nor pain anymore, for the former things have passed away.* (Revelation 21:4)

2. The pain is a vivid reminder that the Lord is very near.

> *The LORD is near to the brokenhearted and saves the crushed in spirit.* (Psalm 34:18)

3. The pain is a vivid reminder to pray to the Lord and always give Him praise.

> *Heal me, O Lord, and I shall be healed; save me and I shall be saved, for you are my praise.* (Jeremiah 17:14)

4. The pain is a vivid reminder that we need and have a Savior, and we can trust Him fully.

> *Consequently He is able to save to the uttermost those who draw near to God through Him, since He always lives to make intercession for them* (Hebrews 7:25). The Greek word that is here translated *save* means "to heal, preserve, save,

make whole." In our pain and always, Jesus Christ is our Savior.

5. **The pain is a vivid reminder that by God's grace we are able to choose to resist the devil, remain firm in our faith, and remember that others are suffering too. Very soon this pain will be finished. In our pain we are reminded of this precious hope.**

> *Resist him* [the devil], *firm in your faith, knowing that the same kinds of suffering are being experienced by your brotherhood throughout the world. And after you have suffered a little while, the God of all grace, who has called you to His eternal glory in Christ, will Himself restore, confirm, strengthen, and establish you.* (I Peter 5:9-10)

To all of this, I say, "Yes, and Amen!" If you should find yourself in pain today or if and when you do in the future, I pray that the truths expressed in these verses may also provide encouragement to you, as they have for me. I experienced firsthand what I attest to you today that in great mercy and love the Lord matures and teaches His children. He holds us close, even in and through our pain.

FOR REFLECTION

As pain is common to us all, what kinds of intense pain have you known, and how did you cope? What pain have you experienced lately, and how has your faith in God helped you in dealing with it? Reviewing again the five biblical reminders listed in this lesson about coping with pain by faith in the Lord, which of these reminders is especially helpful to you right now, and why? What must happen in your heart and daily life for you to receive God's help when pain enters your life? Ask God to help you in this, and He surely will.

61

ON GOD'S WATCH CARE OVER HIS CHILDREN

November 3, 2019

Helen and I are now in Minnesota, and we are settling into our new home. Along our journey and with our arrival, we have experienced and observed the Lord's watch care over us. We give Him praise for watching over us and caring for us in such evident ways. Even as loving parents keep a watchful and protective eye over their little ones, so does our heavenly Father keep a watchful and protective eye over us, His children. He watches over me, and He is watching over you.

We experienced His watch care in three ways since we left Rhode Island:

Safe Travels:
With our son Jonathan's help, we traveled almost 1400 miles in two days without any issues. God was watching over us.

Smooth Transitions:
We have already connected with the church in Northfield where Jonathan and his family attend, and I have connected with the VA Medical Center in Minneapolis, where my chemotherapy treatments will resume tomorrow.

Special Touches:
We have experienced special expressions of God's care for us:

On Monday we went to lunch at a local restaurant where we had a wonderful conversation with our waitress, who is a sister in Christ. She then asked if she could pray over us, and in the middle of that restaurant, she prayed a beautiful prayer of faith and blessing over us. How very special!

A woman from the church we attended last Sunday called us this week and offered to deliver us some meals. Because we were focused on emptying boxes and settling in, and I have not been feeling well, this was an unexpected and special gift to us. Being near our son Jonathan and his family has also been a new and special blessing to us.

I could list many more ways God's watch care has been evident to us. Prayers have been faithfully offered on our behalf from dear family and friends. All of these expressions of love and faith are treasured gifts and reminders of God's continual loving watch care over us.

Do you know God has promised to watch over all of His children continually, wherever we are now and wherever we may yet go? He never stops doing so. As we believe and hold to this promise, our fears and anxieties about our future or current struggles diminish. By His grace it melts away, for by faith we know in our hearts that our God cares for us, and He is carefully watching over us.

Our God is always with us. This is His sure promise for every one of His children. It applied to Joshua. It applied to the disciples of Jesus who watched as He ascended into heaven. It applies to Helen and me. It applies to you and to all who trust in the Lord.

As Joshua was being assigned the monumental task of leading the nation of Israel into the land of promise, Moses knew that they were going to face much opposition, so he declared strong words of encouragement to Joshua: *Be strong and courageous. Do not fear or be in dread of them, for it is the LORD your God who goes with you. He will not leave you or forsake you* (Deuteronomy 31:6). Yes, and these words speak to us now.

Believing this promise and choosing to obey, Joshua went wherever he was led by the Lord to go, thus fulfilling His divine purpose. Whenever you and I believe and choose to obey the Lord, we experience the same blessing.

Jesus made this promise just before He physically ascended to heaven. To His disciples then and to us now, after assigning the Great Commission, to go wherever He sends us to teach and baptize and make disciples for Him, He promised *And behold, I am with you always, to the end of the age* (Matthew 28:20). What wonderful truth to believe and live by! As He is always with us, God's watch care over us is unending.

I thank you again for praying for us during our transition. Thank you for praying about my health. As I had mentioned, a few days before we left Rhode Island, I experienced chest pains, which were resolved by nitro tablets but involved a few hours in the emergency room. Thankfully, a heart attack was ruled out, but further cardiac tests are now required before the SCT can proceed. Also, this week I have been coughing and experiencing other symptoms of a viral infection. Because of this, I could not join Helen at church services today. Continued prayers for my strength and healing are appreciated.

In the midst of our struggles, we are reminded of God's great love and continual watch care over us. Let us rejoice in this.

FOR REFLECTION

As you look back over your life, how have you experienced God's watch care over you? What about lately? How has God's promise to be with you made a difference to you? What will need to change in your heart and daily life for you to recognize more how your Father in heaven is taking good care of you? Ask God to help you in this, and He surely will.

62

ON NOTICING GRACE

November 13, 2019

I have always loved the Thanksgiving story of the Pilgrims who arrived in Plymouth, Massachusetts, on November 11, 1620. They experienced a harsh and sorrowful winter, and by spring half of their number had died. Individually and as a community, they endured profound heartache, disappointment, and grief, but they believed in God, leaned upon Him in faith, and prayed fervently.

Despite their sorrow and pain, they trusted God, and their Father in heaven mercifully heard their prayers and poured out His grace upon them. He gave them comfort in their painful loss of family and friends, as they held to their faith and the sure promises of God.

The Lord heard their prayers and sent to them an English-speaking native named Squanto who helped them survive. Squanto taught them essential lessons to live off the land and open trade with local tribes. They built their homes, and in the spring they planted their first crops. Their new life in the new land began to take shape.

In the fall of 1621, they brought in their first harvest. Despite their many hardships and losses, they received God's blessings and noticed His grace in many ways. They therefore determined to pause to celebrate God's blessings in a feast of thanksgiving. They invited local Wampanoag

Indians to join them, and over ninety came and brought fresh game and food. That festive celebration of thanksgiving lasted three days.

One of the pilgrims at that celebration was Elder William Brewster, who provided spiritual leadership for the pilgrims, and through whom I am able to trace my family lineage. From his example of faith, I have much to learn.

In his excellent book *Chronicles of the Pilgrim Fathers of the Colony of Plymouth from 1602-1605*, Alexander Young researched original records and reported on written accounts of experiences among the Pilgrims and stories told of their leaders.[8] He told of a time several months before that first thanksgiving celebration, when they faced a severe shortage of food. As they sat down one day to a meal comprised of a cup of water and a few clams, Elder Brewster led in prayer. He reportedly quoted words from Deuteronomy and expressed to the Lord humble gratitude for: *the abundance of the seas and the hidden treasures of the sand* (Deuteronomy 33:19).

It blesses me that many generations later, I worship the same Lord he worshipped and revel in the same glorious grace that he declared. Every generation needs to notice God's grace and offer Him our sincere thanks, even in the hardships of life. We need not minimize the struggles we have endured or may be enduring, for God knows our pain. He cares for us and walks with us, even in the pain.

Choosing to thank the Lord for His grace that He has bestowed upon us sets us free to realize our blessings and praise Him from whom all blessings flow. Further, giving God our thanks allows us to receive His promises and perspective with joy. But we must first notice the grace that we are now receiving.

By far the greatest expressions of God's grace are His supreme gifts of forgiveness, salvation, and everlasting life by the sacrificial death and resurrection of our Savior, the Son of God, even the Lord Jesus Christ. These gifts of His grace are not bestowed on us because we have been good enough, for none of us are worthy on our own merit. Rather, grace is freely given by our loving heavenly Father to all who come to His Son, the Lord Jesus Christ, in faith and believe, love, and follow Him.

When such grace is received, we are immediately made spiritually

---

8   Alexander Young, *Chronicles of the Pilgrim Fathers* (New York: Cosimo Classics, 2005).

alive in Christ as God's children and we are spiritually *born again* (John 3:3-8). Thereafter we are blessed to walk in continual, personal relationship with the only God, the Lord of the heavens and the earth, as forever recipients of everlasting life with Him. These promises of God are affirmed often in His Word, but especially in Isaiah 53:1-12; John 3:1-17; Romans 5:1-11; Ephesians 2:1-10; and 1 John 1:1-9. For such grace we can thank and praise God forever.

In addition to God's eternal blessings, day by day and moment by moment He gives His children more grace, whatever we need for each situation. These expressions of His grace must be noticed and, like the pilgrims of old, we must choose to give Him our thanks. I have observed God's grace to me lately in several ways:

Medically – In my cancer battle, recent developments in which I have noticed God's grace to me are:

1. Last week, after some heart tests I was cleared by Cardiology to proceed with my SCT.

2. The cancer cells in my blood are continuing to decrease. The latest measurement was 0.21 milligrams/deciliter, well below the necessary threshold of 0.5 mg/dl.

3. I continue to improve from the viral infection that I have had for three weeks.

4. Yesterday I spent eight hours at the VA hospital in Minneapolis for chemotherapy infusions, and all went well with no negative issues.

5. Last night when I was unable to sleep due to the effect of chemotherapy, God's presence was tangibly real to me.

6. Today a firm date was set for me to report to Nashville for the SCT. Helen and I are to arrive in Nashville on January 5, and I am to check in on January 6.

Relationally – Though it was hard for us to leave Rhode Island and dear friends in New England, I have observed God's grace here in Minnesota as we enjoy family.

1. Helen and I have been blessed through the years of our marriage, even in this challenging season. We are close and grateful for each other. This is God's grace to us.

2. Being in Northfield, Minnesota, near our son's family is a tremendous blessing to us.

3. Seeing our son Carl this past weekend and celebrating his birthday with him was a joy. We now live only a one-and-a-half-hour drive from him, geographically closer than we have been since he lived under our roof in high school. This too is a blessing.

4. Helen and I plan to spend Christmas in Alaska with our daughter and her family. Because of my illness, we have not been together in their home since May 2018. The opportunity to make this trip before my stem cell transplant is a gift of God.

5. We have already connected to a local church family in Northfield, where our son Jonathan and his family attend. In this too we see God's grace.

Domestically – Though we have moved many times, it is never easy and always takes time to settle in. The moving truck arrived two weeks ago and we feel settled. Though these might seem like small things, I can see God's grace in every one of them:

1. Every box is emptied, and my amazing wife has found a place for everything.

2. All the boxes and trash have been cleared from our garage, and we were able to give the boxes to several people in our community who can use them.

3. Because the garage is now empty, today for the first time we were able to park our cars in the garage.

Such blessings and many more have been part of my life lately. Though I could receive them with little notice, God is teaching me to pay attention and notice His grace. And I do. And when we notice His grace toward us, what then? What response should come from those who know and love the Lord and who notice His grace?

In this season of thanksgiving, may our hearts be filled with much gratitude to God for who He is and for all the ways He is blessing us. It is good for us to reflect on how God is blessing us, to make a list, and to thank Him for every blessing on that list. We can ask God to help us learn deeper gratitude for His grace, even if life continues to be hard. In this too, His grace is more than enough.

Grace by its very definition is unmerited favor. Let us revel in the grace of His forgiveness and celebrate the certainty of His promise of life with Him today and everlasting life with Him in glory.

I am increasingly in awe of the ways He bestows grace upon me, even in this season of my life. I am aware that I have not earned His grace, nor could I, nor could any of us. But by God's grace and through our faith we are able to receive it. And as we receive His grace, how grateful we can be!

FOR REFLECTION

Looking back over your life, how has God bestowed His grace on you? If you were to make a list of God's recent blessings, what would you put on the list? How has God's grace changed your life? What will need to change in your heart and daily life for you to recognize more of His grace to you, and for you to respond to Him with gratitude? Ask God to help you in this, and He surely will.

63

ON INCARNATIONAL MINISTRY

November 24, 2019

A theological truth that has powerfully shaped my understanding of Christian life and ministry is the amazing incarnation of Jesus. As Advent and Christmas approach every year in the calendar of the church, followers of Jesus Christ reflect on the marvelous mystery that the eternal Son of the infinite God, at a chosen point in human history, lovingly and with infinite grace entered humanity. How amazing is that! Being fully God, He became fully human, fulfilling the wonderful promise of *God with us* (Isaiah 7:14; Matthew 1:23).

Many Scriptures reveal this truth that was prophesied and at last fulfilled. Seven centuries before the Son of God was born of the Virgin Mary, His birth was foretold in Isaiah 7:14. It was also prophesied in Isaiah 9:6 that *to us a child is born, to us a Son is given; and the government shall be upon His shoulder, and His name shall be called Wonderful Counselor, Mighty God, Everlasting Father, Prince of Peace.* All the names listed in this prophecy concerning the coming Messiah point to the deity of the holy child who was to be born. He would be, He was, and He is forever the incarnate Son of Almighty God. This is Jesus.

The first eighteen verses of John's gospel beautifully describe the incarnation of God's Son. Verses 1 and 14 say, *In the beginning was the Word, and the Word was with God, and the Word was God,* and *The*

Word became flesh and dwelt among us, and we have seen His glory, glory as of the only Son from the Father, full of grace and truth. Eternal God, motivated by love, became incarnate and entered humanity as the Lord Jesus Christ.

The apostle Paul emphasized several qualities of Jesus's incarnation that we who follow Him are called to emulate. He wrote, *Have this mind among yourselves, which is yours in Christ Jesus, who, though He was in the form of God, did not count equality with God a thing to be grasped, but emptied Himself, by taking on the form of a servant, being born in the likeness of men. And being found in human form, He humbled himself by becoming obedient to the point of death, even death on a cross* (Philippians 2:5-8).

Of the virtues mentioned by the apostle as modeled by Jesus for His followers to now emulate, the one that has spoken to me lately is that He came to serve. Jesus emphasized this to His disciples when He said, *the Son of Man came not to be served but to serve, and to give His life as a ransom for many* (Matthew 20:28). Jesus Christ came to serve, and He now sends us out to serve others in His name.

After He washed the dirty feet of His disciples, Jesus explained to them, *You call me Teacher and Lord, and you are right, for so I am. If I then, your Lord and Teacher, have washed your feet, you also ought to wash one another's feet. For I have given you an example, that you also should do just as I have done to you . . . If you know these things, blessed are you if you do them* (John 13:13-15,17). Following Christ's example of incarnational ministry means we will bring His presence wherever we go, and like Jesus, we will serve.

Throughout my years of Christian ministry, this model has motivated me. Wherever He has directed me to go in this world, and in whatever circumstances He has called me to serve, I have regarded myself as a servant of the Lord and of His people. One of the life verses God gave me early in my pastoral ministry was 2 Corinthians 4:5 in which the apostle Paul wrote, *For what we proclaim is not ourselves, but Jesus Christ as Lord, with ourselves as your servants for Jesus' sake.*

Yes! We are given the sweet privilege of knowing and proclaiming Jesus and following His example by serving. I have been reflecting on this aspect of incarnational ministry from the perspective of one who is a recipient of it on a daily basis. For example:

When I had my first appointment with my new primary care physician, I discovered that she too is a follower of Jesus Christ and has a servant's heart. After my exam when she observed that I was struggling to reach my feet to put on my socks and shoes, she said, "Let me do that for you." As she dressed my feet for me, which was very humbling to me, our Lord reminded me that this was incarnational ministry. She was His servant, reflecting His presence and tender care for me.

Several times since we have arrived in Minnesota, our son Jonathan appeared at our home looking for ways to help. With a servant's heart, he and his wife Jackie have done much to help us. Our Lord reminds me that this too is incarnational ministry, as they reflect His presence and personal care.

Because I have been fighting a bacterial infection in my chest and sinuses, earlier this week I was prescribed antibiotics. I am beginning to feel some better, but twice this week I received personal phone calls from medical providers to ask me how I am doing. This too is incarnational ministry, which reflects God's personal care for me.

I now have a PICC (Peripherally Inserted Central Catheter) line in my arm that is used for blood draws and for intravenous chemotherapy. The dressing must be changed weekly and is typically done before chemotherapy is administered. But because no chemo is scheduled for this week, a visiting nurse is coming to my home to change the dressing on my PICC line. This too is incarnational ministry, as God's care comes to us.

I can certainly list many more, and so can you for your life. Our Lord gives all of us opportunities to follow His example and bring His presence and personal care wherever we go. He gives us opportunities to be grateful recipients of His presence and personal care. It is good for us to consider what opportunities He is giving to us to bring His presence and care to others. Consider what ways He has shown us His personal love and care through the incarnational ministry of others.

In the season of Advent and Christmas, as we reflect on the wonder of the incarnation of God in the Lord Jesus Christ, may our heartfelt worship include offering ourselves to Him to be His servants for incarnational ministry. We who know and love the Lord are privileged and blessed to bring His presence to others. With servant hearts, we can speak His truth and show His love and care wherever we go. Let us also be grateful recipients of His incarnational grace, however it is shown to us through others.

Again I want to thank all who have prayed for Helen and me. Your prayers are an instrument of God's incarnational grace extended to us. Please pray with us for His healing and for continued positive response to chemotherapy. Pray too for faithfulness in every divine appointment, so we might bring God's loving presence to others. Pray with us that our home in Rhode Island might sell in God's good time. And as we are now just six weeks from our scheduled departure for Nashville where I am to undergo the SCT, pray for the Lord to direct our every step, that He will receive all glory and praise. Please reflect and rejoice with me now in the wonder of the incarnation of Jesus, for God's wonderful presence and personal care has come to us.

FOR REFLECTION

How have you been impacted by the sweet truth that God Almighty has come to us in human flesh through the Lord Jesus Christ? What opportunities has the Lord given you to serve as His instrument of incarnational ministry to others? What are some ways you have been a recipient of His incarnational ministry through others? What must change in your heart and daily life for you to more humbly and consistently serve others, and for you to gratefully receive His grace through others? Ask God to help you in this, and He surely will.

64

ON CELEBRATING GOD'S GIFTS IN THE FACE OF OUR TRIALS

December 7, 2019

Whenever we are ill, if there is a known remedy, we want it, don't we? We are wise to seek and take the prescribed treatment or medicine to reduce discomfort and speed healing. But does it help us to have available good medicine and proven medical treatments if we do not actually take the prescribed medicine or do what is prescribed? No, it does not! God has reminded me that this principle applies when the struggles and trials of this life cause us to be discouraged or sick in soul. This week I have been learning this important lesson again.

On Monday morning I headed from our home in Northfield to the VA Medical Center in Minneapolis to receive my scheduled chemotherapy. Because of heavy traffic and hazardous travel conditions, the trip took an hour longer than usual. When I finally arrived, my PICC line (a catheter tube used for drawing blood and receiving intravenous infusions) was clogged, so blood could not be drawn from it.

This led to multiple attempts by several people to find a vein in my arms from which blood could be drawn. After fourteen months of chemotherapy, my veins are now so collapsed that this was a huge challenge and led to multiple bruises on both of my arms. After about an hour, blood was finally drawn, and the PICC line was unclogged. Several hours of intravenous treatment were then administered. It was dark out, and I was very tired by the time I arrived home that day. Then, as the week progressed, I became ill with several unpleasant symptoms.

I do not share any of this to elicit sympathy but only to illustrate that on this side of heaven, on this earthly journey, some days are hard for us, and sometimes our struggles plot a course toward discouragement. I have experienced this multiple times this week. Every time this happens, our God cares for us, and He always has precisely what we need.

God has reminded me of a timeless lesson. He calls us to make a faith decision to look beyond our present difficulties, remember His faithfulness, and celebrate His gifts. Such a decision does not come naturally when we do not feel well in body or soul. Rather, it requires an act of faith, a decision to take our "medicine" as God has prescribed it.

So this week I heard my Lord call me again to compile in my heart and mind a list of His blessings to me. My list was quite long. After I reflected on each item, I paused to praise Him and give Him thanks for each gift. In this way I have celebrated His gifts of forgiveness and grace, His continual presence with me, and His sure promises to me. I have celebrated the sweet gifts of His church, the Body of Christ, and many family and friends who mean much to me. I thanked Him and celebrated the treasured gift of the Bible, His written Word that has been and remains timeless and true, relevant and hopeful, and a comfort to my soul. Because of Jesus Christ, I have much to celebrate. As I do this, I am reminded that though trials remain and more struggles may come until I see Him in the fullness of His glory, His powerful medicines of faith, praise, and thankfulness are helping me today.

I invite you to celebrate and rejoice with me for another blessing I received this week. In four weeks Helen and I are scheduled to arrive in Nashville, Tennessee, where I am to undergo a SCT with the hope of achieving prolonged remission. For many long months this has been the goal of my treatment, but because myeloma cells in my bone marrow and blood remained too high, I was not considered eligible.

Because the expected duration of potential remission correlates with the amount of cancer cells that remained at the time of the SCT, the lower the better. In October I learned that the levels of cancer in my blood had at last fallen below the minimum threshold of 0.5 milligrams/

deciliter, so the SCT could be scheduled. Since then I have continued chemotherapy treatments, and at the end of my last treatment cycle, the myeloma cells in my blood had fallen to 0.21 mg/dl. Well, this week Helen and I celebrated when the latest results showed that levels have now decreased to 0.08 mg/dl. Praise God from whom all blessings flow!

Celebrating God's gifts in the face of our trials is very good medicine indeed!

FOR REFLECTION

When have the struggles and trials of your life caused you to be discouraged and sick of soul? When this has happened, have you been able to exercise faith by looking beyond your difficulties and holding on to the truth that God cares for you and has precisely what you need? If not, why not? If so, how did God meet you and show you His love and care? What gifts has God given you that you can celebrate even in the face of trials? How can you celebrate His gifts with more gratitude as a way of life? Ask God to help you in this, and He surely will.

65

ON FACING CONFUSION WITH HOPE

December 14, 2019

We all experience confusion at times; when our minds are clouded, our judgment becomes suspect, and we have no clue what to do. Earlier this week I faced a heavy dose of confusion; admittedly, when it happened, my initial reaction was fear.

I had just completed a medical appointment with a urology specialist at the VA hospital in Minneapolis, for a worsening problem of urinary retention. Prior to the appointment, I had regarded this as a minor nuisance in light of the more serious medical issue of multiple myeloma, and I had presumed that another prescription would soon be forthcoming to address this problem. But after being examined by the doctor, he told me the retention was quite significant, so he recommended additional tests, which needed to be done as soon as possible.

When I explained that I was scheduled to travel next week to Alaska for Christmas and then return and depart a few days thereafter for Nashville to undergo the SCT, he said that though their schedule was very full, they would do their best to fit this in quickly. By the time I departed his office, I was scheduled for a urodynamic study on December 30, with a follow-up appointment with this doctor the next morning – only days before I was scheduled to leave for Nashville.

As I left the doctor's office that day and made my way toward the hospital exit, my head was spinning – really spinning. After fourteen long months of chemotherapy, which has had a cumulative effect on me physically, and waiting so long to be cleared for the SCT and being this close to it actually happening, I was resisting what I had just heard. I rejected any possibility that this could delay my departure. As I walked through the hospital, I felt weak, unsteady, and confused – and a bit afraid.

As I exited the hospital, I made my way toward the handicap parking lot, where I parked my car earlier that morning. Bundled up against the bitter cold, I leaned heavily on my cane and walked as quickly as I could toward my parking spot. But my car was not there. I then slowly patrolled that entire parking lot; I moved up and down, row by row, and searched in vain for my car. I felt confused and fearful that I was losing my memory, fearful that someone had stolen my car, and fearful that this was not going to end well.

Then I remembered the obvious. I remembered to pray. I remembered God's invitation to all of His children. Whenever we are confused or in trouble, He invites us to call out to Him. He said, *Call to me and I will answer you, and will tell you great and hidden things that you have not known* (Jeremiah 33:3). He also said, *Call upon me in the day of trouble; I will deliver you, and you shall glorify me* (Psalm 50:15).

So that is what I did. My prayer was rather short. I simply said, "Dear Lord, please help me." As I prayed, though I remained confused, I knew with certainty and hope that God had heard my prayer and would surely answer. At that very moment, I heard someone calling out to me. It was another veteran.

As I had been wandering around looking lost, another veteran who had just pulled into the same parking lot called out to me, "Sir, are you okay?" Admitting to him my need, my answer was no. I explained to him my dilemma, and he kindly offered to drive me around to search for my car.

His offer was an immediate reminder to me that God had heard my prayer for help; He is always faithful. But sensing that this man was on his way to a medical appointment and not wanting to delay his arrival, I expressed my thanks but declined his gracious offer and determined instead to obtain help from available employees and volunteers who were just inside the hospital.

Escorted by that kind fellow veteran, I reentered the hospital and explained my situation to the security officer and volunteers posted inside the door. They immediately sat me down in a wheelchair, put me in a warm place, and made sure I was okay; then they called for a driver and vehicle to help me search for my car.

Though humbled by this attention and troubled by the confusion, in the midst of it, I was aware of God's personal love for me and that even now He was answering my cry for His help. A few minutes later the promised vehicle and driver arrived to assist me; after a few short minutes of searching, we found my car, though in a different lot than the one I thought I had parked it in.

All of us can experience confusion from time to time, and when we do, we might be afraid. When that happens, we might feel alone, but we are not alone. Our Lord is with us, ready to hear, ready to help, and ready to respond to our cry. The confusion and fear that I experienced that day was by no means fun for me, but my Lord used it to remind me of an important lesson, one I am blessed to share with you now.

The Lord reminded me that in such times we have an open invitation to call to Him in prayer. Every time we do, He hears and answers. He comes to help and save us, just as He promised. Hear the promise of God as recorded in Isaiah, *For I, the LORD your God, hold your right hand; it is I who say to you, "Fear not, I am the one who helps you"* (Isaiah 41:13).

What a great promise! His faithfulness to me this week in the midst of my confusion has further strengthened my resolve to trust and hope in Him in all my remaining days, no matter what may come or the source of my confusion. By His grace I know whom to lean on and whom to call on, and I put my trust in Him. In the Lord Jesus Christ, confusion and fear give way to faith, peace, and hope.

As for the aforementioned medical tests that are scheduled for me just days before our planned departure for Nashville, I request and appreciate your prayers for God to grant wisdom and healing through this and that He will be glorified. My urologist has sent my records and recommendations to the transplant team in Nashville, so they are in consultation. As we continue to pray in faith and believe God for His perfect way in this matter, please pray with me that fear and confusion will give way to trust and hope, all for the glory of God.

If you are facing struggle and confusion, know that I am also praying for you. I pray that by God's grace and faithfulness, as you call out to Him in faith, you will tangibly experience His love for you, evidenced in His help, hope, and peace.

FOR REFLECTION

When have you experienced confusion, and what was it like for you? Reading again God's promise in Isaiah 41:13, when have you ever felt confused or afraid? Did you then call upon the Lord and have Him answer you? Did He take you by the hand, dispel your fears, and provide the help you needed? What should change in your heart and daily living so that calling upon the Lord will be your first inclination when you are confused or in trouble? Ask God to help you in this, and He surely will.

66

ON LEANING UPON GOD'S STRENGTH WHEN WE ARE WEAK

December 29, 2019

Most of the time now I must lean on a cane, for I often feel weak, and I do not want to fall. At first I was self-conscious about this, but not anymore. More than once my cane has kept me from falling and has kept me going when I could not without it.

Friday morning we landed at the Minneapolis airport on our way home after several wonderful days in Alaska, celebrating Christmas with our daughter Amy and her family. What a blessed time we had, celebrating our Savior's birth and enjoying the love and fellowship of family.

As we exited the plane after the nighttime flight, we moved slowly due to fatigue. I leaned on my cane as we walked off the jet way, and almost immediately a driver and electric cart pulled up beside us. He asked, "Would you like a ride to baggage claim?" We sure did, and we said so. That driver carried us all the way!

God often does that for us. He knows when we are weak. He sees when we are weary. He meets us where we need to be met and offers the help and strength we need. This was the testimony of the apostle Paul who, like you and me, struggled with his own weakness. He did what we can do. He prayed and longed for his weakness to go away.

He referred to one area of personal weakness as a *thorn in the flesh* when he described what the Lord taught him through his struggle. *Three times I pleaded with the Lord about this, that it should leave me. But He said to me, "My grace is sufficient for you, for my power is made perfect in weakness." Therefore I will boast all the more gladly of my weaknesses, so that the power of Christ may rest upon me. For the sake of Christ, then, I am content with weaknesses, insults, hardships, persecutions, and calamities. For when I am weak, then I am strong.* (2 Corinthians 12:8-10).

Learning to be content in the face of our weaknesses does not come naturally to us. It comes from knowing God and experiencing His help and strength. Day after day I am learning what this means, and in the days ahead, I expect to learn more of this lesson. The Lord is giving me opportunities to lean upon Him, for which I would appreciate your prayers:

> Today I will preach at St. Lucas Community Church in Lake Elmo, Minnesota. A few weeks ago when my friend Pastor Dan Peterson invited me to proclaim God's Word, I immediately said yes and trusted God to give me the required strength. I know that I am weak, but like the apostle Paul, I know that His power rests upon me, and His strength will be sufficient for me.
>
> Tomorrow morning I will undergo medical tests, particularly a urodynamic study to assess recent problems with urinary retention. I am nervous about this because it could delay my scheduled SCT. But my Lord keeps reminding me to trust Him, *for when I am weak, then I am strong.* My follow-up appointment with the urologist will be Tuesday morning when I should learn what treatment is required or if my SCT is delayed.
>
> God willing, on Saturday Helen and I will depart for Nashville and arrive on Sunday. We will drive so Helen will have the use of a car while we are there. I am scheduled to check into the Bone Marrow Transplant Center of the

Nashville VA Medical Center next Monday morning. Many appointments have already been made for me that week because preparations for my SCT are underway.

This week as I read again the materials about what is going to happen, I became aware again of how profoundly weak I am and how utterly dependent I am upon the Lord. I am dependent on Him for my next breath and next heartbeat, for His strength in my weakness, and for His healing and help.

God knows my weakness and He surely knows yours. God loves when His children lean upon Him in faith and love. When we do this, we always find that His strength is more than enough. He is more than enough for me, and more than enough for you. I pray that this truth comforts you and fills your heart with His joy, as it has done for me.

FOR REFLECTION

When have you been especially weak and found what you needed when you leaned upon the Lord for your strength? What *thorn in the flesh* have you wrestled with that has remained but pointed you to your utter dependence on the Lord for His strength? What should you change so that dependence on the Lord will become a continual way of life? Ask God to help you in this, and He surely will.

67

ON VULNERABILITIES TO VICTORIES

January 1, 2020

On this first day of another brand New Year, we all step off into uncharted territory. In various ways we will all go where we have not gone before, and we will experience things we have not experienced before. If this New Year is like past years, it will include struggles and satisfactions, hardships and happy times, pains and pleasures, vulnerabilities and victories. Sometimes the vulnerabilities and pains will be what is necessary for us to get to the victories and triumphs. Though we might wrestle for a while with this necessity, it remains true.

I know in my soul that this will be my experience in the year that lies ahead. Though I would much prefer for my way to be made easier and smoother, I know that God's plan for me is much better than what I understand or prefer. I know that His plan for me will include struggles and vulnerabilities, but by His grace these will lead to satisfactions and victories, that will be for His glory and praise.

From the depths of my heart, I thank all who have seriously prayed. By praying you have blessed me immensely. The Lord has heard and answered your prayers, and I give Him praise for this. I thank you for partnering with me in faith. God gave me the strength that I needed and brought blessing when I preached His Word last Sunday. He also gave me His presence and peace through the medical tests that I endured

Monday and in my follow up appointment with the urologist yesterday.

When I asked my Lord what He would have me say here by way of an update on my medical situation, He clearly answered that I was to be vulnerable and real. Being vulnerable and real feels risky, and because of pride, we are all prone to resist it. Some of us rarely if ever admit when we feel afraid, weak, or vulnerable. We pretend that things are fine when they are not, and we keep our inner struggles to ourselves. We often discover that people don't really want us to be vulnerable and real, because it makes them feel uncomfortable and reminds them of their own preference for pretense.

But failing to be honest and real can lead to feeling distant from family or friends, and even more so from God. But by His grace, our Lord would help us learn that we can be honest, vulnerable, and real with brothers and sisters and with Him. Doing so allows us to receive His love, understanding, and support, which makes a tremendous difference in our times of struggle.

In obedience to the Lord, I am about to risk vulnerability with you. If this should cause you to feel uncomfortable, I am sorry, but I hope you may consider that this reaction might reflect your own struggles with being vulnerable and real.

I did not like what the doctor told me yesterday. When I heard what he said, I was upset and felt vulnerable, and my eyes filled with tears. Though I knew the report could have been far worse, the timing of what I was hearing made it feel like my heavy load became heavier than I wanted to carry.

Later this week Helen and I will begin our journey to Nashville, Tennessee. And next week, God willing, I begin the long-awaited process of the stem cell transplant with the prayerful hope of a durable remission as the result. I know this will be hard and at times very unpleasant, and I know recovery may be prolonged. But now this too?

The doctor confirmed that because of my significant urinary retention, I was at risk of developing bladder, urinary tract, or kidney infections, which could be very serious and dangerous, especially in light of my pending SCT. So, for this reason he said I must immediately begin doing self-catheterization to fully empty my bladder.

Within a few minutes a nurse entered the room to train me how to do this, and when I departed the hospital, I carried enough catheter supplies to last for a couple months. While I understood what was required of me and why this was ordered, I did not want to do it, and I still do not. But I must endure it, and I will for the hope that is set before me.

I am learning much about vulnerabilities and victories. There are many struggles in this broken world that we would rather not endure, yet we must. Some who will read these words are experiencing huge challenges. You may be facing grief, various struggles, hardships, pains, and vulnerabilities that you wish you did not have to bear.

Others might wonder how you can bear it all, but you know whom to lean on. You know His grace is sufficient for you. You know that you are not in this alone, nor will you ever be. You know that this is a small price to pay for the blessings that are in store for you. You know that by the grace of the Lord Jesus Christ, you will receive sublime satisfactions, joyful times, immense pleasures, and glorious victories. You know this, because you know the Lord Jesus.

The Lord meets me again. He reminds me that I am not carrying my load alone, for He is with me now and will always be with me; He will bear me up and give me His all-sufficient strength. The same is true for you. Believe it. He also reminds me of the great suffering He so lovingly and willingly endured for us. The Lord reminds me of His own struggle with what was required of Him, as is recorded in Matthew 26:39-42.

> *And going a little farther Jesus fell on his face and prayed, saying, "My Father, if it be possible, let this cup pass from me; nevertheless, not as I will, but as you will." And he came to the disciples and found them sleeping. And he said to Peter, "So, could you not watch with me one hour? Watch and pray that you may not enter into temptation. The spirit indeed is willing, but the flesh is weak." Again, for the second time, he went away and prayed, "My Father, if this cannot pass unless I drink it, your will be done."*

The Lord Jesus was at the same time the Son of God and the Son of Man. He was both fully divine and fully human. In the fullness of His humanity, our Lord wrestled with the suffering that was required of Him. Of course He did, for who welcomes horrific pain or the spiritual agony of being separated from our heavenly Father? Jesus's vulnerability was so extreme He sweat drops of blood, and He pleaded with His Father to take away this bitter cup.

But praise be to God, for our Lord lovingly and willingly endured it all for our sake. His suffering and death on the cross led to His triumphant victory over sin and death, as *the Lamb of God who takes away the sin of the world* (John 1:29). Jesus's sacrifice purchased my salvation and yours, for now and forever. Jesus's vulnerability led to His victory and thus to ours.

When Jesus saw the weakness of His disciples, He taught them and now He teaches us that we must always watch and pray, lest we enter into temptation. He observed what He also experienced, and we experience that *the spirit indeed is willing, but the flesh is weak*. But unlike us, in His struggle Jesus never sinned. He owned his vulnerability, and ultimately He won the victory.

By His grace, I know that the same is true for me and for you. So I offer to the Lord my vulnerability. For His sake I offer to Him my struggle and weakness, and I rejoice that He is with me now and will be with me through all that is ahead. I do this with joyful confidence that for His sake and for His glory, the victory will surely come. In this I rejoice.

Thank you again for your prayers and words of encouragement. Helen or I will aim to keep you posted throughout the transplant process. May the Lord watch over you, as He also watches over us. May the Lord remind us all of His constant presence, abiding love, and faithfulness to His every promise.

FOR REFLECTION

How hard or easy has it been for you to be vulnerable and real with another person about your personal struggles, and why? How difficult or easy has it been for you to be vulnerable and real with God about your weakness and struggle, and why? Read again Matthew 26:29-32 and reflect on Jesus's struggle and what He did with it. What lessons do you learn from His example? How can you more freely admit your vulnerability to someone whom you can trust and especially to the Lord? Ask God to help you in this, and He surely will.

68

ON FINDING GOD'S PEACE WHEN HIS PLANS HAVE CHANGED OURS

January 10, 2020

Have we learned yet that our wisdom is limited, but our God's is unlimited? Have we also learned that His plans for us are always loving and good? These lessons are true, even when our life is painful and hard. And these truths can be a sweet comfort to our souls on those hard days when sudden or painful change has come that is not what we wanted or planned.

Many times in my life when sudden change came that I found painful, I have held on to timeless truths that my Lord has taught me. His love has never failed and never will, and He is wholly trustworthy. His wisdom is infinitely greater than mine, and His plan for me and for all of His children is loving and good now and always. He enables me to hold on to these truths, even when life is hard.

I can recall many hard days when I have had to cling to these truths. I recall days of great sorrow – like the day when our firstborn son Matthew was born prematurely and died the next day and the day the following year when our firstborn daughter Joy was also born prematurely. How we held her and each other, weeping, until her heart beat its last. We did not choose or want this pain, but when it came, we leaned on our Lord. He was with us in the pain.

ON FINDING GOD'S PEACE WHEN HIS PLANS HAVE CHANGED OURS

I recall another kind of hard day in Norfolk, Virginia, when I was on my way to Kuwait; I had been recalled from the Navy Reserves to active duty with orders to serve for many months as a Navy chaplain. I was prepared to go. I had said my goodbyes to my family and arranged for my ministry leadership responsibilities while I was gone. I was packed, ready, willing, and expecting to go and serve.

But shortly before I was to depart from Norfolk, a Navy doctor told me, "You are not going." He told me that available medical care in Kuwait would not be adequate in light of my preexisting conditions. Though I did not understand or agree with this decision, suddenly I was on my way home.

A week or two later the reason for cancelling my orders was overruled when the Central Command (CENTCOM) Medical Officer reviewed my records and approved my going. But because the need for a chaplain was so urgent, by then someone else was already on their way. The suddenness of that change was hard. But again, I could lean on the Lord. I knew that His ways are always good, and that I could trust Him. In the midst of these changes, the Lord blessed me with His joy and His peace.

Many such days are burned into my memory and heart. The circumstances of change differed. The heartaches of unexpected change have been plentiful and varied, but the Lord has always been faithful to meet me in my need. Undoubtedly, you also have similar memories of times when unexpected change came to you. Perhaps you received news that a family member or friend had died or suffered painful loss. Maybe your life was headed on a certain trajectory that you desired, when sudden change came, and your path was steered in a different direction, one you neither chose nor desired. In such times we need the Lord. In such times He comes and offers His peace.

Yesterday was that kind of day for me. We are in Nashville, Tennessee, waiting for my long-desired SCT. We have planned and prepared for this for many months, and yesterday was the day I was to meet with my transplant doctor to review the results of recent tests and to confirm that we will now proceed with the transplant. But it did not happen as I had hoped or expected.

A few days ago when I arrived and checked into the Bone Marrow Transplant Center at the Nashville VA Medical Center Bone, I was given a schedule of what to expect. That schedule started this Saturday with four days of a medication to increase my production of stem cells and push them from my bone marrow into my blood stream. Harvesting my stem cells was scheduled for Tuesday and Wednesday, and then on Saturday and Sunday of next week, I would receive mega doses of Melphalan, a strong chemotherapy drug that will wipe my bone marrow clean of remaining cancer cells plus immunoglobulins, immunizations, and all abilities to fight off illness and infections.

Tuesday January 21 is the day when I was to receive my stem cells back into my body via infusion. These would make their way back to my bone marrow to begin doing what God created them to do – make healthy blood cells. I was then to remain in Nashville for several weeks of close observation while I recovered. By the end of February, I hoped to return home to Minnesota for a prolonged period of recovery. This plan was what I expected and desired.

But it is not going to be. The plans have changed because I am now sick. When we arrived earlier this week, I felt like I might be developing a cold. My symptoms quickly worsened with a fever and bad cough. Two days ago tests were done to determine what I am fighting, and yesterday I was informed that two specific viruses have been identified.

So we are now being sent home to Minnesota. Because of my compromised immune condition, it might take three to four weeks for me to fully recover. I am therefore scheduled to return to the Transplant Center in Nashville on February 19. When I heard of this change of plans yesterday, though I understood the reasons, I was upset. This was not what I planned or wanted.

But immediately I was reminded of these treasured verses from Isaiah, which declare a timeless truth I must remember now: *For my thoughts are not your thoughts, neither are your ways my ways, declares the Lord. For as the heavens are higher than the earth, so are my ways higher than your ways and my thoughts than your thoughts* (Isaiah 55:8-9).

This is very true. God's plan for us is far higher and better than our plans, and His ways are always good. His wisdom is infinite, and His love never fails. In light of this, this change of plans no longer upsets me. Helen also has God's peace about it. We know that our Lord has good reasons for this change, and though we do not yet know His reasons, we do know that we can trust Him, and we do, and we will.

My oncologist in Nashville who is a stem cell transplant specialist provided one insight yesterday into God's reason for this change. After describing the two viruses that I have been fighting, the doctor emphatically said that if we had proceeded with the SCT while I was fighting these viruses, I would almost surely have died. When I heard this, my perspective changed, and my heart rejoiced that these viruses were discovered prior to my SCT and not after. We should always praise God that His ways are higher than ours. So I praise Him for this delay.

Whenever God's plans are counter to what ours were, how are we able to find His peace? By choosing to trust Him and believing His Word. By knowing that He loves us and His plan for us is always good. And by resting in Him like a child nestling in his mother's or father's arms. This is what Helen and I are doing now.

Continued prayers are requested and appreciated as I slowly recover from these viruses that have hit me hard. I will spend most of today in bed resting. Please pray with me that by tomorrow I will be well enough to travel, so we can begin our journey home. We have a drive of about 830 miles before us, which we are hoping to do over two days. Pray too for safety along our journey, and for Helen who will do all of the driving. Please pray too that I will shake off this illness entirely, and ask God to protect me from all other illness so I may return to Nashville as scheduled, ready to proceed with the SCT. We ask you to join us in our ultimate prayer, that God's perfect will is done in us for His glory and our good. We pray the same for you.

FOR REFLECTION

When have sudden changes come into your life that were not at all what you desired or planned? In those times, to what extent did you know God's peace? What are some timeless truths God has taught you that can help you find His peace when adapting to disappointment and change? How does Isaiah 55:8-9 apply to dealing with change? How can you find God's peace when unexpected change comes? Ask God to help you in this, and He surely will.

69

ON BEING SICK OF BEING SICK

January 14, 2020

I admitted to Helen this week, "I am sick of being sick." I meant it and I still do. She said she understands why I feel this way and honestly replied that as my caregiver, "Sometimes I am sick of you being sick." There. We have said it.

These are not uncommon sentiments among people who have been sick a long while or for their caregivers as sickness drags on and on. It is hard. So, if you have ever felt this way, or are feeling this way now, please know that you are in good company.

I have battled frequent illnesses for several years now, often sinus infections that required long courses of antibiotics before finally going away. I know that these infections were caused in part by immune deficiencies that were at first a precursor and later a symptom of my developing cancer.

For the last fifteen months as I have battled multiple myeloma itself, both the cancer and the effects of the chemotherapy drugs have presented a tough physical challenge. Much of the time I have not felt well. This prolonged struggle led me to look forward with eagerness to a time of remission post SCT, when I might feel well again, perhaps even for a prolonged period. This was my longing and Helen's when we traveled to Nashville.

Then I got sick again, so they sent us home. And I am still very sick. I am fighting Respiratory Syncytial Virus (RSV) and Human Coronavirus HKU-1. For over a week I have been fighting fever with head and body aches, shortness of breath, and considerable coughing. On our trip home from Nashville, I even considered going to an emergency room, but we decided to wait until we arrived home. So yesterday we went to the ER at the Minneapolis VA Medical Center, where we spent most of the day.

Chest X-rays, CT scans, and numerous lab tests were performed. I received oral medicines, intravenous infusion, and nebulizer treatment. Eventually a bacterial sinus infection was confirmed in addition to bronchitis, and I was released to go home with antibiotics and other medicines. As we departed, they said some blood cultures were still pending, so I would be called if there were any additional findings. I sure hope not.

So I am sick. I don't want to complain because I know how blessed I am. But today I really am feeling sick of being sick. Can you relate to this?

Because today is our youngest grandson Theo's first birthday, Helen is with him now, his big brother Archer, and his parents Jonathan and Jackie. I am glad Helen can be present for his birthday celebration, but I regret that I cannot be there too. When the time came to sing "Happy Birthday" to Theo and watch him eat his birthday cake, mashing it into his face as one-year-old's tend to do, Jonathan made a FaceTime connection with me, so I could at least join from a distance. But I wish I could have been there. I wish I was not sick.

In the sovereignty of God, I have had some alone time today, so I used it to reflect on what God is saying to me in all of this. As I did so, the word that kept coming to my mind is *longsuffering*.

When I was a young boy, the Bible translation that I was most familiar with was the King James Version (KJV). As a boy, I read through the KJV Bible from beginning to end, and I memorized several chapters and verses. Because I was young and the language of the KJV is old, I asked many questions about the meaning of words or phrases that were unfamiliar to me. One such word was *longsuffering*. It means what it sounds like – "suffering long." The Greek word that is translated "longsuffering" in the KJV is translated in most modern translations as "patience."

This particular word appears in several places in the New Testament: Colossians 1:11, 3:12; 1 Timothy 1:16; and 2 Peter 3:15. The verse I have been meditating on today is Colossians 3:12. Here the apostle Paul reminds us that when it comes to enduring hardships, struggles, or any suffering for a prolonged time, as God's dear children, we are given the privilege of putting on God's own characteristic of longsuffering or patience in the same way that we put on a garment.

I am glad that none of us is asked or expected to dig deep and come up with our own supply of longsuffering, because I could not do it, nor could you. Rather, every single day, even on our hardest days, we can look to our Lord in faith and choose to put on His garments of grace. What do such garments include?

Colossians 3:12 says, *Put on then, as God's chosen ones, holy and beloved, compassionate hearts, kindness, humility, meekness, and patience* [longsuffering]. All of these qualities listed by Paul were owned and demonstrated by the Lord Jesus Christ. He is the One who by grace fills our closet with such garments, made to fit us.

As I honestly admit my sickness fatigue, far more do I confess my love and faith in the Lord Jesus who loves me and has done so much for me. So, as the apostle Paul taught Christians to make positive choices in the attributes we wear, I intend to do just that. Prayerfully and by the great grace of my God, I take off my garment of discouragement now and put on His garment of longsuffering. While doing this, I will also put on *a garment of praise, instead of a faint spirit*, as was foretold by the prophet Isaiah (Isaiah 61:3) as something the Messiah would make possible and which the Lord Jesus has done (Luke 4:21).

Though I am still sick, and though I do not like it at all, I remain blessed. My God has always been and is still today gracious to me. So I am going to praise Him, and I am going to continue to praise Him through this storm however long it may last and through whatever trials, difficulties, or sickness may come my way.

I know that my Lord can still heal and restore me. But whether He does or does not, and whether I feel well or not, I am going to praise Him. My greatest longing and deepest prayer has been that He receives the glory in and through my life. If my healing will bring Him glory, I welcome and embrace it. If my continued illness leads to His glory, then let it be. If my death and promotion to heaven can bring Him much praise, then with my final breath, I will praise Him; then I will praise Him forever. To God be all the praise and all the glory.

FOR REFLECTION

When have you ever been sick of being sick and what did the Lord teach you in that season? What is longsuffering and why does the Lord tell us to put on this garment? What have you heard God saying to you through reading this lesson? What will it mean for you to put on a garment of longsuffering? What will it mean for you to put on a garment of praise? What must happen in your own heart for you to know God's peace when life for you is hard? Ask God to help you in this, and He surely will.

70

ON ANSWERED PRAYERS AMIDST SO MANY CARES

January 19, 2020

Though our way can often be hard, in the midst of it, God is still at work, as He reminds us of His love and care. Our part in the struggle is to notice His presence, pay attention to His care, see the answers to prayer, and give Him our thanks and praise. Doing this lifts our focus from the struggles to God's amazing love and saving grace.

This was such a week for me. It was hard physically because I have been sick all week. On Friday I was bad enough to warrant another visit to the emergency room; I was still fighting a fever and coughing more than I ever have. Many more tests were done, because it was clear that the antibiotic was not working. Another one was prescribed and for a longer duration, plus cough syrup with codeine.

I was glad I did not have to be admitted to the hospital, because I rest far better at home, but it has been hard to rest because of my incessant coughing. I have coughed so much that now my ribs, abdomen, and head hurt every time I cough. Being this uncomfortable makes it hard to smile.

But in the midst of this, I fix my eyes on my Lord; I sense His presence; I recognize His mercies; and I give Him praise. When I do this, whatever the degree of my discomfort, my spirit is buoyed, my heart is encouraged, and I know His joy.

A few weeks ago, I made myself vulnerable and shared the news that because of urinary retention, I need to do self-catheterization. I had asked my doctor if my bladder could heal so that doing this would no longer be necessary. I wanted to know what the signs would be that such healing has occurred. He replied that the bladder is a muscle that could heal if given opportunity to do so and he explained how to determine when and if such a healing has occurred. So I did what was prescribed, while praying that God would heal my bladder and prostate so that self-catherization would not be necessary.

I want to report now for the glory of God that He has answered that prayer. This week I called my urologist to discuss it. Based on the careful records I have kept and my answers to his questions, he told me that I am now free to stop the self-catheterization. In the grand scheme of things, this might seem like a small matter, but it is more than that to me. In this specific answer to prayer, God reminded me that He is still a prayer-answering, miracle-working God who cares about us. No detail of our lives is ever outside His loving concern or His ability to bring healing and grace. So I give to the Lord my praise, and as I do, His joy fills my heart.

As I have been reading the book of Genesis, I am reminded of Hagar and her troubles. Though God did not remove all of her troubles, He did something better. God met her personally and gave her a hope and a future. Hagar then fixed her eyes on the Lord. Declaring to Him her praise, she joyfully proclaimed, *You are a God of seeing . . . Truly here I have seen Him who looks after me* (Genesis 16:13). Hagar then returned to Abraham and Sarah. God had met her and promised her a son, so she gave Him her praise. Because she now knew that God saw her and watched over her, she was able to carry on.

After Hagar returned, she bore Abraham's son Ishmael. But after the birth of Isaac, she suffered from the disdain she received from Sarah; once more she ran into the wilderness, and there God met her again in the deep valley of her suffering. The Bible says Hagar lifted her voice and wept. Knowing the faith of Abraham, who would have been concerned for Hagar and his child, we might presume that he was praying for her too.

So, we can carry on too. I have been reminded again that God always watches over me, and He always watches over you. In so many ways, He shows us that it is so. The Lord has not, nor will He, remove all of our struggles, for He uses these for His glory and for our good. But when we open our eyes of faith to see, like Hagar, we too can see that He is watching over us. I have seen it this week in the healing of my bladder. How have you seen the Lord's watching over you? Where have you witnessed answered prayer in the midst of your many cares? When you do see it, give Him your praise.

FOR REFLECTION

Amidst your recent struggles, how have you noticed God's presence? How have you noticed God's care for you? What answers to prayer have you seen? To what extent have you given God your thanks and praise? What will enable you to more readily notice God's blessings to you, even amidst your struggles, and for you to give Him your thanksgiving and praise? Ask God to help you in this, and He surely will.

71

ON SEEING NO ONE BUT JESUS

January 26, 2020

Sometimes we feel so overwhelmed by our circumstances or by our own smallness and weakness that we despair and become fearful. This has happened to me at various times and in various ways, but over and over, by God's grace, He has taught and reminded me of what I must do. Sometimes I remember and obey, and at other times I forget and become afraid. Can you relate?

I spent most of this week in bed feeling weak and miserable. I doubted I would ever be well enough to proceed with the SCT or regain sufficient strength and health to resume the kind of active life I used to know. Further, as I watched television and saw some of the things going on in our nation's capital and throughout the world, I felt despair for America and for our world. There is much in this world that can evoke fear.

Though I knew what I needed to do, I still had to be reminded to fix my eyes on the Lord and put my whole trust in Him. How loving and merciful is our God. On Friday I again went to the Minneapolis VA Medical Center. First I saw the nurse practitioner who oversees the stem cell transplant patients. When she saw my condition, even after I have been fighting these infections for two and a half weeks, she was concerned. This prompted phone consults with an infectious disease (ID) physician and with an ear, nose, and throat (ENT) physician, which led to a change in my prescriptions and additional follow-up appointments.

I was then given an infusion of intravenous immunoglobulin (IVIG) treatment, which is immunoglobulins my body does not sufficiently produce that have been harvested from plasma donors. While all of this was going on, I rested in the Lord and felt His presence; I knew I was being well cared for, and I heard His gentle reminder that He always has, is now, and always will take good care of me, for He loves me. He does the same for all of His children. What love, and what grace!

Our Lord beckons us to fix our eyes not on our trying circumstances, which might call us to despair or fear, but on Him, for He is with us now and will be with us always. He is more than able to prevail over every seemingly insurmountable problem and to lead us to victory, healing, and hope. The Lord showed me this truth in the Scripture lessons I read today, as part of my schedule to read and reflect on the entire Bible in a year.

The Old Testament lesson today was Exodus 14-15. The Israelites were understandably afraid, because their circumstance seemed hopeless to them. In front of them was the Red Sea and behind them were chariots of the advancing Egyptian army. Humanly speaking there was no possible way to escape. They were terrified and filled with despair. But in this situation, God had a perfect plan. He sought to teach them and us that nothing is impossible for God, for He is able in every situation. It is important to remember this when we are in a situation that feels impossible.

God wanted the Israelites, and He wants us, to look beyond seemingly ridiculous circumstances that caused us to fear. He wanted them to see Him and fully trust Him, so He did what only He could do. He parted the sea, and miraculously His people crossed through with a wall of water on both sides. Before that night was over, they were all on the other side, and the enemy they had feared was destroyed.

Sometimes we find ourselves in a situation that feels that impossible. If and when this happens, our God is still with us, loving us, and teaching us to trust Him; He desires us to open our hearts of faith to see what He will do.

The New Testament lesson I read today was from Matthew 17, which is the amazing account of the transfiguration of the Lord Jesus Christ. Peter, James, and John were with Jesus at the top of that high mountain. Suddenly Jesus was transfigured; He revealed His majesty and heavenly glory. His face shone like the sun, and his clothes were as white as brilliant light. Moses and Elijah appeared too, and they conversed with Jesus. Then a bright cloud of glory covered them all, and God the Father spoke from the cloud saying, *This is my beloved Son, with whom I am well pleased; listen to Him* (Matthew 17:5).

Verse 6 says, *When the disciples heard this, they fell on their faces and were terrified.* I can understand this response, can't you? What they had just seen and experienced was far beyond their comfort level. They did not comprehend, and they were afraid. Their eyes had been opened to see the Lord in His heavenly glory. They heard God's voice tell them who Jesus is – the beloved Son of our heavenly Father. And they heard God's personal invitation that they should *listen to Him.*

Haven't you heard this same invitation from God? I rejoice, for I have! But for Peter, James, and John, their hearts were still afraid, because of what they had seen and heard; they now knew with vivid awareness of how weak and unworthy they were. I have often felt this way, especially this week.

But then something wonderful happened to Peter, James, and John, and our Lord has done the same for me. Verses 7 and 8 say, *Jesus came and touched them "Rise, and have no fear." When they lifted up their eyes, they saw no one but Jesus only.*

When we despair and are afraid, our Lord comes and personally touches us. He touches us and directs us to *rise* from wherever we are. Because we recognize that He is with us, we can release to Him all of our fears; He tells us so.

How was this possible for Peter, James, and John, and how is it possible for you and me? Verse 8 tells us: *When they lifted up their eyes, they saw no one but Jesus only.* When we move our focus from whatever causes us to fear and place it upon the Lord Jesus Christ who has personally touched us, and whom we know and love, our fear is overmatched by His love, our dread is overwhelmed by His hope, and our despair is overcome by His joy. Again today I am blessed, for in faith I see no one but Jesus.

FOR REFLECTION

When have you ever felt overwhelmed by your circumstances or by your own smallness and weakness, such that you despaired or became fearful? When has God reminded you to fix your eyes on the Lord and to put your trust in Him? As you reflect on the passage from Exodus 14-15, what is the Lord teaching you about trusting Him in the face of situations that seem impossible? As you reflect on the passage from Matthew 17, what is the Lord teaching you about His presence and personal touch? What is He teaching you about opening your eyes and seeing only Jesus? What needs to happen for you to see Jesus whenever you are facing struggles and fear? Ask God to help you in this, and He surely will.

72

ON ACCIDENTS AND PROVIDENCE

January 29, 2020

Accidents happen with some frequency in this broken world, often suddenly and with sad results. People die or are injured, and pain is left in the wake. Most of us have experienced this in one way or another. As a clergyman, I have walked with many through such tragedies, some of which are traumatically and indelibly planted in my memory, for the pain was so great. Some are left with deep grief, others with profound pain, and others with enduring questions like "How could this happen?" or "Why did God allow this?" Have you ever wrestled with these questions?

I wrestled with these issues yesterday, because Helen and I were involved in a car accident. Thankfully, no one was seriously injured, but the suddenness of it and the pain of it, on top of everything else I am dealing with, left me feeling confounded and confused.

Helen was scheduled for oral surgery yesterday, and she was not allowed to drive because of pain medicines, so I was driving her to her appointment. Soon after we left home, as I drove around a corner on a twisty country road, a car appeared in our lane, heading directly at us. I swerved toward a ditch, and the other car broadsided us; it hit just behind my driver's door and pushed us off the road.

When this happened, I hit my head hard. I was bleeding and the world began to spin. I rejoiced when, in spite of my fog, Helen said she was okay and was calling 911 to request an ambulance. We rejoiced to see the other driver extract herself from her car, as her airbags had all deployed. She walked to our car, reported that she was fine, and asked if we were okay. A few minutes later, an ambulance arrived, and we were on our way to the nearest emergency room. I had a horrible headache, significant back pain, and stiffness and pain in my neck and shoulders.

I was treated to CT scans and x-rays, which confirmed that nothing was broken, but I had suffered a concussion. Thankfully, no other serious injuries were found. Several hours after our arrival, I was released. When our son Jonathan came to pick us up, he told me that I reminded him of Job.

I did not argue with this comparison, but of course Job's suffering and losses were far greater than mine. Job did not appreciate his suffering, nor did he feel that he had done anything to warrant it. He wrestled with it and wondered why. I can relate to this. Sometimes, even for God's people, it can feel like everything is going wrong.

But is it? Are our struggles merely random difficulties without purpose or meaning? Or does God have providential reasons for our struggles that are intended for His glory and our good? Are we able to trust God even though we cannot fully see?

From prison, the apostle Paul faced hard circumstances, and he undoubtedly did not want to be there. In spite of that, the Holy Spirit inspired him to write to Christians in Philippi and urge them to *rejoice in the Lord always* and *in everything, by prayer and supplication with thanksgiving, let your requests be made known to God* (Philippians 4:4, 6). Then Paul declared a promise that is fulfilled in us when we choose to put our trust in Christ: *And the peace of God, which surpasses all understanding will guard your hearts and your minds in Christ Jesus* (Philippians 4:7).

Rejoicing in the Lord *always*? In *everything* praying ... with *thanksgiving*? Experiencing God's *peace, guarding our hearts and minds in Christ Jesus*? Is this actually achievable for us, even when accidents and losses come into our lives, or we are feeling miserable and do not yet understand,? Is it possible when the unpleasant circumstances that assault us seem to be out of our control? These are real questions.

Because God's Word invites us to this, and because God never calls us to anything that He does not equip us to do, I know that yes, by God's love and grace it is possible.

All of us experience struggles in this life. I know that you do and you are. And so am I. My recent struggles have included cancer, immune deficiencies, reduced stamina and strength, and the inability to do the work I love. In addition to prolonged chemotherapy treatments and postponement of the SCT, I am now fighting viral and bacterial infections with significant coughing and feeling generally miserable. And now this car accident, a concussion, a pounding headache, and a destroyed car.

As I reflect on Jonathan's reference to Job, this does feel like a test. When I think of Paul's exhortation to Christians in Philippi, I do not think I have done so well on this test, or at rejoicing, being thankful, or experiencing God's peace through it all.

As I was tempted to grumble and complain, I heard the Holy Spirit remind me that I could choose to complain if I really want to, but by His grace, I am able to make a better choice. So I have asked God to help me make a better choice. And He is answering my prayer.

When the car accident happened, my glasses flew off my head; they were not immediately found. So after I was released from the hospital, I asked Jonathan to take us to the garage where our car had been towed, so we could look for my glasses. Jonathan looked for them inside the car and found them underneath the driver's seat. Meanwhile, I looked at the exterior damage done to our car. As I did so, my Lord spoke to me and revealed that this could have been much worse. We could have been seriously injured or even killed. When I realized this, my perspective changed, and I determined in my heart that I will rejoice. I will give God thanks, and I will celebrate His grace, even in this.

Today my head and neck hurt a lot, and my body aches – remnants of yesterday's accident. But I know in faith that this too shall pass, and in the sweet providence of God, I know that there is a bright side. The Lord is with me, and something good will come of this, as I thank my God and allow Him to have His way in me.

When we cannot yet see a bright side in the darkness of our current struggles, let us choose to fix our eyes firmly on the Lord who is wonderfully with us in this and every situation. Let us rejoice that our God has cared for us through every trial we have endured or are now enduring, even in our pain and uncertainties about the future. He will be with us to the very end of our earthly journey and then forevermore.

Though we may not yet understand God's plan, because of His great love and for His great glory, we can know that He will fulfill His purpose in us and through us. For this we can give Him our praise.

FOR REFLECTION

When have you ever wrestled with the questions "How did this happen?" or "Why did God allow this?" When and why have you struggled to trust God in the face of pain and hardship and unanswered questions? What is your reaction to the suggestion that grumbling and complaining is a choice that we make, and that by God's grace we can make a better choice? How can you more readily trust God even when life for you is painful or hard? Ask God to help you in this, and He surely will.

73

ON DEALING WITH UNEXPECTED DELAYS

February 2, 2020

Often we establish in our minds a time frame of when certain things will happen. Then something outside of our control occurs that changes the plans. When this happens, we must cope with the delay.

It happens with military deployments. We can have a particular date in mind by when we will return home to reunite with our loved ones. Then a delay is announced, which we have no control over. We may be disappointed, as are those who await our return, but we must push through the disappointment and deal with the delay.

This also happens regarding illness and other human struggles. We look ahead with longing to when things will improve. But then an interruption comes. A setback occurs, and we have to find a way to cope with the delay. This happens to all of us.. It happened to me again this week.

My scheduled SCT was already delayed once, when soon after we arrived in Nashville on January 6, I became sick with two confirmed viruses, which later led to a bacterial sinus infection. The SCT was therefore postponed, and we returned to Minnesota until I am well enough to try again. We had been scheduled to go back to the SCT Center at the Nashville VA Medical Center on February 19. But because we were in an automobile accident, this has forced yet another delay. I have been driving nearly fifty years now, and this was the first time I have ever been hurt in a car accident, so I definitely did not see it coming. But it happened.

At the hospital emergency room I was diagnosed with a concussion. That was five days ago, and I am still dealing with headaches. I also have lingering pain in my neck, shoulders, and back. For this reason I have pursued chiropractic care, and I will most likely need physical therapy to recover from my injuries. Because of the pain and my slow movement, the bone marrow biopsy that I was to have done this Monday has now been postponed, and my return to Nashville for the SCT is again delayed. This lingering pain must be behind me, and I must be as strong and mobile as possible before I am able to proceed.

I've already admitted that I was sick of being sick. Today I admit that I am frustrated by yet another unexpected delay in my recovery. Yesterday Helen could join our son Jonathan in taking our young grandsons to the zoo. I was glad she could do this, and she reported that they had a great time. But I could not go, though I long to be well enough to do such things. As the SCT is part of the path I expect to follow in order to get there, experiencing another delay is hard to take.

Coping with the unexpected delays is not easy for us. Though there might be nothing we can do about the delay itself, the Lord reminded me there is something we can do about our responses.

What can we do? We can choose to take a deep breath and let go of our frustrations and our insistence on controlling the future. We can make a faith decision to choose to trust God, even in this deep valley. After all, we know God loves us, and we know He is forever faithful. We also know that His plan is always good.

So we can ask God to guide us through this disappointment and grant us sufficient faith and peace to rest in Him. When I reflect on certain precious and timeless truths, they get me through:

Reflect and accept that God loves me.
Psalm 36:5-7 says, *Your steadfast love, O LORD, extends to the heavens, your faithfulness to the clouds. Your righteousness is like the mountains of God; your judgments are like the great deep; man and beast you save, O LORD. How precious is your steadfast love, O God! The children of*

mankind take refuge in the shadow of your wings. Yes. Thank you God for loving me. I know that you do, so I draw closer to you now, beneath the safe and protective shadow of your wings.

Reflect and accept that God has been, is now, and will forever be faithful.
Deuteronomy 7:9 says, *Know therefore that the LORD your God is God, the faithful God who keeps covenant and steadfast love with those who love Him and keep His commandments, to a thousand generations.* 2 Timothy 2:13 says, *If we are faithless, He remains faithful – for He cannot deny Himself.* Yes. Thank you God for your faithfulness. I believe and know that you remain faithful to me.

Reflect and accept that God's plan for me is good, and He will lead me in it.
Jeremiah 29:11 says, *For I know the plans I have for you, declares the LORD, plans for welfare and not for evil, to give you a future* and a hope. Proverbs 3:5-6 says, *Trust in the LORD with all your heart, and do not lean on your own understanding. In all your ways acknowledge Him, and He will make straight your paths.* Yes. Thank you God for your good plan for me and for your promise to lead me in it. I believe and I trust you, and I rest in your promise.

Coping with disappointments and unexpected delays requires that we make a faith decision to rest in God's love, faithfulness, and His promise that His plan for us is good. I am making that decision now, even as I deal with my current situation that includes unexpected pain and as I ask and trust God to lead me on the path of His peace and His will. If you are dealing with similar frustrations, I pray that you too will make a faith decision to rest in Him – cling to His love and faithfulness and the assurance that His plan for you is still good.

Toward this end Helen and I appreciate your prayers – prayers for His healing, prayers for His leading, and ultimately prayers for His purpose and glory. Thank you for standing with us along our journey. It is wonderful to know that in Jesus Christ we never walk alone. We are blessed by your encouragement and prayers.

FOR REFLECTION

When have you faced unexpected delays that upset your plans and for which you struggled to cope? In what ways are you facing such delays now? What does it mean for you to make a faith decision to choose to trust God, even in this? How will it affect you in the days ahead to reflect and accept that God loves you? How does it bless you to reflect and accept that God has been, is now, and will be forever faithful? How will it impact you to reflect and accept that God's plan for you is good, and He will lead you in it? Ask God to help you in this, and He surely will.

74

ON ENCOURAGEMENT FOR OUR DISCOURAGEMENT

February 7, 2020

Sometimes we need to hear words of encouragement. We all experience seasons of discouragement. This has been that kind of week for me. These health-related things have discouraged me this week:

- I continue to deal with pain from the car accident that I was in last week. At times the pain is intense and distracting, which causes me to move slowly.
- I am still fighting infections that I have had for over a month, and I have had a fever again.
- The SCT I was scheduled to undergo in early January and rescheduled for mid-February is now postponed until April 20.
- Because of this delay, the chemotherapy treatments that were halted in December must resume, which means dealing with the side effects again.
- Because of collapsed veins from prolonged chemotherapy treatments, I need to have a PICC line (peripherally inserted

central-line catheter) installed from my arm to just above my heart.

- Yesterday my new infectious disease physician urged that because my immune system is compromised, until I arrive in Nashville for the SCT, I must be very careful to avoid places or people where I could be exposed to illness, including my grandchildren.

Just one of these things could discourage me, but experiencing all of them together has been discouraging to me. In my heart I know that these problems are not insurmountable. I also know that my God is able, for nothing is too difficult for Him. Throughout my life as I have walked with God, I have witnessed and experienced His faithfulness, and I know that He has not changed, nor will He. I have received a long litany of blessings from God for which I give Him my thanks. Yet I face discouragement.

In this broken world, discouragement comes to us all. Even people of strong faith face it. When life is hard and things transpire that are out of our control and we do not understand, discouragement mounts. When our grief is great or our pain is intense, when loneliness overwhelms and our hope has dissipated, discouragement can roll over us like the unstoppable tide.

But God has reminded me this week that when discouragement comes to His children, He is not unaware. God is not unconcerned or unable to meet us in our need. God always knows, He always cares, He always speaks, and He always comes.

This week I have been amazed at how God has used His children to encourage me. He works in this way to care for His discouraged ones. We have been given the privilege and responsibility of being simultaneously an instrument of God to deliver encouragement and to be a blessed recipient of His grace of encouragement.

This week I have been a grateful recipient of such blessings. I received my Lord's encouragement through a number of people, and my soul is lifted. My dear wife Helen reads me very well. She knows when to take my hand, hold me close, pray with me, or speak words of love, faith, and affirmation. She has done this for me throughout our forty-three plus years of married life together, and she has done so this week. What a blessing from God she is to me! She has encouraged me greatly.

And two days ago when my heart was especially heavy, I received two wonderful phone calls from friends in other states who love the Lord and love me. They were stirred by the Lord to listen, to love, and to share words of encouragement that I needed to hear. They prayed with me, and my heart was lifted.

This week I also received via mail, email, and text message several personal messages from family and friends who shared kind and loving words; they reminded me of God's love and theirs and of God's faithfulness and their prayers. Through these I received words of affirmation, gratitude, and faith, and I have been encouraged.

Yesterday I received a personal message from a friend on another continent who said he had been interceding for me before God's throne. As he prayed for me, he received a message of faith, promise, and hope from the Lord, which he then passed along to me. His words of encouragement from the heart of God refreshed me.

On my way home from a hospital appointment yesterday, I listened on the radio to a Christian worship song that pointed me to the promises of God. As I heard this, and as I sang along, the Lord used that songwriter and those gifted musicians to meet me in that car and fill my heart with praise and joy in His presence and promises. My heart was greatly encouraged.

I have been filled with joy this week by how my Lord knew that I needed encouragement and how He met me in my need. He knows the same about you. Whenever one of His children is discouraged, God knows, and He cares. He speaks to us by the Holy Spirit through His Word, and He gives us brothers and sisters who can bring God's presence and speak His truth. Such personal encouragement from the Lord God Almighty is powerful and medicinal to heal, help, and restore.

Many Scriptures teach us to encourage one another and to receive God's encouragement. I have been especially blessed this week by these:

Anxiety in a man's heart weighs him down, but a good word makes him glad (Proverbs 12:25). Yes. How true!

Let us consider how to stir up one another to love and good works, not neglecting to meet together, as is the habit of some, but encouraging one another, and all the more as you see the Day drawing near (Hebrews 10:24-25). Yes. Doing this requires intentional obedience, and it requires that we look beyond our needs to the needs of others. Doing this brings great reward in our giving and receiving. As God's children, we are blessed to look ahead to that great day that is soon coming when we will see the fulfillment of God's promises, and we will behold Him in the fullness of His heavenly glory.

Encourage one another and build one another up, just as you are doing (1 Thessalonians 5:11). Yes. Encouraging one another is an integral part of following Jesus Christ. We are blessed to be both instruments and recipients of His personal encouragement.

By God's great grace to me and despite my current struggles, I am encouraged. This does not mean that my way is easy, nor does it mean that I will not face discouragement when my path is hard. In fact, I expect that in coming days there will be times when my path is difficult. Psalm 46:1 presumes that trouble will come to all, but when it does come, we can turn to our God who is with us and who will be our refuge and strength: *God is our refuge and strength, a very present help in trouble.*

Jesus declared that His disciples will face trouble, but when the trouble comes, we can turn to Him in faith and enjoy His peace. He said in John 16:33, *I have said these things to you, that in me you may have peace. In the world you will have tribulation. But take heart; I have overcome the world.*

And so the Lord assured me again this week that He is with me now, and He will never forsake me. I know that He will continue to provide the encouragement I need and that others may need along the way. I pray that He might use me and you as His instruments to encourage others.

I want you to know that whenever you have prayed for me or shared heartfelt words with me, you have encouraged me. I thank you for this. I also pray for you that when you face discouragement and whatever you may need, you too may receive encouragement from the Lord whose love for you will never fail.

FOR REFLECTION

When have you faced much discouragement but received the Lord's encouragement through the words and presence of others? Who has the Lord placed upon your heart that you might bring His encouragement to them? Prayerfully read again Proverbs 12:25; Hebrews 10:24-25, and 1 Thessalonians 5:11. What action steps would the Lord have you take to be a giver or recipient of His encouragement? Ask God to help you in this, and He surely will.

75

ON BEING FOREVER FAMILY

February 17, 2020

What a change four decades brings. Forty years ago, while I attended Bethel Theological Seminary in St. Paul, Minnesota, Helen and I were part of a wonderful local church that was called University Avenue Congregational Church. During our seminary years, this congregation was family to us. We have many treasured memories of people there whom we loved and who loved us. We experienced then the blessing of being part of God's eternal family. Many of those dear people are now in heaven's glory, while some remain.

I was privileged to serve that local congregation as the director of youth ministry, and Helen served beside me. How we loved those teenagers, and how blessed we were to see God working in their young lives. Soon after I graduated from seminary, we moved from St. Paul, Minnesota, to Pawtucket, Rhode Island, when I answered God's call to serve as pastor of another local church family called Darlington Congregational Church.

So much has transpired and many things have changed in the last forty years, but some things remain. People who were family then are still family now, and because of Jesus Christ, we know that we will be family forever. Helen and I celebrated this truth yesterday when two friends who were part of our youth group forty years ago came to visit us. Forty years ago these were young teenagers, and Helen and I were young adults in our twenties. It was wonderful yesterday to share precious memories and recount God's faithfulness to us all through the years. Though we have noticeably changed, some things have not changed at all. We are still family, and we know that, because of Jesus Christ, we will be family forever. This is true cause for celebration.

As my body has aged, and my health has diminished, I have increasingly focused my mind and heart on what will long endure, which includes God's immeasurable grace to all who know and love the Lord Jesus Christ. Though we cannot hit a rewind button to restore the years of our youth, we can surely make a faith decision to treasure what mattered most then and prioritize now what will matter most in eternity. We can choose to love the Lord our God above all and to value the blessings of His grace and love, including the sweet joy of being part of His family for time and eternity.

This week I have reflected on these biblical truths about being God's children and thus forever His family with one another:

1. In Jesus Christ we are God's own children:

> *But to all who did receive Him, who believed in His name,*
> *He gave the right to become children of God.* (John 1:12)

2. Christ has made us family together:

> *So then you are no longer strangers and aliens, but you are*
> *fellow citizens with the saints and members of the household*
> *of God.* (Ephesians 2:19)

3. We are blessed to carry the family trait of God's primary characteristic, which is love:

> *A new commandment I give to you, that you love one*
> *another: just as I have loved you, you also are to love one*
> *another.* (John 13:34)

4. We who are God's family now by faith in Jesus Christ, will be His family forever:

> Beloved, we are God's children now, and what we will be has not yet appeared; but we know that when He appears we shall be like Him, because we shall see Him as He is. (1 John 3:2)

5. God's love for His dear children is for time and eternity:

> The steadfast love of the LORD is from everlasting to everlasting on those who fear Him, and His righteousness to children's children, to those who keep His covenant and remember to do His commandments. (Psalm 103:17-18)

As these past forty years have so quickly gone by, I know the next forty will too. Moments, days, and years pass us by and we cannot regain them. What we can do is treasure every day while we have it, and treasure each relationship that is entrusted to us. We can treasure most our relationship with God and that we are blessed to be His children. We can rejoice that the relationships we now enjoy with others through Jesus Christ will endure for time and eternity. How blessed we are to be forever family.

FOR REFLECTION

How have you experienced the joy and blessing of being forever family? Review the five biblical truths that were listed here about being God's children and forever His family with one another. Which of these speaks to you today, and why? What changes do you need to make to more fully know the joy of being His forever family? Ask God to help you in this, and He surely will.

76

ON STAYING POSITIVE WHEN FEELING NEGATIVE

February 24, 2020

When we are feeling negative, it is not easy to remain positive. I know this firsthand, and I know that you do too. Seventeen months of dealing with active multiple myeloma with significant lifestyle changes, disappointments, and prolonged periods of not feeling well has not been easy. Yet, I am experiencing God's grace in countless ways.

I had hoped that it would be easier by now to stay positive, no matter how negative I may feel. But I have seen again this week that I remain a work in progress. God is not finished maturing me in Christ. Nor is He finished with you. Because remaining positive in the face of adversity is not an automatic response for us, the Lord reminds us to exercise our faith by choosing to look to Him.

I have not felt well this week. Wednesday I experienced an allergic reaction during my chemotherapy treatment. The primary symptom was significant nausea, which led to a pause in treatment while I took medicine to address those symptoms. Chemotherapy was resumed, though administered slowly. I was at the hospital twelve hours that day. The past few days I needed to stay near a bathroom, and I have felt generally weak and tired.

I also continue to receive treatments for the pain in my neck and back from the car accident. Though there has been some noticeable improvement, it still hurts. Further, following four weeks on a current course of antibiotics to fight a sinus infection, my infectious disease physician has determined I should remain on antibiotics for eight more weeks, until I report again to Nashville for the SCT. Though staying on antibiotics is hard on my system, the doctor said this is necessary, so I can be infection free when arriving for the SCT.

So how are we to stay positive when feeling negative? How are we to overcome the negative feelings we have from our weakness, hard circumstances, and struggles to find and experience God's help, hope, and confidence? The answer is by faith. God never asks or expects us to ignore our weakness and pretend that all is well when it is not. Rather, He calls us to exercise our faith by lifting our eyes and shifting our focus from ourselves to Him. This can be our proactive decision.

A particular verse of Scripture that has been ringing in my heart lately is our Lord's exhortation in Hebrews 12:2. The KJV renders it, *Looking unto Jesus the author and finisher of our faith; who for the joy that was set before Him endured the cross, despising the shame, and is set down at the right hand of the throne of God.* The NIV introduces this verse with, *Fixing our eyes on Jesus.*

In this verse God calls us to turn our gaze from ourselves to the Lord Jesus; that is, to make an intentional shift in our focus. We are called to fix our eyes on *Who* Jesus is (He is *the author and finisher of our faith*), and on *What* Jesus endured for us (He *endured the cross, despising the shame*), and on *Where* Jesus is now (He *is set down at the right hand of the throne of God*).

When we fix our eyes on Jesus, we cannot remain focused on our own struggles and negative feelings. Our focus becomes increasingly filled with the Lord – Who He is, What He has done, Where He is now, and thus on what He will yet do for our good and for His glory.

My friend, Pastor L. David Green, recently sent me a wonderful book on this theme that has blessed me – *I Shall Not Die, But Live.*[9]. The author, Douglas Taylor, was for fourteen years Assistant Editor at the Banner of Truth Trust in Edinburgh, Scotland. In 2011 he was

---

9   Douglas Taylor, *I Shall Not Die, But Live,* (Banner of Truth, 2016).

diagnosed with inoperable liver cancer. Rather than focus on his own struggle and terminal diagnosis, he made a faith decision to fix his focus on the Lord.

A theme verse for Taylor was Psalm 118:17, *I shall not die, but live, and declare the works of the Lord* (KJV). He maintained a daily blog he called *Works Worth Declaring*, in which he took his eyes off his own struggle and pending death and looked instead toward the living hope that is ours in Jesus Christ. He determined to point others toward the source of His comfort and strength, the One whose presence is real and whose promises are assured. The lessons in his blog articles were compiled into his inspiring book.

This is the key for me now and for all of us when we struggle with negative feelings or circumstances. We can choose to focus on our struggles if we wish. I know because I have faced that temptation this week. But by God's grace, we can also choose to exercise our faith and fix our eyes on Jesus.

Douglas Taylor quoted Dr. Samuel Johnson who said, "Depend on it Sir, when a man knows he is to be hanged in a fortnight, it concentrates his mind wonderfully."[10] Applying this principle to his own situation, Taylor wrote, "Something similar may be said of a man who is diagnosed with an incurable disease, which normally carries a prognosis of about six months. But if that is true, what kind of self-delusion would lead him to the text that heads this blog: *I shall not die, but live*? Certainly not any thought of dodging the arrow that has brought down every man since the fall of Adam. Rather, the thought that he must now focus on the things that really matter with the conviction that in sober reality, he will not die until his work is done, until the things that God has intended for him to accomplish are accomplished. Till then, *I shall not die, but live*; and what could be more worth doing than what the psalmist speaks of next: *and declare the works of the Lord*?" Yes, and Amen.

So how are we to stay positive when we are feeling negative? How can we continue to accomplish God's purposes even when our bodies fail us or circumstances are assail us? How?

- By exercising our faith in the Lord Jesus Christ

---

10 George Birkbeck Hill, ed., *Boswell's Life of Johnson*, vol. 6, (New York: Macmillan and Co., 1887), 296.

- By fixing our focus not on our struggles and disappointments but on Christ
- By believing and holding on to the sure promises of God
- By determining to declare the works of the Lord as long as we have breath
- By knowing with joyful certainty that by the grace of our Lord we will surely live with Him forever.

I attest to you today, as my Lord has been teaching me, that when we ask Him to help us with these things, He surely does.

FOR REFLECTION

In what ways and for what reasons have you struggled with staying positive when feeling negative? What does it mean to shift your focus from yourself to Jesus? Review again Hebrews 12:2. How does it help you to fix your eyes on *Who* Jesus is (He is *the author and finisher of our faith*)? How does it help you to fix your eyes on *What* Jesus endured for you (He *endured the cross, despising the shame*)? How does it help you to fix your eyes on *Where* Jesus is on your behalf now (He *is set down at the right hand of the throne of God*)? Knowing these things about Jesus, how can you more easily stay positive when negative feelings assail you? Ask God to help you in this, and He surely will!

77

ON WANDERING AIMLESSLY OR PURPOSEFULLY

March 1, 2020

Sometimes we feel like we are wandering around in circles, getting nowhere. Sometimes that is precisely what we are doing, because we have no clear direction. At other times we feel like we are wandering aimlessly, when in fact the unseen hand of God is guiding us.

Often the people of Israel had no direction. They wandered about in the wilderness for forty long, frustrating years as a direct consequence of their failure to believe and obey the Lord. When we choose to disregard the Lord and go our own way, we meet with painful consequences. Still, the Lord extends grace and mercy, as was expressed in Deuteronomy 2:7 – *For the LORD your God has blessed you in all the work of your hands. He knows your going through this great wilderness. These forty years the LORD your God has been with you. You have lacked nothing.*

When we feel like we are wandering aimlessly, our Lord is watching over us with infinite affection. He meets us in our need, and He longs for us to notice, believe, and receive His love and grace.

The Scriptures commend some people of faith who experienced much affliction while wandering about in this harsh world. The eleventh chapter of Hebrews was an early Hall of Fame that gave tribute to faithful people who preceded us and lived their lives walking with God by faith.

We read of such exemplary faith-filled wanderers: *They were stoned, they were sawn in two, they were killed with the sword. They went about in skins of sheep and goats, destitute, afflicted, mistreated – of whom the world was not worthy – wandering about in deserts and mountains, and in dens and caves of the earth* (Hebrews 11:37-38). Yes, they wandered, but not aimlessly. Their wandering was purposeful, for the Lord their God was with them; He guided and sustained them, as they walked with Him by faith even in the deep valleys of affliction.

A qualitative difference exists between wandering aimlessly and wandering purposefully. We who love and follow Jesus Christ by faith are not among those who wander aimlessly. We have a God who is always with us and guides us, even when we do not see it. No matter how it might feel in the midst of our afflictions, we are led by the Lord who has an excellent plan. He knows our ultimate destination and the best path that will lead us there. Our Lord has been with us. He is with us now on our journey, and He will be with us until the end.

I have been prayerfully reflecting on these things because at times I have felt like I am wandering aimlessly. I feel like I am not getting better and am no closer to healing and remission. Sometimes I feel like I am wandering around as in a wilderness. Perhaps you have felt this way at times. Of course, our perceptions are not always true.

Though such feelings have been real to me, my Lord reminds me that such feelings do not reflect His truth. His Word is true, and His Word says He has always been with me, and He is with me now. His Word says that because He is watching over me, I have lacked nothing that I have really needed. His Word tells me that a life of faith in God means there may be seasons of struggle, hardship, and loss, but He is and will be forever faithful.

My Lord has reminded me that there has been purpose in my wanderings. Physically, I have made progress, for which I rejoice. As I have rested, my body has been healing. Because the post-accident pain in my neck and back has decreased, beginning this week I can reduce my chiropractic visits to once weekly. Also, I noticed that today I am half way between the day that Helen and I returned from Nashville and the day that we are scheduled to return to proceed with the SCT. Reaching this halfway milestone encourages me.

The Lord also has reminded me of what He is doing in my life spiritually. I thank Him for the lessons He is teaching me, for the wonderful sense of His presence that I have known, and for the ever-growing assurance of His promises. I thank Him too for the joy of every divine appointment and for every opportunity that He has given me to express His truth and show His love. Though I would not have chosen this road, and though wandering through a desert is difficult, having seen some of the loving purposes of God, I would not trade this course for another.

FOR REFLECTION

When have you felt like you were wandering but getting nowhere? Has there been a time when you felt like you were wandering aimlessly, when later you perceived that you were actually being guided by the unseen hand of God? What is the difference between wandering aimlessly and wandering purposefully, and how can you experience the latter? How can God help you fulfill and appreciate His purpose? Ask God to help you in this, and He surely will.

78

ON COMING TO JESUS FOR ALL THAT WE NEED

March 8, 2020

One of my longtime favorite narratives in the gospels is the account of a blind man named Bartimaeus as told in Mark 10:46-52. I love this story because I can relate to Bartimaeus. Though I have never been physically blind, I have been blind in other ways, and I have experienced profound needs that no one but Jesus could meet. I too have called out to Him and been amazed at His love and mercy to me.

The Lord Jesus was on His way toward Jerusalem where He intended to lay down His life as the Lamb of God, the perfect sacrifice for the sins of the whole world. In Mark 10:32-34, we hear Jesus foretelling what He would experience in Jerusalem. This is the third time in Mark's gospel where Jesus foretells His death (Mark 8:31-33; 9:30-32).

Why did Jesus repeat Himself like this? Surely, this repetition was so His disciples might know that His mission was not to set up an earthly kingdom by overthrowing Rome, as they had expected. Rather, His mission was to provide forgiveness of our sins and to bestow on us His perfect righteousness. He wanted us to know that it was out of great love that He gave His life for our salvation.

So before it happened, Jesus repeatedly described to His disciples the suffering that He would endure and the death that He would die.

He told them that on the third day He would rise from the grave. As the Righteous Lord, the Son of the Living God, what Jesus foretold is what happened.

So on the day described in Mark 10, Jesus passed through Jericho on his way toward Jerusalem. He had just sixteen more miles to walk along His journey to that city, where He would endure for all of humanity the suffering and death that He foretold. But in Jericho that day a divine appointment awaited Him, one that still blesses us today and reminds us all that we too can come to Jesus for all that we need.

Bartimaeus, son of Timaeus, was a blind man in Jericho who had longed for an opportunity like this. He was a beggar who spent his days along the side of that road. Day after day and year after year, he sat there and called out for alms, pleaded for pity, and hoped against hope that enough coins would be given to him so he could survive.

What a hard life he lived, and what dismal prospects he had. Humanly speaking, he had no reasonable hope for a better future. But when he heard about Jesus, hope was born in his heart. He probably heard about Jesus from people who had been in the Lord's presence and had heard His teachings. Perhaps he heard personal testimonies of people who had witnessed or experienced a miracle performed by the Lord Jesus.

Bartimaeus heard about Jesus healing many people with all kinds of diseases. He heard about His raising somebody from the dead, His restoring hearing to the deaf, and best of all, His giving sight to the blind. And by the grace of God, Bartimaeus believed what he heard about Jesus, so he determined in his heart that He must be the Messiah, the long awaited Son of David.

Bartimaeus dreamed of Jesus and longed for an opportunity to meet Him. He imagined what he would say if he ever met the Lord personally. He knew only Jesus could meet his need, so he longed for Jesus to pass by. Bartimaeus intended to cry out to the Lord and plead for His mercy. He was going to ask Jesus to meet his need.

And on that day, it happened. As a crowd passed by on the road through Jericho, much excitement was in the air. Bartimaeus sensed it and heard it, so he asked someone, "What is going on?"

That was when great excitement gripped his heart, for he heard the wonderful news that *Jesus of Nazareth is passing by* (Luke 18:37).

When Bartimaeus heard this, his heart may have skipped a beat or two. Could it be? When he realized it was true, that Jesus was passing by, he immediately cried out, not in a whisper but in a shout: *Jesus, Son of David, have mercy on me!* He did not yell it once. He cried it over and over: *Jesus, Son of David, have mercy on me!* Someone told him to be quiet and stop annoying everybody, but Bartimaeus was undeterred. He continued calling out to Jesus.

Our Lord heard his cry, just as He has often heard ours. Verse 49 says, *And Jesus stopped and said, "Call him."* Bartimaeus then received the wonderful, joy-giving, life-changing news that was intended for him, the same good news that changes lives today. *They called the blind man, saying to him, "Take heart. Get up; he is calling you."*

When Bartimaeus heard this, he wasted no time. Verse 50 says, *And throwing off his cloak, he sprang up and came to Jesus.* I love the picture this conveys; there was no hesitation or delay. There was only eagerness to come to Jesus right here and right now. How often I have done this at my Lord's invitation, running to Him, filled with joy at the privilege, in awe of the opportunity, and so glad to be in His presence.

As the Lord welcomed Bartimaeus that day, and as Jesus gave Bartimaeus His full attention, Jesus then asked a question that must be answered in faith (v. 51). He asked, *What do you want me to do for you?* What an awesome question to be asked by the Lord.

Bartimaeus was prepared with his answer, for he had dreamed of this moment. He replied to the Lord, *Rabbi, let me recover my sight* (v. 51). Bartimaeus knew only Jesus could do this, so he asked Him to restore his sight. The Lord's answer was immediately yes. Jesus said to Bartimaeus, *"Go your way; your faith has made you well." And immediately he recovered his sight and followed him on the way.*

And what was Bartimaeus's response to the Lord's wonderful provision that day? We can imagine there was much joy with shouting and praise. Did Bartimaeus return to his place of begging? No, his life was changed by Jesus, so he joined the crowd of Christ-followers and went with the Lord to Jerusalem. When they arrived, and the triumphal entry occurred, I picture Bartimaeus in the midst of the crowd, joyfully singing and shouting from the depths of his grateful heart, *Hosanna to the Son of David! Blessed is He who comes in the name of the Lord!* (Matthew 20:9).

My Lord has reminded me lately that I too am invited to come to Him for all that I need. I can also believe in His power to save, and heal, and strengthen, and provide, and lead, and help. The Lord Jesus is able to provide all that we need. He invites us to come to Him and to keep coming again and again.

As my body has been slowly healing, and as I am nearing the time when the SCT might be accomplished, my Lord reminds me of my many needs that only He can fill. I often feel vulnerable and weak, but like Bartimaeus, I know my Lord can provide what I most need. I often feel the seriousness of my sin, and I know I need His mercy and forgiveness. I often feel troubled and sorrowful, and I know I need His comfort and peace. I often feel discouraged, tempted, and weak, and I know I need His strength to endure and His protection from temptations and dangers. I often feel downcast and ill, and I know I need His hope and His healing. I know I need His anointing for whatever He calls me to do, and I need His eternal perspective. I know that I need Jesus more than my next breath or heartbeat. I need the Lord more than anything. Do you know that you need Him too? We all need the Lord.

Jesus invites us to come to Him, and when we do, we can hear Him ask us the same question he asked of Bartimaeus, *What do you want me to do for you?* He longs for us to answer this question as Bartimaeus did – with true faith in Him. No matter what happens around us, He does not want us to worry or despair. He wants us to trust Him and know that His will and ways are always loving and good, even when we walk through deep valleys. Our Lord invites all of us to bring Him our needs.

A worship song that has lately ministered to me on this theme is one by Lauren Daigle called "Everything." The lyrics reflect my own testimony of God's faithfulness because they speak of how He loves me more than the sparrows and roses, the oceans and seasons and gives me everything I need. Particularly the last verse mentions that He carries me when I can't stand and He is mighty when I am weak. This is what my Lord is doing for me now; He is everything I need.

Yes, and Amen! May the Lord of all bless and lead us, just as He blessed Bartimaeus that day. May we call out to Jesus and come in faith to the One who so mercifully and lovingly gave His life for us and who forever gives us everything we need.

FOR REFLECTION

In what ways have you been blind, and what needs have you had that only Jesus can meet? What do you learn from Bartimaeus's example about bringing your own need to Jesus? What must change so you can come often to Jesus and trust Him for everything you need? Ask God to help you in this, and He surely will.

79

ON GOD'S RESTORATION OF WHAT IS BROKEN

March 16, 2020

When we look at something that is broken, we may think it can never be restored, but our God teaches us otherwise. He reminds us of what He can do and what He is doing.

I can never forget that day when I smashed my first bicycle into a tree. I was six or seven years old and learning to ride an old bicycle that had been passed down from my big brother David. I had not yet mastered the all-important skill of braking, so as I rode down a hill, I went faster and faster but couldn't stop or slow down. I smashed full speed into a tree, and there my bike and I came to a full stop. I came away with scrapes and bruises, but even more upsetting to me, my bike appeared to be smashed beyond repair. The frame and wheels were bent, and I cried because my bike was destroyed.

But my dad looked at the tangled mess, and he saw what I could not see. He saw what was possible. My father took my broken bicycle and put it in the skilled hands of a friend who was the shop teacher at the local high school where they had a machine shop, tools, ability, and time to fix it. Under the watchful eye of that skilled teacher, those students repaired and restored my bicycle. Later, to my amazement, they returned it to me, and I gratefully rode it again.

Something similar has happened to our car. A few weeks ago when another car hit us, I was physically hurt, though I thank God that I have largely recovered. Our car however appeared to be damaged beyond repair. Yet, it was repaired. Extensive work was done, and a few days ago, the car was returned to me. Driving it now, I cannot help but smile because it is fully restored. It looks, rides, and smells as good as new.

The COVID-19 pandemic that now affects our world reminds us all that we are living in a world that is broken. In many ways, life the way we knew it before has suddenly smashed against a tree. We look at the damage of this pandemic and of other crises in our world, and we experience some of the pain of it, but we do not see how or if it can be fixed. Some of us are scared. The ripple effects of the brokenness in our world upon us and upon countless individuals, families, communities, and nations are far greater than we have grasped or imagined.

Much important work is being done locally, regionally, nationally, and internationally to manage the crises and provide help; we would all do well to encourage and pray for those who are sacrificially giving and helping. Words, human interventions, and promises can help for a time, but these will not be sufficient to restore what is damaged and broken.

For calm in the storm, peace for troubled hearts, and strength for the weak, we all need the Lord. For hope for the hopeless, wisdom for those who lack it, protection from unseen dangers, and restoration of what is broken, we need the Lord. More than we know it, we need Him. In His great mercy, God will use our personal and collective brokenness to point us toward Himself and His love, for He is the only One who is able to restore.

As we perceive the anguish and trouble of so many, and as we prayerfully share the heart of God, our hearts may ache because of the pain and struggle that is so prevalent. But walking with God through faith in the Lord Jesus Christ means that we are blessed to know that for ourselves, for those that we love, and even for all of humanity, our greatest and enduring treasure and hope is the Lord.

We know that He is with us in these days of uncertainty, and we know that He alone is able to heal and restore what is broken. We also know that He would use us in these days to reflect His compassion and care to people who need Him.

These are lessons I have been learning through my illness. Many of the life changes urged for everyone because of COVID-19 were nothing new for me, for I have been living this way since I first received my cancer diagnosis. Safe practices of frequent hand washing, social distancing, avoiding crowds and public transportation, wearing gloves and masks in public, disinfecting hard surfaces, staying away from anyone who might be sick, not touching my face, and being careful about what I eat: this has been my way of life since October 2018.

I can tell you that it is not easy, but I am reminded that all of this is temporary. As with my first bicycle and my car, my broken life and yours, and this broken world –all are proverbially in the shop – in the hands of the only One who can restore them. He alone can restore us. He alone can restore this world. By His great grace through the Lord Jesus Christ, He will do just that. This hope is a secure anchor in these trying days.

I do not know if my Lord will fully restore my diseased body, the tent that I now dwell in. I do not know if I will have the SCT, or if I will survive it and achieve prolonged remission and renewed strength. But I know that my God is able, and I know that He will accomplish His purpose in me and for me. He will bring glory to His name. I also know that ultimately He is going to restore my body and yours to be perfect and new. It will not be like the perishable body we have now, with frailty and weakness. It will be an imperishable body, far better than we have known or imagined.

In His Word God has promised this: *I tell you brothers, flesh and blood cannot inherit the kingdom of God, nor does the perishable inherit the imperishable. Behold! I tell you a mystery. We shall not all sleep but we shall all be changed, in a moment, in a twinkling of an eye, at the last trumpet. For the trumpet will sound, and the dead will be raised imperishable, and we shall be changed. For this perishable body must put on the imperishable, and this mortal body must put on immortality. When the perishable puts on the imperishable, and the mortal puts on immortality, then shall come to pass the saying that is written: "Death is swallowed up in victory." "O death, where is your victory? O death, where is your sting?"* (1 Corinthians 15:50-55). Yes! Hallelujah and Amen!

As we ponder the brokenness of our own lives and of this hurting world, and if our hearts become discouraged, or hopelessness pervades, let us remember in faith the sure promises of God. Let us know with deep conviction that our God is able, and He alone restores. Let us humbly and prayerfully seek Him for ourselves and for the people of this broken world whom God loves, and who need Him so.

Let us anticipate with heartfelt wonder and firm assurance that one day God will make all things new. Until that day comes, let us enjoy the sweet blessings of walking with Him, for He loves me and He loves you with an everlasting love; we are blessed to love Him too. Let us cling to the sweet promise that our God is with us now, and He will be with us to the end.

Oh, how I have loved walking with God through the storms and deep valleys of life, for He has been ever faithful to me! He comforts, guides, and sustains me through it all. All of us are invited to enjoy this great privilege through faith in the Lord Jesus. We are all invited to joyfully and prayerfully answer His call to show His love to others and share His great news, so that His hope and peace might reign in their hearts too.

Let us remember and believe the end of God's restoration story, for this is our story too by the grace of the Lord Jesus Christ: *And I heard a loud voice from the throne saying, "Behold, the dwelling place of God is with man. He will dwell with them, and they will be His people; and God Himself will be with them as their God. He will wipe away every tear from their eyes, and death shall be no more, neither shall there be mourning, nor crying, nor pain anymore, for the former things have passed away." And He who was seated on the throne said "Behold, I am making all things new." Also He said, "Write this down, for these words are trustworthy and true"* (Revelation 21:3-5).

Yes. Hallelujah and Amen! Let us be glad, for our God restores what is broken. Even now He is restoring me and you.

FOR REFLECTION

When have you ever seen something broken that you thought could not possibly be restored, but God taught you otherwise? What lessons if any have you learned from the Lord through the COVID-19 pandemic, or any other recent hardship concerning God's restoration of what is broken, even in your life? How can you increasingly gain strength from God when you are weak and facing hard situations? Ask God to help you in this, and He surely will.

80

ON MAKING THE MOST OF SOCIAL DISTANCING

March 22, 2020

As we are relational and social beings by our created nature, the requirement to stay apart for a season can be a hard thing. Beyond the physical risks and real medical consequences of COVID-19, compulsory social distancing was one of the most difficult parts for many people. For some, including me, required social distancing continues to be a heavy burden to bear.

Contagious illnesses can lead to this requirement and struggle. When I was a young boy, members of our family were diagnosed with scarlet fever. We had a guest in our home when the diagnosis came, so our entire family and our guest were quarantined in our home for two weeks. Required social distancing is a hard thing.

Children and students cannot go to school or be with their friends. It is stressful and financially painful for employers and small business owners who cannot operate their businesses. Workers become anxious when they cannot work, and their income is reduced or gone, or future employment is uncertain. Social distancing hinders travelers when they are restricted and must remain at home.

For congregations that cannot safely gather for fellowship and corporate worship, the loss is tremendous. For extended families and friends who cannot safely gather to enjoy a wedding or graduation or to grieve and celebrate life in a funeral service, the pain of social distancing is great indeed. In many ways and for many reasons social distancing is hard.

But in the worldwide pandemic of a virus that is so contagious and dangerous, some social distancing was needed for a while. In such circumstances, wisdom demands that everyone be careful and social distancing be our daily practice. Proverbs 27:12 offers this wisdom: *The prudent sees danger and hides himself, but the simple go on and suffer for it.*

Though social distancing can be needed for a season, it is not easy. I know because I have been practicing social distancing for eighteen months now. I did this because of immune deficiencies related to multiple myeloma and exacerbated by chemotherapy drugs.

Helen and I are scheduled to arrive again in Nashville, Tennessee, in four weeks. God willing, I will undergo an autologous stem cell transplant, a process that will wipe clean the "hard drive" of my bone marrow, killing any cancer cells but in the process removing all immunoglobulins and the protections of every immunization I have ever received. For a while thereafter, I will have no natural abilities to fight infection. For months thereafter, until my bone marrow and blood are restored, I will need to practice extreme social distancing, because exposure to any infection could be life threatening.

So social distancing makes good sense for me. I would be foolhardy to ignore the realities of my illness and risk going out in public as though I faced no danger. I understand that I must take careful precautions, for I have learned this lesson the hard way. Sometimes I have not been sufficiently careful, and as a consequence I became quite sick.

Because of COVID-19, people have learned and lived lessons that I learned earlier about required social distancing. Though hard for a while, social distancing is necessary at times. So this week I have prayerfully reflected on primary lessons the Lord has taught me about making the most of social distancing.

First, we would all do well to remember that all of God's promises are true all the time, even in the deepest valleys and hardest times of our lives. One of His precious promises that has been a treasure to me through the years is the promise revealed in Romans *And we know that for those who love God all things work together for good, for those who are called according to His purpose* (Romans 8:28).

But does *all things* really mean all things, including our present difficulties and heartaches? Yes, it does. I memorized this Scripture promise when I was a young boy, and my Lord has often brought it to my memory, especially in times when life was hard. When I did not appreciate or understand why such painful troubles were happening to me, this promise has remained true. And sure enough, in the sovereignty of God and in the certainty of His love, I have experienced that God has been, is now, and will forever be entirely faithful. I have often seen the glory of God and the good fruit that He produced through it all.

The season of COVID-19 has been the same, even in the social distancing. In this restricted time, the Everlasting Creator of the universe, who loves this world and all of humanity, aims to draw a people to Himself whom He will nurture, so we might grow closer in Him.

But for this to happen in us, when social distancing is required in our lives, we must in faith turn our focus from the crisis to the Christ. We must look to Him with increasing spiritual hunger, receive and believe His Word, and then obey the principles He calls us to. May we not see seasons of social distancing as a curse but as an opportunity given to us by God for His glory and our good.

The Lord has taught me five simple lessons for making the most of social distancing. Though I have long aimed to practice them, doing so in my circumstance has required intentional creativity. I have grown in my walk with Christ, and in ways that have often surprised me, the Lord has blessed me to bless others.

To make the most of social distancing, our Lord calls us to continue seeking, praying, trusting, connecting, and loving. If you know you have not succeeded in these practices, the Lord may bless you and help you see a season of social distancing as His mercy in your life. This can be a life-changing opportunity to seek, trust, connect, love, and pray. And as you live this way, God will bless your socks off, and you will be a blessing to others.

1. Continue Seeking
God tells us to seek Him. He calls us to desire Him, not a little, but

more than we desire anything else in this world. In His Sermon on the Mount, Jesus observed what so many have experienced; we can become anxious about material provisions like what we will eat, drink, or wear. To His disciples He said, *Your heavenly Father knows that you need them all. But seek first the kingdom of God and His righteousness and all these things will be added to you. Therefore do not be anxious about tomorrow* (Matthew 6:32-34). Our Lord calls us to continue seeking Him.

In the Bible we often see the Lord command and invite His people to seek Him, even as they faced hard circumstances, including painful consequences of their corporate sin. Such a passage is found in Deuteronomy 4. Looking ahead to when the people of Israel would be settled in the land of promise, Moses foresaw that as a nation they would forsake the Lord and therefore experience much pain.

Then we hear these inviting and hope-filled words: *But from there you will seek the LORD your God and you will find Him, if you search after Him with all your heart and with all your soul. When you are in tribulation, and all these things come upon you in the latter days, you will return to the LORD your God and obey His voice. For the LORD your God is a merciful God. He will not leave you or destroy you or forget the covenant with your fathers that he swore to them* (Deuteronomy 4:29-31).

What was true of Israel then, and is true of nations now, is also true of congregations, families, marriages, and individuals. God calls us to seek Him first and to continue seeking Him. When life is easy, seek Him. When life is hard, seek Him. When social distancing is required for a while, continue seeking Him.

2. Continue Praying

God also calls us to pray and to keep on praying. Praying is a foundational part of seeking and knowing the Lord. Through prayer, we prioritize our relationship with Him, because He is our first love. We can enjoy the privilege of sharing with our Lord all that is on our heart through prayer. We hold nothing back from Him. We desire to hear from Him and carefully listen to Him in our times of prayer. The problem for many is that we know we can pray, or even that we should pray, but we actually pray very little. Our Lord can use the struggles we are in, even the requirement of social distancing, to remind us to pray and keep on praying.

In the days of King Solomon, in the triumphal night that followed the dedication of the new temple, the Lord appeared to Solomon with prophetic instruction for what His people must do in future seasons of painful calamity. He said, *When I shut up the heavens so that there is no rain, or command the locust to devour the land, or send pestilence among my people, if my people who are called by my name humble themselves, and pray and seek my face and turn from their wicked ways, then I will hear from heaven and will forgive their sin and heal their land* (2 Chronicles 7:13-14).

In the sovereign plan of God, the crises of our lives remind us of our need to pray and to keep on praying, for thus we acknowledge and express our complete devotion and dependence upon Him. And the Lord says we are to pray in humility and with true repentance, which means turning from our sinful ways.

In my prolonged season of social distancing, I have been blessed to pray and to keep on praying. Having time and opportunity to devote to prayer as I desire closer communion with Him, I have sought His face, and He continues to meet me. This is His wonderful promise to all.

3. Continue Trusting

What is the point of claiming faith in God if we do not fully trust Him? And how real can our trust be if we only apply it when life is going well? Trust flows out of trustworthiness. We learn to trust someone when we see and experience that they have been faithful.

Hasn't God always been trustworthy and faithful to us? Has He not faithfully provided, directed, protected, and forgiven us? Has He not promised to be with us always and to care for us? And so the Lord invites us and tells us to not be anxious (Matthew 6:25-30), for He has promised to take good care of us. God calls us to keep trusting.

After the attack against America on 9/11, for me personally, trusting God in a season of great trouble was a primary focus of my own spiritual growth. Our nation was in much turmoil. Fear and uncertainty abounded. We did not know when or if another attack would come or what might happen next. At that time I was serving a local church in New Hampshire and also serving as a chaplain in the U.S. Navy Reserves. Then suddenly, along with tens of thousands of reserve soldiers, sailors, and airmen, I was back on active duty.

I received a phone call late one night to inform me that I was recalled to active duty and must report the next day. With only a few hours warning, I had to leave my family and congregation and serve for a year in the U.S. Navy. That year, in the midst of much national and personal turmoil, the Lord wonderfully met me and continually challenged me to trust Him. By His grace I determined to do just that. God had always been faithful to me, and I knew He would still be faithful, even in that hard time.

I have learned this same lesson as I have dealt with cancer. We were privileged to learn it again as we faced ripple effects of COVID-19. The repercussions of this virus presented uncertainties and requirements of social distancing, but God is forever faithful, and we can trust Him.

In a time of national calamity, the prophet Jeremiah declared, *Blessed is the man who trusts in the LORD, whose trust is the LORD. He is like a tree planted by water, that sends out its roots by the stream, and does not fear when heat comes, for its leaves remain green, and is not anxious in the year of drought, for it does not cease to bear fruit* (Jeremiah 17:7-8). Yes, how true!

This is a lesson our Lord wants all of us to learn. He teaches this when we call upon Him in a time of storm. Matthew 8:23-27 describes the time when Jesus's disciples were in a ferocious storm on the sea, and they were afraid. They called out to Jesus and He calmed that storm, vividly teaching them that they could trust Him. There are many lessons for us in this account, for we too can find ourselves in a storm.

Like the disciples in that boat, we must own our fears and then bring them to the Lord. We must recognize that Jesus is with us now in this boat and in this storm, and we can call upon Him and trust that He will help us. Thus, we must come to Him. And notice how Jesus responded when they did call upon Him. All the disciples in that boat were utterly exhausted, flustered, and afraid, just as we can be when facing the storms of life.

But was Jesus anxious? No way! In the midst of the storm, He was calm, so much so that He had fallen fast asleep. And when they woke

Him, He did not join them in the fear. Instead, with peace, power, and authority, He calmed that storm, and He calmed His disciples too. In that storm our Lord taught them, what He has been teaching me – that no matter what is going on in the world around us, and no matter the strength of the wind and waves, He is with us in this boat, and we can continue trusting Him.

4. Continue Connecting

We must stay connected to God and others. We connect with the Lord as we continue praying, seeking, and trusting Him, and as we listen to Him by the Holy Spirit and through His Holy Word. Connecting with others is also important, for God connects us together. When we have to practice social distancing, we must be intentional about connecting with others.

When we cannot be together, we can and must find ways to be spiritually present with each other. Local churches and small groups can utilize social media and other means to make connection, to have real conversations, and to express love and show that we are connected with one another. We must go beyond thinking about it to actually doing it. The same intentional effort is needed for families when we are apart from each other.

When we are separated from people whom we know and love, we are still called by God to connect, so that we can love and serve each other. These commands of the Lord are not cancelled by the requirements of social distancing:

> Galatians 6:2 – *Bear one another's burdens, and so fulfill the law of Christ.*

> 1 Corinthians 12:25-27 – *That there may be no division in the body, but that the members may have the same care for one another. If one member suffers, all suffer together; if one member is honored, all rejoice together. Now you are the body of Christ and individually members of it.*

What does this mean? It means we must continue to seek and find ways to reach out and connect; we must ask the Lord to show us how we can tangibly care for others, carry their burdens, and demonstrate His love. It might be via proactive phone or video calls, as we pray for and with each other from a distance. We could send notes or cards, or pick up and deliver groceries for someone who cannot get out. As we ask our Lord, He shows us how.

Social distancing and being physically apart from others has been hard for me these past eighteen months, but my Lord has provided ways for me to stay connected. As we are linked together in Christ, as we seek Him, He shows us how to continue connecting.

5. Continue Loving

If we belong to Jesus Christ, we must continue to love. Jesus said, *This is my commandment, that you love one another as I have loved you. Greater love has no one than this, that someone lay down his life for his friends* (John 15:12-13). This commandment is not suspended or postponed because of required social distancing.

In the article "Removing the Coronavirus Mask: May This Crisis Reveal Us as Christians," Ed Stetzer tells the famous example in church history of Christians showing God's love during a fourth century epidemic that swept through the Roman Empire.[11] The historian Eusebius recorded that rather than fleeing the cities or shutting off their homes from others, "all day long [Christians] tended to the dying and to the burial, countless numbers with no one to care for them. Others gather together from all parts of the city a multitude of those withered from famine and distributed bread to them all." As a result, Eusebius concluded, "[the Christians'] deeds were on everyone's lips, and they glorified the god of the Christians."

This was the church living out God's commandment to love, even in a time of societal turmoil and danger. How are we doing that in our generation? How will we do it? What is our responsibility in a season of trouble? Is it not to ask our Lord to show us how we can proactively and tangibly show His love to hurting people, and then to do it? In this too, if we ask Him, He surely shows us.

---

[11] Ed Stetzer, "Removing the Coronavirus Mask: May This Crisis Reveal Us as Christians," *USA TODAY*: www.usatoday.com/story/opinion/2020/03/19/during-pandemic-cornoavirus-christians-act-as-jesus-taught-column/5055427002/ (March 19, 2020).

This can include loving people we know as directed by the Lord in 1 John 4:7, which says, *Beloved, let us love one another, for love is from God; and whoever loves has been born of God and knows God.* It might also include loving neighbors and people whom we do not yet know, as our Lord taught us in His parable of the good Samaritan.

In this remarkable story recorded in Luke 10:25-37, Jesus answered a question about who the neighbors are that we are called by God to love. Jesus's answer was this parable of a Samaritan who sacrificially gave of his time and resources to help a hurting stranger in need. This is loving our neighbor, and Jesus calls us to do this. Required social distancing does not remove us from this command, so we must proactively ask our Lord to show us how and for whom we can proactively demonstrate His love. I know firsthand that this is a prayer He will answer.

How then can we make the most of our social distancing?

By continuing to pray, seek, trust, connect, and love.

FOR REFLECTION

Do you tend to regard your seasons of required social distancing as a curse or an opportunity afforded by God for His glory and your good? How have you experienced the truth of Romans 8:28, even in difficulties and trials? In practical terms, for each of the five lessons shared here, what has it meant, and what will it mean for you to continue seeking, praying, trusting, connecting, and loving? Which of these has already been a source of great joy for you? Which of these has been hardest for you to faithfully practice and why? Ask God to help you in this, and He surely will.

81

ON PRAYING LIKE JESUS

March 28, 2020

With all that is going on in my life, the lives of family and friends, our community and nation, the church of our Lord, and throughout the world, I have been compelled to pray. I hope you have too. One of the blessings of required social distancing that I have enjoyed is increased time and opportunity to pray. But this is a blessing to us only when we seize it.

Recently someone asked me some excellent questions about prayer, why it is important, and how we can pray as God intends. This brought me back to the request of Jesus's disciples – to teach them to pray. Of course, they had prayed before, but the prayer life of Jesus was attractive and compelling to them. They wanted to pray like He prayed.

Often Jesus encouraged prayer by His words and by His example. After reading Luke's gospel, I was astounded at how often I saw Jesus in prayer. Then I was amazed to see how often the apostles and the early church prayed in the book of Acts. They faithfully followed Jesus's teaching and example. Jesus prayed in many situations. Have you pondered why the Son of God prayed so often? After all, did He not possess the perfect divine nature?

Yes, He did, for He was and is fully God. Colossians 1:15-20 describes His divinity: *He* [Jesus] *is the image of the invisible God, the firstborn of all creation. For by Him all things were created in heaven and on earth, visible and invisible, whether thrones or dominions or rulers or authorities – all things were created through Him and for Him. And He is before all things, and in Him all things hold together. And He is the head of the body, the church. He is the beginning, the firstborn from the dead, that in everything He might be preeminent. For in Him the fullness of God was pleased to dwell, and through Him to reconcile to Himself all things, whether on earth or in heaven, making peace by the blood of His cross.* And Colossians 2:9 succinctly states concerning Jesus: *For in Him the whole fullness of deity dwells bodily.* Jesus was fully God.

He was also fully human, thus making Him the perfect sacrifice for our sins and the perfect Mediator between God and humanity. Jesus was and is the perfect God-Man. If this were not true, there would be no salvation for sinful people.

Many biblical passages reveal the fullness of Jesus's humanity. He was hungry (Matthew 21:18), and He was thirsty (John 19:28). He grew weary and required sleep (Mark 4:38), which God does not do (Psalm 121:4). At times His knowledge was finite (Matthew 24:36), thus reflecting His human nature. Like us, Jesus faced temptation, but unlike us, He never succumbed to temptation. Unlike Adam and Eve and all of their descendants throughout history, Jesus never sinned. And because He faced temptation and became like us in all respects except for sin, He is able to help us when we are tempted (Hebrews 2:17-18), and He taught us to pray for deliverance from temptation and evil (Matthew 6:13).

As the Son of God, the Lord Jesus was determined to do His Father's will. Thus, He was compelled to live a life of prayer in full devotion and dependence on His Father. Jesus had to pray, as we all do. All of humanity was designed by God to pray. Learning and living in accord with Jesus's example of prayer, we are blessed to pray as He prayed.

In answer to why Jesus prayed, consider with me five examples in Luke's gospel. These are important to me because they reveal why Jesus prayed and why I must follow His example:

1. Jesus Prayed to Seek Divine Fellowship
In Luke 5 Jesus appears extremely busy with countless demands upon Him, for multitudes followed Him wherever He went. Can you relate

to busyness and constant demands? But our Lord never allowed the demands of this world to determine His priorities or to decide how and where He would spend His time. Verse 15 beautifully reflects the ongoing prayer life of Jesus: *But Jesus often withdrew to lonely places and prayed* (NIV).

His relationship with His heavenly Father was His most important priority. As the eternal Son of God, He had enjoyed perfect fellowship with God the Father and God the Holy Spirit throughout eternity, and this relationship was more important to Him than the many demands He faced day by day. So also with us. If Jesus needed to prioritize prayer in order to seek close fellowship with God, how much more must we.

2. Jesus Prayed Before Important Decisions

Desiring to do His Father's will, Jesus prayed before making a critically important decision in Luke 6. Of the multitudes who followed Him, Jesus chose twelve to be His apostles. And though He was fully God, He was also fully Man, having *emptied himself by taking the form of a servant, being born in the likeness of men* (Philippians 2:7). Because of His great love, our Lord condescended to take upon Himself limitations of our humanity.

Our Lord's divine nature and His human nature were in the words of the Council of Chalcedon (AD 451): "without confusion, without change, without division, and without separation."[12] In this perfect union, our Lord revealed to us what it means to desire only the Father's will and thus to pray to discern and do it. Although sinless from conception and without sin all his life, His human mind was necessarily finite. So when the incarnate Lord Jesus did not know what to do, He prayed.

Verse 12 of Luke 6 says Jesus prayed the entire night before choosing His twelve apostles. Then He was prepared to proceed. The Holy Spirit tells us that if Jesus prayed fervently to discern His Father's will in important decisions,, how much more must we.

3. Jesus Prayed When He Faced His Heavy Cross

Jesus went up on a mountain to pray and took Peter, James, and John

---

12 William J. Abraham, *Divine Agency and Divine Action: Systematic Theology*, Vol. 3 (Oxford University Press, 2018) 78.

with Him (Luke 9:28-36). As His time was approaching, the focus of His prayer seems to be the fulfillment of His mission, which would include His sacrificial death on the cross to atone for the sins of the world. This would be the culminating event in the history of redemption. Knowing this would be a lonely and heavy cross to bear, our Lord was compelled to pray and seek His Father's face.

As He prayed, Jesus was transfigured to His heavenly glory. Two great servants in God's redemptive history appeared to Jesus and discussed with Him what He was about to accomplish in Jerusalem, for He would accomplish the great exodus for humanity out of the bondage of sin into the liberty of salvation. Moses and Elijah represented respectively the Law and the Prophets, thereby indicating that Jesus was the complete fulfillment of both. Jesus affirmed to Moses and Elijah and to us that He is the One to whom their ministries were directed, for in Christ, God's plan of salvation is now completed.

The Lord Jesus blessed Moses and Elijah that day, and they glorified their Lord. Then God the Father spoke audibly; He commended His beloved Son and impressed upon Peter, James, and John the radiant splendor of His Son, the Lord Jesus Christ, who is the fulfillment of all that God promised in Holy Scripture. The affirming words of God the Father were *This is my Son, my Chosen One, listen to Him* (Luke 9:35). God the Father was magnified; Moses and Elijah were rewarded and fulfilled; Peter, James, and John were blessed; and the Lord Jesus Christ was exalted and encouraged to complete His great mission of bringing salvation to the world. All of this happened as our Lord prayed.

As Jesus prayed when approaching the heavy cross that He would bear for our salvation, so must we pray and seek our heavenly Father to endure whatever crosses we must bear for His glory.

4. Jesus Prayed to Teach Others to Pray
As Jesus prayed, His disciples asked Him to teach them to pray like He prayed (Luke 11). They had long witnessed the prayer life of Jesus; they could see that He prayed like no one they had ever known. He prayed with faith, fervency, confidence, and intimacy, and His prayers were answered. They longed to pray as He did, so they asked Him to teach

them. And He did. Now if Jesus prayed to teach others to pray, how much more must we.

I learned to pray as a young boy when I watched and heard my parents pray, and my grandparents and other Christians whom I knew and loved. If we want our children and grandchildren to learn to pray, they must see and hear us pray and live a lifestyle of prayer. This follows Jesus's example. Living a life of persistent prayer was Jesus's way of life, and it was a theme of His teaching, as we see in Luke 18 in His parable of the persistent widow.

5. Jesus Prayed To Do the Father's Will

Perhaps the most compelling prayer of Jesus is in Luke 22, when He prays on the Mount of Olives. He knows that He is about to be arrested, tortured, and crucified for the sins of the whole world. This was a very heavy load for Him, so He prayed. He asked His disciples to pray with Him, for He desired their prayer support, but they did not.

What did Jesus pray for exactly? Ultimately, and in great anguish, our Lord prayed for His Father's will. Of course, in His flesh He did not want to endure this cruel suffering, yet He was willing to do so because of His great love for His Father and His deep love for us. By God's mercy, we will never bear a cross as heavy as Jesus bore for us, for He bore the judgment our sins deserved. But He said if we wanted to follow Him, we must bear our crosses of suffering, sacrifice, and hardship (Matthew 16:24-27).

So Jesus taught us to pray according to God's perfect will. How then are we to pray when we are not entirely sure what His will is? When we know for sure that something is God's will, then we are to pray accordingly. I thank God that by the Holy Spirit's revelation and the revelation of Holy Scripture, I have often known God's will, so I have been able to focus my prayers accordingly. I have seen God work in many marvelous ways in answer to prayer and for His glory.

But at other times, I realize the limits of my own wisdom and am not entirely sure what God's perfect will is. I then humbly tell Him how I see it and what I desire; I add my complete trust that His will is good and right and that His will is what I most desire. This is praying like Jesus.

This reflects my prayers regarding my stem cell transplant and its outcome. I would love to come through it well, regain my health, and be able to travel and serve my Lord and His church again, perhaps for several years. So this is what I ask. But I do not know with certainty if this is God's will for me. I do know that God alone sees the whole picture, and that He alone knows what will best accomplish His purposes. So, as the Lord Jesus prayed, I am bathing it all in a prayer for His perfect will. Trusting God fully, I am excited however He may answer.

Praying like Jesus is powerful and life transforming:

1. *Jesus Prayed to Seek Divine Fellowship*

2. *Jesus Prayed Before Important Decisions*

3. *Jesus Prayed When He Faced His Heavy Cross*

4. *Jesus Prayed to Teach Others to Pray*

5. *Jesus Prayed To Do the Father's Will*

We need to pray for these reasons and more. As we ponder these things, will we ask our Lord to teach us to pray as He prayed? He has given us the opportunity, and He has set an example for us. He has given us the Holy Spirit to help us, and He has invited us to pray. He waits for us to retreat with Him often, to seek His face, and to enjoy His presence. We will discover what Joseph Scriven affirmed in what later became the hymn called, "What a Friend We Have in Jesus." *What a privilege to carry everything to God in prayer.*

Helen and I sincerely thank you for your prayers for us, and we ask you to please continue praying with us for God's glory and for His perfect and gracious will. We are now just three weeks from arriving in Nashville for my SCT. We are resting in His promises, assured of His faithfulness and confident that He is a prayer-answering, miracle-working God, for us and also for you.

FOR REFLECTION

After prolonged observation of Jesus's prayer life, His disciples asked Him to teach them to pray like He prayed. Whose example of prayer has motivated you to pray? What prompted Jesus's disciples to ask Him to teach them to pray? Have you ever asked Him to teach you to pray, or will you ask Him now? How might your life be changed if you more consistently prayed as Jesus did to seek divine fellowship? Before important decisions? When you face a heavy cross? To teach others to pray? To do the Father's will? Ask God to help you in this, and He surely will.

82

ON RUNNING TO THE FINISH LINE

April 2, 2020

I miss running. I really do. With spring-like temperatures in Minnesota for several days, I see many people running by, some young, some middle-aged, and some seemingly as old or older than me. I have longed to run again. I have many good memories of trails along winding paths through lovely woods, on majestic mountain trails with panoramic views, and through lush valleys. I remember running in early mornings through sleeping villages and still-quiet urban neighborhoods and watching the sun rise with sparkly diamond reflections by scenic shores of beach-rimmed or rock-bound seas. I have run in large formations, huge crowds, with a few others, and all alone. I miss running.

But in recent years, I have not been able to run. All I can do is remember running I have done before, watch others run, and perhaps cheer them on. If you are still able to run, or if you are able to stay physically active in other ways, I exhort you to count your many blessings and run on.

As I reflect on running and address my frustrations, the Lord has reminded me of several Scriptures in which He reminds His people to keep running well for as long as we can as far as we can for Him. The Lord has brought these seven Scriptures to my attention for reflection:

1. *You were running well. Who hindered you from obeying the truth?* (Galatians 5:7)

This is our Lord's call to never stray from the gospel of grace that is in Christ Jesus or to wander onto a path of religious legalism but to return and run again on His trail of biblical grace, freedom, and fellowship with Him. The Lord says to *keep persisting* and keep running well.

2. *And the Lord said to me, 'Write the vision; make it plain on tablets, so he may run who reads it. For still the vision waits its appointed time; it hastens to the end – it will not lie. If it seems slow, wait for it; it will surely come, it will not delay. Behold, his soul is puffed up; it is not upright without him, but the righteous shall live by his faith* (Habakkuk 2:2-4).

This was the Lord's word in a time of national calamity and struggle, which surely speaks to our own chaotic world. The Lord says that He will unfold His plan, and He calls the righteous to believe this, to wait upon Him, and to live by faith in Him. And we who have received this message of grace and hope are not to keep it to ourselves, but we are to run with it and bring His extraordinary good news to others. The Lord says to *keep waiting*, trusting, and running by faith.

3. *I will run in the way of your commandments when you enlarge my heart* (Psalm 119:32, ESV), or *I run in the path of your commands, for you have broadened my understanding* (NIV).

The phrase that is translated *enlarge my heart* or *broadened my understanding* conveys an expanded ability to perceive God's truth. Don't you love it that God increases our ability to perceive His truth? The psalmist teaches here that as we grow in our faith, our God expands our understanding of His truth. As this happens within us, we are motivated to continue running in the way of His Word and His will. Our Lord says *keep growing* and thus keep running on the path of my Word and will.

4. *They who wait for the LORD shall renew their strength; they shall mount up with wings like eagles; they shall run and not be weary; they shall walk and not faint.* (Isaiah 40:31)

This is God's holy promise of fresh supplies of renewed strength.

Strength for what? Strength to continue in faithful service to Him – even flying as on wings like eagles, running without weariness, and walking without fainting. That sounds fantastic to me. The Lord says to believe and wait for Him. *Keep moving* and continue in the strength He provides.

5. *Do you not know that in a race all the runners run, but only one receives the prize? So run that you may obtain it. Every athlete exercises self-control in all things. They do it to receive a perishable wreath, but we an imperishable.* (1 Corinthians 9:24-25)

Corinth was the site of the biennial Isthmian games, which at that time were second in fame only to the Olympian games, so Christians in Corinth would have been familiar with Paul's reference to a *perishable wreath* (ESV) or *a crown that will not last* (NIV) made of greenery, which the victor received after a public athletic contest.

This picture speaks to me, for my given name is Stephen, which comes from the Greek word *stephanos,* meaning "crowned one." I have long loved this picture, for I know that I have already received the sure promises of God, and that all who belong to the Lord Jesus by faith will soon be crowned ones with our imperishable crown of glory that will never fade away.

In the days when Paul used this illustration to describe his future and ours, he reminded his readers that receiving a crown of greenery was the goal of every runner in the big race Corinth was famous for, but it would soon fade. And, it would be awarded to only one winner. Our Lord says that we who know Him are also running a race, and we too are in pursuit of a prize.

We know that all who faithfully run this race to the end will receive the victor's crown; a crown that will not perish; it will be imperishable and endure forevermore. Our Lord says to us to *keep going*, keep running, keep your eyes on the prize, and know that soon it will be yours.

6. *I have fought the good fight, I have finished the race, I have kept the faith. Henceforth there is laid up for me the crown of righteousness, which the Lord, the righteous judge, will award to me on that day, and not only to me but also to all who have loved His appearing.* (2 Timothy 4:7-8)

In the apostle Paul's final letter, he includes athletic imagery of crossing the finish line into heaven and receiving the victor's crown, the crown of righteousness. He says he has finished the course by His grace and encourages us to do the same.

Our Lord says to get up and *keep running* for Jesus Christ, confident of the prize He has promised us, which will be the crown of righteousness. And let us be fully determined to run faithfully until we cross the finish line into heavenly glory.

7. *Therefore, since we are surrounded by so great a cloud of witnesses, let us also lay aside every weight and sin which clings so closely, and let us run with endurance the race that is set before us, looking to Jesus, the founder and perfecter of our faith, who for the joy that was set before Him endured the cross, despising the shame and is seated at the right hand of the throne of God. Consider Him who endured from sinners such hostility against Himself, so that you may not grow weary or fainthearted.* (Hebrews 12:1-3)

The saints who have gone before us are the cloud of witnesses who cheer us on. Because we want to run this race well, we are called to discard our sins and every distraction that slows us down. We are to run this race not haltingly but for the long haul with patient endurance; we are to look to our Lord and Savior Jesus, who gave His all for us and is now in heavenly glory at the right hand of the throne of God. Motivated by the endurance of Jesus, we are to press on through all weariness and faintness of heart.

Our Lord says to us to *keep enduring*; don't stop now, get rid of whatever slows us down, and press on with endurance. Be encouraged and motivated by the saints who have gone before us, looking always to our Lord and Savior.

So my Lord has been reminding me to *keep persisting, keep waiting, keep growing, keep moving, keep going, keep running, and keep enduring* – for this is His will for all His children until He calls us home to glory in heaven. Hearing this again has convicted me. In truth, I have focused considerably more on my longing for heaven, the victor's crown, and the inexpressible joy that will soon be mine when I behold my Lord in the fullness of His glory. I am looking forward to that day.

But some days I have focused more on this promise than I have on the race that I am still running with and for my Lord. Can you identify with this at all? Have your physical struggles or hardships in this broken world led you to pay less attention to the race God still has marked out for you, for His glory, for your good, and for the blessing of others?

The apostle Paul could confidently testify that He had *finished the race* and *kept the faith*; he was now looking forward to the crown of glory which He would very soon receive (2 Timothy 4:7). But even still, He was faithfully passing to Timothy the things God had spoken to His heart.

And in Jesus's High Priestly Prayer, He prayed to His Father, *I glorified you on earth, having accomplished the work that You gave me to do* (John 17:4). Our Lord knew that He was about to complete the work He was assigned to do to purchase our eternal salvation, yet He was still focused on accomplishing His mission.

As God gives to each of us a finite number of days that He alone has determined (Psalm 139:16), let it be our continued desire to complete all the work He has given us to do every single day. And let us faithfully run our race until by His great grace we have crossed the finish line into glory.

In his book, *I Shall Not Die, But Live: Facing Death With Gospel Hope*, Douglas Taylor said that those who know they have a limited time to live might focus too exclusively on the things of heaven and forget there may still be more things to do for God's purpose and His glory. He added that we must run to the finish line and accomplish every bit of work God may give us.[13]

In this regard Taylor told a story of the great evangelist George Whitefield who spoke with a group of ministers during the Great Awakening in America. Perhaps tired or even discouraged, he emphasized to the ministers the great comfort he felt that soon his labors would be over and he would be with Jesus Christ in glory. Though the people present agreed with Whitefield in the sweet promises of God, one older minister named William Tennent, Jr. disagreed with Whitefield's emphasis. Tennent said, "I have nothing to do with death. My business is to live as long as I can, until He shall think proper to call me home."[14]

---

13 Douglas Taylor, *I Shall Not Die, But Live*, (Banner of Truth, 2016).
14 William Buell Sprague, *Annals of the American Pulpit*, Vol. 3 (New York: Robert Carter & Brothers, 1859) 61.

I understand Tennent's point, for this speaks to me of running my race all the way to the finish line – of keeping on *persisting, waiting, growing, moving, going, running,* and *enduring* for and with Jesus Christ to complete the entire course He has marked out for me. It also reminds you to keep running the race He has marked out for you.

With this in mind, let us continue to ask our Lord to lead us on the path He has chosen for us, all the way to the finish line. Though we might not run as fast or as far as we once did, we are still walking and running with our Lord, and He will be with us until the end, and then, *Praise God*, forevermore!

In closing, I will share with you a praise and a petition, so you might rejoice with me and join again in praying for God's perfect will to be done:

A PRAISE:
Rejoice with me for answered prayer and for God's healing grace. When I was first diagnosed with active multiple myeloma in October 2018, my bone marrow was measured at 80% plasma monoclonal (cancer) cells, which is very high and an indicator of advanced disease. This week, after eighteen months of chemotherapy, no measurable cancer cells were found remaining in my bone marrow – from 80% to 0%! Praise God with me! This means I am now considered as ready as I can be for SCT with significantly increased potential for a prolonged and durable remission.

A PETITION:
Our scheduled departure for Nashville is still Saturday April 18, arriving on Sunday April 19, and checking in to the Bone Marrow Transplant Center at the VA Medical Center in Nashville on Monday April 20. I have received calls this week from the Nashville VA and the Minneapolis VA Medical Centers; because of COVID-19, they are uncertain if they will be able to proceed with my SCT. At a minimum, the plan is for my stem cells to be harvested and frozen for potential future use. If upon my arrival, the hospital is swamped with treating COVID-19 patients, they may have limited space or staffing to proceed with my SCT. They will then send me home to Minnesota and put me on a maintenance

chemotherapy drug until I am cleared to return to Nashville for the SCT when the pandemic has passed.

In a phone call from a health care provider yesterday, I was directly told that if I were to contract COVID-19 or another virus soon after the SCT, I would not be expected to survive, so the risk is considered much higher now. But I am trusting my Lord and at peace with this, and after I've waited so long and faced so many delays, and because I am now as physically ready as possible to proceed, I am hoping we can go on with the SCT this month. But I also know that God alone sees the complete picture: past, present, and future. He knows what will bring Him the greatest glory and what is best for Helen and me and for the sake of His kingdom. I know that His will is always good and right. Will you please pray with me for our Lord's perfect will to be done in this and for peace and protection for Helen and me through it all? Thank you so much!

FOR REFLECTION

Why do you think the Scriptures include so many references to running as a metaphor for our lives? Reflect on the various passages quoted in this lesson; which of these has spoken to you? What have you heard from the Lord? As you continue to run your race for the Lord until you cross the finish line into heavenly glory, what will it mean for you in practical terms to persist, and wait, and grow, and move, and go, and run, and endure with and for Jesus Christ? Ask God to help you in this, and He surely will.

83

ON UNCERTAINTIES AND CERTAINTIES IN TIMES OF STORM

April 5, 2020

As we look to the future, by faith we can be entirely sure of some things, and there are other things that we simply cannot know with absolute certainty. We can be sure, for example, that the sun is going to rise tomorrow morning, that the earth will keep rotating on its continuing journey around the sun, that Almighty God will still rule over heaven and earth and His infinite creation, and that He is and will forever be faithful to every promise He has made.

Everyone who knows and believes in the Lord has a secure anchor of hope in times of storm, when so many worries abound. The Lord has spoken to me lately on this as our nation and the world face painful uncertainties due to the awful pandemic of COVID-19 and other tragedies in our world

Large scale uncertainties abound with regard to how long these horrible "storms" might last, how many may die, and what might be the lasting impact on the world's economy. Many personal uncertainties multiply about the risk to our own health and well-being, and to the health and future of our loved ones. Many throughout the world are facing the hard reality of their own mortality, and many are afraid. We face both certainties and uncertainties.

My battle with multiple myeloma has sometimes felt to me like a prolonged storm. For the past eighteen months I have been, as it were, at sea. Sometimes the waters have been rough, and I have been batted about by winds of physical weakness and malaise, of immune deficiencies, and the hard isolation of required social distancing. I have been tossed by waves of unpleasant reactions to chemotherapy and by showers of discouragement from postponements of a potential remission through the SCT. At first my slow response to chemotherapy caused the delay, then an infection, a car accident, and COVID-19.

Two weeks from today, I expect to arrive again in Nashville where, God willing, my stem cells will be harvested and frozen. I do not know yet if I will be allowed to proceed with the SCT. This decision will be made when I arrive, based on the COVID-19 case load and the impact on hospital space and staffing at that time. So many uncertainties remain.

Throughout this prolonged storm, the Lord has reminded me to trust Him in the uncertainties and hold on to the certainties. Toward this end, I have found myself singing an old hymn that I learned when I was a boy called "A Shelter in The Time of Storm." The lyrics were written by Vernon John Charlesworth, a British pastor, and based on Psalm 32:7, which says, *You are a hiding place for me; you preserve me from trouble; you surround me with songs of deliverance.*

Ira Sankey, who later composed the most popular tune for this hymn, observed that this was a favorite song among fishermen on the north coast of England. They often sang it as they approached their harbors in the time of storm. As you read these lyrics, prayerfully consider if this expresses your own faith-filled experience, as it does mine – that in the raging storms of our lives, even in the uncertainties of living in a weary land, that in the Lord Jesus Christ, we have a shelter in times of storm.

> The Lord's our Rock, in Him we hide,
>   A Shelter in the time of storm;
> Secure whatever ill betide,
>   A Shelter in the time of storm.

ON UNCERTAINTIES AND CERTAINTIES IN TIMES OF STORM

Refrain:
Oh, Jesus is a Rock in a weary land,
    A weary land, a weary land;
Oh, Jesus is a Rock in a weary land,
    A Shelter in the time of storm.

A shade by day, defense by night,
    A Shelter in the time of storm;
No fears alarm, no foes afright,
    A Shelter in the time of storm.

The raging storms may round us beat,
    A Shelter in the time of storm
We'll never leave our safe retreat,
    A Shelter in the time of storm.[15]

This is holding on to the certainties of faith in the Lord Jesus Christ, no matter what storms may rage around us. A beautiful example of this in the Scriptures is Acts 27:13-44, where the apostle Paul displayed tremendous peace in the midst of a violent storm at sea. Yes, there were surely uncertainties, for such is the nature of storms. But in the midst of it, knowing and trusting the Lord Jesus Christ, there is shelter and peace.

I recall a time during my career in the Navy when we were at sea during a storm. The waters were rough, the wind was violent, and the sky was ominous. I saw waterspout tornadoes all around us. The Captain ordered all hands to clear the weather decks, thus to enter and remain within the skin of the ship. I can tell you, I did not have to be told more than once to do this, for I knew that in the skin of that ship I was safe. So did the apostle Paul know that despite the strength of the storm raging all around them, by faith in the Lord Jesus Christ and within His protective arms, he was as safe as he could possibly be. And so are we today.

And just as the people on that ship watched the apostle Paul in the midst of that storm, marveled at his faith, and wondered at his calm, so people watch us, for everyone longs for peace in the storms of life. God

---

15   Vernon J. Charlesworth, "A Shelter in the Time of Storm," (1880).

provides His children with opportunities to be His faithful witnesses in this world. By grace He allows us to experience and model what it means to know and trust the Lord Jesus through all of life, even in the storms. As we hold to the certainties of our faith, we find Him faithful.

If we never encountered the storms, even furious storms, we would not know the sweet blessing of finding God faithful in the storms. I have observed that God has often instructed me in the light and then tested me in the night. He lovingly pours into our hearts His wonderful truth and His promises. Then He puts us in places where we have the privilege of stepping out in faith and living what He has taught us. Our God bestows much grace in the storms of life.

So the question each us must answer in the times of storm is where our faith is. In the storm that is described in Acts 27, the apostle Paul held to the certainties of his faith in the Lord Jesus Christ, so he was at peace. In the uncertainty of the storm, he clung to the certainty of Jesus, so he experienced shelter in the time of storm.

In this biblical account, we see two insights on how peace is known in times of storm:

Peace is found in the certainty of God's presence.
As the storm raged against that ship and everyone aboard it, the apostle demonstrated God's peace by saying, *Yet now I urge you to take heart, for there will be no loss of life among you, but only of the ship. For this very night there stood before me an angel of the God to whom I belong and whom I worship.* (Acts 27:22-23).

How was Paul able to have peace in the midst of that violent storm? By knowing His Lord was with Him. Paul knew with certainty that he was not alone in the storm, for God Himself had sent His angel to remind him of this. When we know that our Lord is with us, we know that we have no reason to fear. Consider young David facing the giant warrior Goliath, Daniel in the lion's den, Shadrach, Meshach, and Abednego in the fiery furnace, and Elijah on Mount Carmel opposing four hundred priests of Baal. Peace is still found in the certainty of God's presence. Do you know that the Lord is with you now?

Peace is found in the certainty of God's promises.
The apostle had heard the sweet promise of God, and he believed it. By faith he knew that all of God's promises are guaranteed. They are as sure as tomorrow's sunrise.

So Paul demonstrated the certainty of his faith in the Lord Jesus by quoting the words he had heard the Lord say, *Do not be afraid Paul; you must stand before Caesar. And behold, God has granted you all those who sail with you* (Acts 27:24). Then, based on the promise of God, Paul exhorted the men on that ship who were terrified by the storm and said, *So take heart, men, for I have faith in God that it will be exactly as I have been told* (Acts 27:25). And of course, the promise of God is precisely what occurred, and so it will always be. Peace can be found in the certainty of God's promises. Do you know that all of God's promises to you are true and guaranteed?

As I look to the future, many things are uncertain. But because I know and trust the Lord, my confidence is in Him, and I have no cause for worry or fear. I am blessed to enjoy His peace.

Peace is found in the certainty of His presence and in the assurance of His promises. No matter what storms may be raging in your life, may the Lord richly bless you to know and enjoy the sweet shelter of His peace and the great joy of pointing another toward Him and His peace.

FOR REFLECTION

What "storms" have you encountered in which you faced uncertainties? What effect has your faith in the Lord had? When and in what ways have you experienced God teaching you in the light and then testing you in the night? In recent or current storms, how has the certainty of God's presence affected your peace, and why? What promises of God speak to your current situation? How is your faith in the certainty of God's promises affecting your peace now? Ask God to help you in this, and He surely will.

84

ON PRAYING TODAY FOR GOD'S WILL TOMORROW

April 6, 2020

None of us can see tomorrow, but we can know with certainty that God will be there and that He will be faithful tomorrow even as He was yesterday, and as He is today.

Today I received a phone call from the transplant team at the Nashville VA Medical Center. They asked if I could please arrive a few days earlier than scheduled. So Helen and I now expect to depart from our home next Monday April 13 and arrive in Nashville April 14 to check in on Wednesday April 15.

While in Nashville, we expect my stem cells will at least be harvested and frozen for future use, a process that could keep us there for seven to ten days. If this is the extent of what can be done, we will return to Minnesota with plans to come back to Nashville when the COVID-19 pandemic is behind us.

Tomorrow the transplant team in Nashville will convene and discuss my case to make a decision on whether or not to proceed. For several reasons my strong personal preference is to proceed, though I certainly do understand the hesitancy, as COVID-19 is a significant risk, and the effect on that hospital, its staffing, and the potential precautions in the near future must be considered.

But I ask for and desire only God's will in this matter. His perspective is complete and mine is partial. His wisdom is perfect and mine is imperfect. I see as through a glass darkly, and He sees clearly and completely. So I pray for God's will in this matter to be made known to the transplant team when they convene tomorrow. I pray that they will be united in their decision, and it will be right for them and for me, and God will be glorified. I also pray that when I learn of the decision of the transplant team, I will have a full measure of God's peace and will give Him the praise He is due.

Proverbs 3:5-6 promises, *Trust in the LORD with all your heart, and do not lean on your own understanding. In all your ways acknowledge Him, and He will make straight your paths.* I am determined to do this, confident that my Lord will be faithful to His promise.

I will trust the Lord. I will lean on His understanding and not my own. I will acknowledge Him in all things, even in this. So I trust, knowing that He goes before me and will make my path straight as He guides this decision for His purpose and glory.

Will you please join me in this and pray today for God's will tomorrow? Thank you so much. I will let you know how the Lord answers.

FOR REFLECTION

Of what can you be entirely confident when you pray for yourself or on behalf of others? Why did Jesus teach us to pray, *Your kingdom come, your will be done, on earth as it is in heaven* (Matthew 6:10), and why is it important and helpful to pray this way? How have you experienced the truth of Proverbs 3:5-6? When have you been blessed as others prayed with you and for you, and when have you been blessed as you joined in prayer for others? Ask God to help you in this, and He surely will.

85

ON REJOICING IN ANSWERED PRAYER

April 7, 2020

The story that is told in Luke 7 of Jesus healing the centurion's servant is very precious to me. It speaks of the power of faith and intercession before the Lord Jesus heard and received the petitions that were brought to Him on behalf of the centurion, who had sent messengers to intercede for his servant who was very ill. Clearly, the centurion had faith that Jesus would hear the petitions and was able to heal his servant, even from a distance. I love that the centurion asked others to intercede for him, which they did. And our Lord heard and answered.

The gospel account says the centurion did not wish to presume upon Jesus to enter his home. He knew he was a sinner and did not feel worthy of the Lord's presence. He did not yet know the depth of the Lord's love and mercy, but he did believe in His power to heal and to answer requests brought to Him in faith. So the centurion sent a messenger to say to Jesus on his behalf, *But say the word, and let my servant be healed* (Luke 7:7).

The Bible says Jesus was astounded at the centurion's faith, and he immediately answered his prayer. *Turning to the crowd that followed him,* [Jesus] *said, "I tell you, not even in Israel have I found such faith."*

And when those who had been sent returned to the house, they found the servant well (Luke 7:9-10).

I can picture great rejoicing in the centurion's house that day. I know that faith grew in his heart and in his home with praise to the Almighty and love for the Lord Jesus. I expect that thereafter the centurion and his servant loved testifying to others about what Jesus had done for them. I love to do the same.

This gospel account speaks to me today because as with the centurion:

1. Faith in Jesus leads us to bring our problems and petitions to Him.
Though the problems are bigger than we are, we know our Lord is able.

2. Faith in Jesus leads us to ask others to intercede with us and for us.
The Lord calls us to intercede for one another, and He hears and answers when we do.

3. Faith in Jesus leads us to rejoice in answered prayer and give Him our praise.
As there was rejoicing in the centurion's home that day, today there is rejoicing in mine.

Yesterday I asked for prayer, and today I thank all who interceded for us. I knew that my own perspective is limited, but our Lord's is limitless and complete. I also knew that our Lord can change minds and hearts to accomplish His will. After waiting for eighteen months and being physically ready, I desired to proceed. But I have only wanted whatever God's will is, and I have learned from the Lord to pray, *Thy Kingdom come. Thy will be done, on earth as it is in heaven.*

And as with the petitions of the centurion's friends, so also with yours. Our Lord has heard, and He has answered. The transplant team informed me by phone today that they have agreed to proceed with my SCT. So it is a go! When I heard this news, I rejoiced, knowing this was an answer to your prayers and mine, and peace settled upon me that this is the Lord's answer. May God be praised!

For your ongoing prayer support, here are some of the scheduling dates I was given today:

- April 15: Arrive and check-in, to be followed by a few days of tests and medicine to increase my production of stem cells.
- April 23-24: Stem cell harvesting.
- April 27-28: Mega-doses of chemotherapy.
- April 30: Stem cell transplant.

This will be followed by a few weeks of careful monitoring while I lay very low, being careful to not be exposed to anything while the stem cells make their way to my bone marrow and do what God created them to do – make healthy blood cells and regenerate my immune system.

So, rejoice with me now! Helen and I thank you for standing with us in prayer. The sweet adventure of *Walking With God Through Deep Valleys* continues.

FOR REFLECTION

What astounded Jesus about the centurion's faith? Have you prayed and longed for the same depth of faith? Write or share your reflections and experience concerning each of these lessons: (1) Faith in Jesus leads us to bring our problems and petitions to Him. (2) Faith in Jesus leads us to ask others to intercede with us and for us. (3) Faith in Jesus leads us to rejoice in answered prayer and give Him our praise. If you have struggled with any of these, ask God to help you with this, and He surely will.

86

ON EASTER AND EVERLASTING JOY

April 12, 2020

On the evening of that day, the first day of the week, the doors being locked where the disciples were for fear of the Jews, Jesus came and stood among them and said to them, "Peace be with you." When He had said this, He showed them His hands and His side. Then the disciples were glad when they saw the Lord. Jesus said to them again, "Peace be with you. As the Father has sent me, even so I am sending you." (John 20:19-21)

The resurrection of Jesus Christ brings new life and resurrection joy to all who believe. He did this for His disciples on that glorious day. He has been doing the same throughout history for all who have believed in Him. The risen Lord Jesus Christ brings forgiveness, help, hope, everlasting life and joy. How so?

The Resurrection brings His Presence into Locked Rooms

His disciples were afraid – very afraid. They hid from threats lurking outside, shuttered behind locked doors, afraid of unseen dangers.

Then the risen Lord Jesus Christ came to them and stood in their midst. They could see Him. They could touch Him. They could hear Him. They could believe, rejoice and love Him again. And they did. The Lord Jesus died on the cross to atone for our sins. He was the perfect Lamb of God, who suffered and died in our place, bearing the judgment we all deserved. His body was then taken down from the cross and buried.

But the grave could not hold Him, and death could not defeat Him. On the third day, as He had repeatedly promised, up from the grave He arose.

The resurrection of the Lord Jesus Christ changes everything for those who believe. He forgives all who come to Him in faith, and He breathes upon us the breath of new life. The risen Lord breaks through the closed and locked doors of our sinful lives. He comes to people who are fearful and hiding from lurking dangers. His life and presence with us now changes us.

His presence has changed everything for me. In my own sinful condition and in my physical struggles, I was withdrawn, hiding behind closed doors. I have been afraid. And at times I have closed my heart. Have you ever done the same? But oh, how wonderful is His grace to meet us, love us, forgive us, restore us, and help us.

Though I have known my Lord many years, recently I have hidden myself behind closed doors of fear and doubt regarding the SCT process. But by the sweet grace and resurrection power of our risen Lord and Savior, He has met me where I am, entering my home and heart. By faith I have beheld Him. I have touched Him, and heard Him, and been changed by Him. The great truth of Easter and of His triumphal victory over sin and death has changed everything for me. His resurrection life and joy has brought the wonderful confidence of His presence into my heart, no matter the circumstances in my own life or in the world around me. I hope and pray that by His grace and by your faith in the risen Lord Jesus Christ, you too may enjoy the sweet assurance of His living and abiding presence.

The Resurrection brings His Peace into Troubled Hearts
The disciples of the Lord had troubled hearts. They grieved over His death and all their grand dreams for a beautiful kingdom on earth in which they would rule beside their Master. With the death of Jesus, their dreams had also died. They were distressed and afraid of what might happen to them.

They had all witnessed Jesus's arrest, and to their great shame, they had all run away. They hid, trembled, and wept as their Lord and friend was mocked, scourged, and horribly crucified. Their hearts were troubled.

But then the Lord Jesus came to them. On the evening of that glorious Resurrection Day, Jesus appeared to them. He knew what they needed, just as He knows exactly what we need. His first words to them offered His peace. He said, *Peace be with you."* Shalom.

Every troubled heart needs His peace. We often long for it. The risen Lord Jesus Christ comes to us speaking peace, bringing peace, and restoring peace. For all who hear and believe that He lives and is Savior and Lord, peace floods into our dry souls like a rushing, refreshing river of life.

We have that wonderful and delightful peace, because Jesus lives; He has conquered sin and death once and for all. Resurrection joy brings His peace to our troubled hearts.

How blessed I have been to know His peace in my life and heart. Because He lives and His constant presence is with me, His shalom has been real to me, even when I have been troubled and have called upon Him. The risen Lord does this for those who believe in Him.

Tomorrow Helen and I will depart for Nashville where my transplant team will harvest my stem cells, which will be returned to my body later. This process will cause me to feel vulnerable, weak, and physically miserable for a while.

And though it might feel as though my life hangs in the balance, because the risen Lord Jesus Christ is with me and with Helen, we are enjoying His peace now and will to the end, and forevermore. Our Lord's resurrection joy has brought such peace to my own heart, no matter what the circumstances are in my life or in the world around me. I hope and pray that by God's grace and through your response of faith in the risen Lord Jesus, you too may enjoy such peace.

The Resurrection brings His Purpose into Aimless Lives

After Jesus died, the disciples did not know what to do. They did not know where they should go or what they should do. The world as they had known it had entirely changed and left them with grief and without clear direction or purpose. Across the USA today and around the world many feel similarly, for the world as they have known it has changed and left them without clear direction or purpose.

On that Resurrection Day, the risen Lord Jesus came to His aimless disciples. When He stood among them, they saw Him and by faith knew that He lived. Jesus was dead, but now He is alive. And He is with us now and brings His presence and peace. To every aimless life, Jesus Christ brings His purpose. He said, *As the Father has sent me, even so I am sending you* (John 20:21). Then Jesus equipped them, and now He equips us by breathing on them the person, presence, and power of God the Holy Spirit.

What a holy privilege is ours now, and what a responsibility and purpose has been entrusted to us by our Lord – to go into this world in His great name, to do His work and accomplish His will by sharing His good news of everlasting life and joy. We are now His ambassadors (2 Corinthians 5:20). We are now His instruments, His servants, His witnesses, His proclaimers of what we have come to know concerning Jesus Christ – that He is Lord, He is Alive, and He is Savior for all who believe and receive Him by faith.

His resurrection joy has brought purpose to me. The risen Lord has long been my life purpose, and He remains my purpose still. I live to love, serve, honor, and proclaim Him for all my days, and forevermore. I pray that He has become your purpose too.

I therefore understand and concur with the apostle Paul who said, *For to me to live is Christ, and to die is gain* (Philippians 1:21). This is my conviction too. If the risen Lord should give me more years in His service, my continuing purpose will be to love and serve Him however He directs me until He calls me home. And when the Lord promotes me to glory, I will enjoy His glorious presence, and I will give Him praise forever.

When our risen Lord appeared to His disciples on the evening of that first Resurrection Day, He brought His Presence, His Peace, and His Purpose. The Bible says, *The disciples were glad when they saw the Lord* (John 20:20). They were overjoyed for the rest of their days and forever. Because He lives, we are now granted the privilege of sharing the gladness that flows from resurrection joy for all of our remaining days and forevermore.

On this Easter Sunday 2020, though COVID-19 has mandated social distancing and we may be huddled in our homes, our risen Lord comes to us today, just as He came to His earliest disciples that glorious day. This changes everything for us. Our Lord still brings His presence into locked rooms, His peace into troubled hearts, and His purpose into aimless lives. The victory of the Lord Jesus Christ over sin and death for all who believe and receive Him in faith is resurrection joy.

The risen Lord Jesus has done this for me. Hasn't He done the same for you? He will if you seek Him and ask Him, for He comes to all who will welcome Him. May the risen Lord Jesus Christ bless you this Resurrection Sunday and always.

Helen and I again thank you for your love and prayers for us, as we extend to you our love and Easter greetings. As we join today in celebrating our Lord's great love and His victory for us over sin and death, let us revel together in His resurrection joy.

FOR REFLECTION

Read again John 20:19-29. If you had been in that upper room either of those evenings with the door locked, and suddenly you saw, heard, and touched the risen Lord, what do you imagine your reaction would have been? What has been your actual reaction to the resurrection of Jesus Christ? To what extent and in what ways has the risen Lord brought His presence into your locked rooms, His peace into your troubled heart, and His purpose into your aimless life? In what ways have you known everlasting life and joy because of faith in the risen Lord? If you ask God to help you with this, He surely will.

87

ON KNOWING WE ARE NOT ALONE

April 15, 2020

Greetings from Nashville! Helen and I had a safe trip and arrived yesterday. We enjoyed the journey, as we sensed our Lord's presence along the way and appreciated each other's company. We talked a lot on our shared journey, but today when I checked into the Bone Marrow Transplant Center at the Nashville VA Medical Center, she was not allowed to accompany me due to visitor restrictions because of COVID-19.

Today was a full day with several medical tests throughout the day. Relatively speaking, I feel good, and everything went well, except I missed Helen's presence as I navigated my way from place to place through the hospital. Friday morning I am scheduled to review all of today's test results with the physician who is the Chair of the Bone Marrow Transplant Department.

I feel a bit overwhelmed at times, but even though Helen and I cannot be together, we know that we are not alone. This is God's promise to us and to all who belong to Him by faith (Psalm 23:4; Psalm 46:1-3; Deuteronomy 31:6; Joshua 1:9; Matthew 28:20; Hebrews 13:5). In everything we will face, we know and rejoice that we are not alone now, nor will we ever be alone. Our Lord is with us.

The current treatment plan here is that I will receive injections on four consecutive days next week, Monday through Thursday, to increase my stem cell production and release into my blood stream. Stem cell harvesting is scheduled for Thursday and Friday, April 23-24. Mega-doses of chemotherapy will be administered Monday and Tuesday, April 27-28, and my stem cell transplant is scheduled on Thursday, April 30. After that I will be monitored while my immune system slowly rebuilds.

Because of COVID-19, both the hospital and the hotel are taking careful precautions to insure that no viruses are communicated from person to person. Helen and I appreciate these precautions and see them as a blessing now, because they are creating a safer environment for me. As exposure to any communicable illness is life-threatening for me, the precautions people are taking make it much less likely that I will be exposed. I see this as a small part of the good that God has brought from the tragedy of this horrible virus (Romans 8:28).

We are also doing our part in being wise and careful; we wash our hands often, wear masks in public, and keep our distance from other people. Ultimately, of course, we put our trust in the Lord, who is with us to keep us safe and steer us through these troubled waters. In His care, we know we could not be safer.

So that is it for now. We thank you again for praying with us along our journey. Your prayers are a treasured ministry for the Lord and a powerful gift to us. Our Lord is hearing and answering; He reminds us often of His love and yours. How sweet to know we are not in this alone, for He is with His children through everything. We know that He is also with you, and He will be through all the days and years to come. Grace and peace to you through our Lord Jesus Christ.

FOR REFLECTION

Have you ever been isolated from people you love and felt alone? Read the Scriptures listed in the third paragraph of this lesson about God's promise to be with us always. How has this affected you in your life, especially lately, to know in faith that you are never alone? As you look ahead to an uncertain future, how does it affect you to know that no matter what may come, God will always be with you? If you lack peace about the future or feel alone, ask the Lord to help you with this, and He surely will.

88

ON PEACE AMIDST UNCERTAINTY

April 16, 2020

In the face of uncertainty, what can we do to find peace? We can plant a flag of faith in what we know. I recall various struggles and victories of my own life and remember the importance of planting a flag of faith in the Lord to celebrate life and to continue until the end.

At Parris Island, which was my final assignment as a military chaplain, there is a larger than life monument of United States Marines raising the flag of the USA on the summit of Mount Suribachi during the battle of Iwo Jima in the final stages of World War II. At Marine Corps Recruit Depot Parris Island, before this monument precious memories are planted in the hearts of young men and women.

Ceremonies take place there, when drill instructors give recruits the Eagle, Globe, and Anchor emblem of the United States Marine Corps, for they have completed their grueling recruit training, which concluded with an arduous fifty-four-hour test of endurance called "the Crucible." Their time as recruits has ended, and they are now United States Marines.

Every time I stood there to witness this momentous event, I wept for the joy of the new Marines and their well-earned sense of accomplishment because they endured and pushed through to the finish line. At last this reward is theirs. It was all incredible to me.

The most memorable of these times for me was when my Navy enlisted Religious Program Specialist (RP) and I joined the particular battalion of recruits with whom we had spent much time. We had encouraged them and built relationships along the way. That day we hiked with them the final nine miles of their Crucible. I was thrilled to cross the finish line with them and join them in celebrating that they were now United States Marines. And because I would soon complete my own military career, in some ways their accomplishment and completion symbolized my own.

As I recall the solemn joy of that day as we stood before that Iwo Jima monument of a flag being raised, I am reminded of the importance of raising a flag of faith to commemorate what we stand for and know. Though new Marines could not possibly see what the future held for them, they could celebrate and hold on to what they did know and what it meant for them to be U.S. Marines.

We also have uncertainty about our future. None of us know how life will unfold for us, whether our path will be smooth and bright or if our journey will be through deep and dark valleys. By God's grace and through faith in Him, we can know that whatever comes, our Lord will be with us, because we belong to Him. Of this we can be sure.

As Helen and I prepared to leave our home in Minnesota, I learned that several appointments that had been made for me in Nashville had been cancelled. Because this happened without any explanation, I was unsure if my scheduled SCT had also been cancelled. As we prayed together about this, we determined that we would trust our Lord and rest in Him. By faith we knew that if He determined for my SCT to proceed, nothing could deter it.

We then journeyed to Nashville and arrived two days ago. Then yesterday, in my first day at the Bone Marrow Transplant Center in the hospital, I was blessed to learn that at this point my SCT is still a "go." Hearing this brought us much joy, for we know that our lives have always been, are now, and will always be in His hands.

But like new Marines, I too face uncertainties about what my future holds. Will my way be relatively easy and my physical healing be rapid and complete? Or will my way be hard with many struggles to come, but with eventual renewed health? Or will the Lord soon promote me to heaven to enjoy the glory of His majesty? I do not know. But I do know that God holds my life and yours in His hands, and I can trust Him. I pray that you may have the same confidence through faith in the Lord.

Whatever the future holds for me, I am at peace now, for I know and I trust my Lord. How is it possible to have peace in the face of uncertainties? It is possible by holding on, standing on, and planting a flag of faith on what we know about God. Doing this brings His peace, no matter our circumstances or our uncertainties about the future.

Four attributes of God that I hold to and stand on to plant a "flag" are these:

God is Faithful

God is faithful by whom you were called into the fellowship of His Son, Jesus Christ our Lord (1 Corinthians 1:9). *Let us hold fast the confession of our hope without wavering, for He who promised is faithful* (Hebrews 10:23). My God has always been faithful. He is faithful now, and we know that He will be forever.

God is Loving

But God shows his love for us in that while we were still sinners, Christ died for us (Romans 5:8). *For I am sure that neither death nor life, nor angels nor rulers, nor things present nor things to come, nor powers, nor height nor depth, nor anything else in all creation, will be able to separate us from the love of God in Christ Jesus our Lord* (Romans 8:38-39). God has always been loving to us, even when life has been hard. His love for us is greater than we can fathom. He loves us in this moment, and we know He will love us forever.

God is Able

And God is able to make all grace abound to you, so that having all sufficiency in all things at all times, you may abound in every good work (2 Corinthians 9:8). *Now to Him who is able to do far more abundantly than all that we ask or think, according to the power at work within us, to Him be glory in the church and in Christ Jesus throughout all generations, forever and ever. Amen* (Ephesians 3:20). Absolutely nothing is impossible for God (Genesis 18:14; Matthew 19:26). The Lord has always shown Himself able to meet me and to provide whatever I have needed in every season of life and in every situation. He is able now, and I know He will be able forever for all. Do you also know this by faith?

God is Good
Oh, taste and see that the LORD is good! Blessed is the man who takes refuge in Him (Psalm 34:8). *Oh give thanks to the LORD, for He is good, for His steadfast love endures forever! Let the redeemed of the LORD say so, whom He has redeemed from trouble* (Psalm 107:1-2). God is always good, so His plans for us are good too, even when life is hard, for in our trials He brings His grace and blessings.

If you face uncertainties but desire to know God's peace, I invite and encourage you to plant your flag of faith in the truth and character of God who has been, is now, and will forever be faithful, loving, able, and good. Amen.

FOR REFLECTION

When have you ever faced uncertainty and lacked peace? And when have you faced uncertainty but experienced peace through faith in the Lord? What does the picture of "planting a flag of faith in the Lord" say to you? Even in the face of uncertainties, how does peace come from knowing and trusting that God is faithful? That God is loving? That God is able? That God is good? If you struggle with any of this, ask God to help you, and He surely will.

89

ON ENDURING TRIALS WITH JOYFUL ANTICIPATION

April 19, 2020

Greetings again from Nashville. On Friday I met the physician who will be overseeing my SCT. She is Director of the Nashville VA Medical Center Bone Marrow Transplant program. We spoke at length about what I am likely to experience and what the outcome may be.

She answered all of my questions and described the risks and physical struggles that are in store for me. Beginning on the day of my transplant, I will be an inpatient at the hospital for at least two weeks while my immune system reboots and begins to rebuild. All of this sounded hard and unpleasant to me. But thankfully, she told me more.

She described a time in my future when my strength will be renewed with a restored immune system, and I will be more active than I have been. I imagined a time when I can safely travel again and be close to people I love, even in crowds. Though she admitted there are no guarantees of how this will turn out, she assured me that she and her team will do everything possible to get me through this successfully, toward the brighter future she described. She encouraged me greatly.

I was drawn to the portrait she painted for me of my future health, mobility, and lifestyle. I have hung this picture in the gallery of my mind and heart. Looking at it increases my joyful anticipation, so I am more motivated to endure whatever suffering and hardships I must endure to reach such a beautiful reward.

The Bible has painted for us a lovelier picture of a coming day when our trials will be over, and we will be with Him forever in the beauty of His heavenly glory. We will then grasp that *this light and momentary affliction* was *preparing us for an eternal weight of glory far beyond all comparison* (2 Corinthians 4:17). Then, *we shall be like Him, because we shall see Him as He is* (1 John 3:2). This glorious picture inspires me even more, and it hangs in a most prominent place in the gallery of my heart and mind.

The Holy Spirit reminds us that joyful anticipation preceding suffering and trials was the experience of the Lord Jesus. The incarnate Son of God lived, loved, served, and cared compassionately for people. He taught wonderful life-giving truth, and in the anointing of God the Holy Spirit, He ministered powerfully with healing, forgiveness, and love. Encountering much sinfulness and pain, as is common in this broken world, our Lord longed for and prayed for God's kingdom to come, and for God's will to be done on earth, as it is in heaven (Matthew 6:9-10; Matthew 9:36; John 5:6; Luke 19:41-44).

The Lord Jesus envisioned and prophesied a grand church portrait of what will be. So, just prior to His great suffering and death, Jesus prayed to His Father with deep longing for our salvation and eternal life, for the unity of His bride the church, and for the glory and will of God, His Father (John 17).

The Lord Jesus envisioned us receiving His love, forgiveness, restoration, and everlasting life. He envisioned us walking with Him through all of life, enjoying His presence and our personal relationship with Him even in the deep valleys. He envisioned our being with Him forever in paradise. What a glorious thought.

But our Lord understood that for such blessing to become reality for His disciples, He must *humble Himself by becoming obedient to the point of death, even death on a cross* (Philippians 2:8). The Lord Jesus did this in infinite grace and love for our eternal blessing and for the glory of His Father.

The Bible says joyful anticipation motivated Him to endure the suffering that was before Him. The writer of Hebrews says all who believe in the Lord are to be *looking to Jesus, the founder and perfecter of our faith, who for the joy that was set before Him endured the cross, despising the shame, and is seated at the right hand of the throne of God. Consider Him who endured from sinners such hostility against Himself, so that you may not grow weary or fainthearted* (Hebrews 12:2-3). What a sweet and hopeful invitation! I pray that we will do this today and every day, until He calls us home.

Christ's great love for all humanity and His joyful anticipation of our salvation motivated Him to endure horrendous suffering, even to endure death on the cross. His amazing example of love and faith beckon all who love Him to endure every trial in faith with complete dependence on our Lord.

So, as this week begins, I picture the portrait portrayed by my doctor of my improved health and mobility. I do this with understanding that if I should recover my health in this way, my improved condition will only be for a while. Our Lord reminds us that our days in this mortal body are finite and numbered by God (Psalm 139:16), and that there will still be trials and trouble along our way (John 16:33).

But I also envision the time when I will see my Lord face to face in the fullness of His heavenly glory. And oh, what a wonderful day that will be!

Our Lord reminds us that joyful anticipation of what is coming is not found in achieving circumstances that please us, for disappointments and trials come to us all. Rather, joyful anticipation and enduring satisfaction are found in personal relationship with the Lord and believing in His promises.

Ezra and Nehemiah understood this in their time, when God's people were in extreme trouble and pain because of personal and collective sin. They had strayed far from His will, and the resulting consequences included much sadness and many tears. So Ezra read the inspired Word of God to the people, and Nehemiah exhorted them to believe in the Lord and remember that *the joy of the Lord is your strength* (Nehemiah 8:10).

I love this because the joy of the Lord is my strength now. I can relate to the people of Israel in the days of Nehemiah and Ezra. As with the people of that day, I have much sadness at the condition of our nation, the world, and even His people the church. There is personal sadness too because of my own sin and broken condition. But by God's grace, I have heard the precious Word of God, and I believe it.

I rejoice today, for I believe His promises, and I have received His forgiveness. I therefore share the joyful anticipation of the Lord Jesus and of the thief who was dying on the cross who believed (Luke 23:43). Like that dying thief, whoever turns to Jesus Christ in faith will soon be with Him in paradise. And our Lord has promised that we will be with Him, not only for a little while, but forever (John 10:28-30). This assurance fills me now with joyful anticipation. How about you?

Do you have joyful anticipation regarding what is ahead for you through faith in the Lord Jesus Christ? I am praying that you do. Believe in the Lord Jesus Christ, and fix your eyes on Him, holding on to His promises, and you surely will.

By His grace, I know that on the other side of my SCT, I may gain a measure of restored health and strength with the blessing of more opportunities to serve my Lord. I also know that whether it is soon or several years from now, I will soon be welcomed into His presence in the sweet glory of heaven. This motivates me.

I praise Him because my joyful anticipation of these things is high today. Our Lord is the One who walks with us and shows us the way. He is the One who walks with us through the deep valleys of life, and He is the One who enables us by His grace to endure every trial with joyful anticipation of what is to come.

Helen and I thank you again for your prayers. We know that our God hears and answers those prayers. Please know that we are praying for you too, that you may share with us the blessing of joyful anticipation in our Lord and that you may also give Him praise.

FOR REFLECTION

What pictures hang in the gallery of your mind and heart regarding your future? Read again Hebrews 12:2-3. How does the Lord's amazing example of enduring the cross *for the joy that was set before Him* speak to you now as you face the future? How high has your joyful anticipation been as you look to the fulfillment of the promises of God? If you struggle with these things, ask God to help you, and He surely will.

90

ON NEVER BEARING A CRUCIBLE ALONE

April 26, 2020

A crucible is a container in which metals or other substances may be subjected to very high temperatures and melted, or a situation of severe trial. I have mentioned the crucible experienced by recruits going through a Marine Corps Recruit Depot, a fifty-four-hour test of endurance at the conclusion of their recruit training.

After they complete this crucible, they are awarded their eagle, globe, and anchor, for they are now United States Marines. Though this crucible is hard, and though it requires tremendous endurance, one of the greatest blessings is that they go through it together and complete this arduous journey with those who walked with them through it all. They travailed together, encouraged each other along the way, finished together, and shared one another's joy. At Parris Island, each time I attended a celebratory breakfast with new Marines, I witnessed much shared joy among them.

The apostle Paul taught the church to *rejoice with those who rejoice, weep with those who weep* (Romans 12:15) and to *bear one another's burdens, and so fulfill the law of Christ* (Galatians 6:2). This is what love does. These scriptural injunctions imply our coming alongside one another in times of distress, so that no one walks through a crucible alone. Healthy churches do this; healthy Christians and families also do it. When this happens as our Lord intends, we are encouraged to keep pressing on no matter how hard our crucible may be. We are not in this alone.

So what happens when we must enter into a crucible without family and friends? I have been pondering this, because it is what I am about to do. After nearly nineteen months of dealing with multiple myeloma, I am at last ready to enter the crucible of my stem cell transplant.

Two days ago my stem cells were harvested, and it was a successful day of harvest. The goal had been to harvest four million stem cells, but that evening my team informed me via phone call that they had collected 7.5 million cells. Amazing. Many thanks to all who prayed for a successful outcome. Your prayers were surely answered.

My doctor also informed me that because my white blood cell count is high now, my scheduled dates for receiving heavy doses of chemotherapy, which will wipe clean my bone marrow, have been moved to Tuesday and Wednesday, April 28 and 29. My new date for receiving the transplant is Friday May 1. He also told me that I will be admitted to the hospital on Tuesday, the same day I will begin chemotherapy treatments, and I must remain as an inpatient for at least two weeks.

The hardest news was that I will be unable to receive any visitors while I am an inpatient. This includes my wife. This precaution is because of the continuing risk of COVID-19, which is highly contagious and could be carried in by persons who do not yet have symptoms. If this or any other virus were transmitted to the bone marrow transplant floor of the hospital, lives would be put at risk, as every patient has a severely compromised immune system.

Though I understand this restriction, and I applaud and appreciate the extraordinary efforts to protect patients and staff, it is still hard for me and for Helen to go through this crucible apart from each other. When we discussed this, Helen compared it to going through another deployment. We have done long deployments before. But this time, though we must be apart for a while, we know it will not be for long. This perspective helps us now, and it helps all Christians who must say goodbye for a while.

In a week or so, I will likely have lost all of my hair and feel quite sick; this is the expected response to the chemotherapy I will receive. I do wish I did not have to enter this crucible alone. Helen's sweet presence and strong encouragement have meant so much to me through the years along with the comforting presence and love of family and friends. Perhaps you can relate to this, for you too have probably faced hard challenges and felt alone.

So I want to share the comforting reminder our Lord has given me, as my crucible draws near. This promise is for me, and for Helen, and for you too. God has promised that we will never for one single moment be alone. He says, *I will never leave you nor forsake you* (Hebrews 13:5), and *Be strong and courageous. Do not fear or be in dread of them, for it is the LORD your God who goes with you. He will not leave you or forsake you* (Deuteronomy 31:6). Amen! What calming assurance God's Word brings!

While I am an inpatient, pushing through my crucible, I am comforted to know that Helen and other family and friends will be standing beside me in prayer. Thank you so much. Perhaps we can connect with one another now and then via phone, FaceTime, or Social Media. But in the times when I really need someone to be with me, my Lord has assured me that He has me covered. He will be there. He will use nurses and doctors and care providers to help me along the way. But He is the One who has always been with me. He will be with me still, with love, and strength, and promise, and hope. Helen has the same sweet assurance – that our Lord will never forsake her, not even for a moment.

Do you know that He is with you too? He surely is. Through faith in the Lord Jesus Christ, we can know He will always be with us for all our days and forevermore. God continues to hear and answer our prayers for one another and for all from whom we must be apart for a while. For this, let us give thanks to our God, and let us continue faithfully in prayer.

At the hospital yesterday I had another divine appointment while I waited to have my blood drawn and for the central line to be removed from my neck. I shared heart to heart with a dear woman who is the wife and caregiver of another multiple myeloma patient who is also being prepared for a stem cell transplant. Like Helen and me, she and her husband are walking through a crucible now. I know God put us together yesterday so we could pray for and encourage each other.

This lady loves her Lord, and her heart is filled with praise for His love and faithfulness. But she tearfully admitted that it has been hard for her to witness her husband's suffering. Then she said to me, "But the Lord is seeing us through." Amen. Helen and I understand and we agree. All of us can attest that life is not always easy. It may not be easy for us now, but the Lord is seeing us through. Though coming days may be hard for us, we will still say, "But the Lord is seeing us through." Whatever you are going through now, can you also say, "But the Lord is seeing us through"?

Our Lord is the One who sees us through. He walks with us through every deep valley, in every crucible, in every struggle, even when we must journey through the valley of the shadow of death. Our God is forever with us, and He is forever faithful. I am so encouraged by this.

Your continued prayers are appreciated for me and for Helen through the days that lie ahead. I do not know whether or how often I will have strength or opportunity to update you while I am an inpatient, but I will try when I can. If necessary, Helen will update you through this venue on my behalf and hers. Let us all continue to trust our Lord who is ever with us. He is forever faithful, loving, able, and good. Grace and peace to you all in our Lord Jesus Christ.

FOR REFLECTION

When have you ever been in a crucible (a situation of severe trial) in which you were blessed to know that you were not alone? What are we to do as Christians when we are aware of brothers and sisters who are facing a crucible? In what ways lately have you faithfully responded? How and when were you blessed to know the Lord is with you, and He is seeing you through your personal crucible? If you struggle and feel alone, ask God to help you, and He surely will.

91

ON ENDURING THE STRUGGLE TO EXPERIENCE THE MIRACLE

April 28 to May 13, 2020

The days of my hospitalization were hard. They included two days of receiving mega-doses of chemotherapy, which completely destroyed my immune system and wreaked havoc on my gastrointestinal tract. They included the day of harvesting my stem cells, which were frozen for future use, followed by multiple days of weakness, exhaustion, and feeling physically miserable.

It also included the day when a miracle began within me – the day of my stem cell transplant. More than 3.7 million cells were thawed and then returned to my body. These cells were miraculously directed by God our Creator to return to my bone marrow and begin creating new and healthy blood cells to restore my depleted immune system. This is truly a miracle, and this miracle is still underway. Many days when I have felt physically miserable, my God has reminded me that He is still working a miracle within me. Believing this in faith has motivated me to endure the struggle.

Science offers no reasonable explanation for how each entirely identical stem cell knows what type of cell it must now become in order to restore health and bring new life. Each stem cell is a blank slate, awaiting orders on what to become; when those orders are received, it becomes what it is meant to be. This miracle is happening within me, and in you, every single day. The only reasonable explanation is that Almighty God who loves us is accomplishing such miracles within us. Why? Because He is God, and He sustains and renews what He creates, and because of His very great love for me and for you.

As each of us looks back over the years of our lives, are we not able to perceive many miracles that our Lord has done for us and in us? I know He has accomplished many miracles in me, for me, and through me. I could write many volumes to testify of His miraculous grace in my life. I have received and witnessed immediate answers to prayer for God's healing. I have witnessed and received miraculous provision for material needs. I have seen God intervene to bring repentance, change hearts, and restore relationships. Like every stem cell, I have received God's miraculous direction in times when I had no idea which way to go or what to do. So many times and in so many ways, I have received and been blessed by God's miracles of grace.

But upon prayerful reflection, I now see that often, before I could receive and recognize God's miracle of grace and provision, I first had to endure a struggle. What I have experienced in my struggle with cancer, stem cell transplant, hospitalization, and isolation, and what I will affirm in the years to come, is that God meets us in our struggles, which we must endure for a season to rejoice in the miracles He brings.

Have you experienced this? Haven't you found that God's healing, hope, release, or joy after the storm is far greater than it could have ever been without enduring the storm? I have. So, as we endure our struggles now, let us remember in faith that God loves us, and He intends to bring us through to experience yet another miracle of His grace. Let us rejoice together in this hope.

FOR REFLECTION

When have you ever had to endure a struggle in order to experience a miracle? Have you witnessed this in someone else? What does our Lord want us to do when we face a difficult trial? Why is this not easy? How easy or difficult has it been for you to trust the Lord in the midst of a hard struggle? What blessings may be in store for you if you trust Him in your current circumstance? If you struggle with trusting God when life is hard, ask Him to help you, and He surely will.

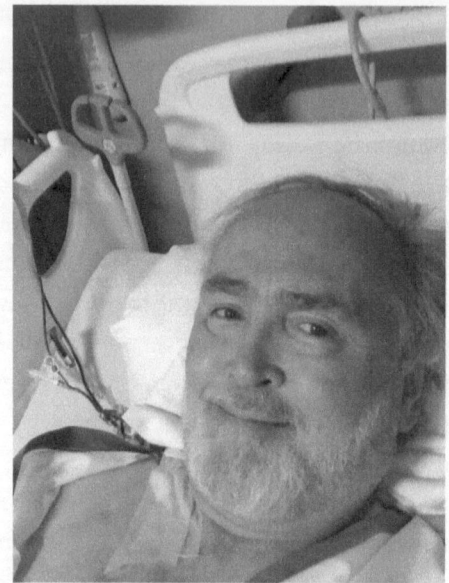
My stem cells being harvested

The joyful day of my hospital discharge when Helen and I were reunited

92

ON SETTING GOD-PLEASING GOALS

May 15, 2020

As I am progressing toward the end of the deep valley through which I have sojourned, and as I see the sun and clear skies ahead, I have allowed myself the luxury of beginning to make some plans. For some time I was unsure if I would survive this ordeal, because of the cancer, the reduced ability to fight off potential infections, and the extreme risk of the stem cell transplant process itself, which suppressed my immune system to near zero for a while.

I was spiritually prepared and excited in faith about whatever outcome our Lord had determined for me. But now that I am out of the hospital and my immune system is being slowly restored, I perceive that God's will for me is to carry on for a while longer in this mortal body. This realization has led me to reflect on some goals for the future that honor, glorify, and please my Lord – goals of things I would love to do. In several ways the Holy Spirit has prompted me to proceed in this way.

When I was an inpatient in the hospital, for several consecutive days I was very weak and had little or no energy or motivation. One day when I had been in bed the whole day, feeling sick and weak, I fully intended to stay in bed for the remainder of that day, but I received a word of encouragement via email from my friend, Pastor David McDowell, who is also a cancer survivor. David encouraged me to "set a goal every day, and do it." Because of this encouragement, I prayerfully set a goal to arise from my bed, go to the recumbent exercise bike that was in my room, and pedal the bike for the number of minutes I had determined in my heart as a goal for that day. And so I did it.

I also set a personal goal of increasing the amount of time I exercised on that bike by one minute each day I remained an inpatient. This may seem like a very small thing, but because I set this goal and did it every day, I slowly became stronger, and I was ultimately released from the hospital two days earlier than was originally expected.

Through a book I have been reading, the Lord spoke to me about setting God-pleasing goals. That book is *The Life and Diary of David Brainerd*, edited by Jonathan Edwards, *With a Biographical Sketch of the Life and Works of Jonathan Edwards*, by Philip E. Howard Jr. David Brainerd and Jonathan Edwards are powerful examples of true disciples of the Lord Jesus Christ.

Brainerd and Edwards were contemporaries and friends in eighteenth century America. They knew our Lord and served Him wholeheartedly. David Brainerd gave his life in service to God as a missionary to Native Americans living in New England. Though he died of tuberculosis when he was only twenty-nine years old, his story stands as a powerful testament of walking with God through trials in order to accomplish a greater purpose. David Brainerd set biblical goals, and he kept them – to the glory of God.

Jonathan Edwards was a renowned New England pastor, theologian, and revivalist preacher who was used of God in the First Great Awakening in American History. In reading the aforementioned book, I was led to pause for a while in the section of Howard's biographical sketch of Jonathan Edwards to prayerfully ponder Edwards's *70 Resolutions*.

Sometime after completing his studies at Yale College where he earned undergraduate and graduate degrees, Jonathan Edwards penned seventy resolutions or life goals. He was living at the home of his father, Pastor Timothy Edwards, in East Windsor, Connecticut. He introduced his resolutions in this way: "Being sensible that I am unable to do anything without God's help, I do humbly entreat Him by His grace, to enable me to keep these resolutions, so far as they are agreeable to His will, for

Christ's sake." Then he made a note to, "Remember to read over these resolutions once a week."

Jonathan Edwards made these resolutions while a young man, but by faithfully living out these prayerful goals according to the will of God, this man was prepared, powerfully anointed, and used as God's instrument in the First Great Awakening in America. I have prayerfully adopted several of Edwards's *70 Resolutions* as personal goals for my own remaining days, including these seven:

6. Resolved: To live with all my might while I do live.

7. Resolved: Never to do anything, which I should be afraid to do if it were the last hour of my life.

17. Resolved: That I will live so, as I shall wish I had done when I come to die.

28. Resolved: To study the Scriptures so steadily, constantly, and frequently, as that I may find, and plainly perceive, myself to grow in the knowledge of the same.

29. Resolved: Never to count that a prayer, nor to let that pass as a prayer, nor that as a petition of prayer, which is so made, that I cannot hope that God will answer it; nor that as a confession, which I cannot hope God will accept.

52. I frequently hear persons in old age say how they would live if they were to live their lives over again. Resolved: That I will live just so as I can think I shall wish I had done, supposing I live to old age.

70. Resolved: Let there be something of benevolence in all that I speak.[16]

---

[16] Jonathan Edwards, *The Life and Diary of David Brainerd with a Biographical Sketch of the Life and Work of Jonathan Edwards by Philip E. Howard Jr.*, (Ada, Michigan: Baker Books, 1989).

The ultimate goal I have set for my remaining days is to become more like Jesus Christ who said, *Whoever finds his life will lose it, and whoever loses his life for my sake will find it* (Matthew 10:39). I want to LOSE my life for Christ, always finding the fullness of life in Him. Using the acrostic L-O-S-E, my goal of being more like Christ includes: Love more, Obey more, Serve more, Enjoy God more:

I want to **Love more** and thus fulfil what Jesus declared to be the first and second greatest commandments – to love God most and to love others as we love ourselves. I want to reflect the character of my Lord who taught that *on these two commandments depend all the Law and the Prophets* (Matthew 22:37-40). I want to love more.

I want to **Obey more**, for the Lord Jesus said, *If you love me, you will keep my commandments* (John 14:15). In my remaining days, I want to Obey more.

I want to **Serve more**, as our Lord taught us. He said, *Whoever would be great among you must be your servant, and whoever would be first among you must be slave of all. For even the Son of Man came not to be served but to serve, and to give His life as a ransom for many* (Mark 10:43-45). I want to serve more.

I want to **Enjoy God more**. The most famous question of the Westminster Confession, composed in 1646-1647, describes this prayerful aim. The question is "What is the chief end of man?" And the answer: "Man's chief end is to glorify God, and to enjoy Him forever." Our God created me and you for personal relationship with Himself, and living in such relationship is to be enjoyment forever. Having walked with God many years now, I have enjoyed Him so much. As I glorify God with all that I have and am, it will be my aim to enjoy God all my remaining days, and forevermore. I want to enjoy God more.

By loving more, obeying more, serving more, and enjoying God more, I want to LOSE my life for Christ, thus I will find it in Him. Parallel with this desire, I hope to do specific things on this side of eternity for God's glory; for these I am setting prayerful goals, knowing that if our Lord wills, it will surely come to be.

Such plans are always to be made tentatively, per the inspired teaching of James who said, *You do not know what tomorrow will bring. What is your life? For you are a mist that appears for a little time and then* vanishes. Instead you ought to say, "If the Lord wills, we will live and do this or that (James 4:14-15). Desiring God's will and trusting Him fully is the way we are to make plans.

With all this in mind, I want you to know what a joy it is for Helen and me to be able to make some plans now. It is wonderful to do this, trusting God for the outcomes and knowing that the One who has walked with us through the deep valleys is the same God who never fails and is with us now. He will surely lead us every step until He leads us home. If you belong to the Lord Jesus Christ by faith, the same is true for you.

Are you in a deep valley now? The Lord is with you. Are you coming out of a deep valley now? The Lord has brought you through. Are you looking ahead to an uncertain future? You can know that the Lord will direct your steps. Are you looking to the future with hope for all your remaining days and for eternity? This is God's gift to all who believe in Him.

Helen and I are so grateful to all who have prayed, and who continue to pray for us in our journey through the deep valley. Thank you so much! Let us trust Him together for our remaining days and yours, until we gather before His glorious throne.

Recently when I was an inpatient, one of the nurses who cared for me mentioned that her son's name was Jude. This reminded me of the sweet benediction of Jude that my father so often recited at the conclusion of gathered worship. My nurse and I then recited together the words of this benediction from Jude 24-25. I conclude with these words as my benediction over you: *Now unto Him that is able to keep you from falling, and to present you faultless before the presence of His glory with exceeding joy, to the only wise God our Savior, be glory and majesty, dominion and power, both now and ever. Amen* (KJV).

I have one more piece of good news to share with you today. My scheduled discharge date from the Bone Marrow Transplant Unit of the Nashville VA Medical Center is Wednesday May 27. Helen and I are now scheduled to depart on Thursday May 28 to arrive home in Minnesota on Friday May 29. Your continued prayers are appreciated, as much patience and protection will be required while my immune system rebuilds. But we know our God is with us now and always! Amen? Amen!

FOR REFLECTION

When have you benefitted from setting a small goal and doing it? Of the resolutions of Jonathan Edwards quoted above, which of these can you adopt as your own prayerful goals? Of the author's stated desire to LOSE his life for Christ's sake by loving more, obeying more, serving more, and enjoying God more, which speaks most to you now, and why? As you look to the future prayerfully, making plans and setting goals, what will it mean for you to "make God-pleasing goals"? How does the benediction of Jude 24-25 speak to you now?

93

ON DYING IN CHRIST

Can we all admit now what we have always known to be true but have too often preferred to ignore? We are going to die. To use the first person pronoun, "I am going to die." If you have not said those words lately, go ahead and try. In my journey with cancer, I have been reminded of this reality.

There have been times when I thought I could die soon. In August 2018, I was hospitalized with a serious case of bacteremia (blood infection), and I knew I could die. In January 2020, just prior to when my SCT was scheduled, I was diagnosed with two viruses. My doctor told me if this had occurred after the SCT, I would have died. In April and May 2020, when the SCT was finally accomplished, I knew if I were to contract an infection, I would likely die.

Planted firmly in my memory is a Sunday morning in 2018 when I stood in front of the congregation I loved, and I spotted my precious wife Helen. Tears came to my eyes then, as the reality of cancer settled upon me with the awareness that my days on this earth could be cut short, and I would be leaving her and everyone I loved. In those moments, my Lord wonderfully reminded me to trust Him in this.

None of us know when or how we will die, but we all know that we will die. There is no doubt about it. The only exception to this are Christians who remain alive on the day of our Lord's return as described in 1 Thessalonians 4:13-18. Everyone else will die. No one can escape.

So how are we to prepare for our death? Until that day comes, how should we then live?

The COVID-19 pandemic reminded many throughout the world of their mortality, because this virus could infect anyone who has been exposed. Many have suffered and some have died, and more will die. The hard reality though is that we are all going to die. I will, and so will you. It is good for us to admit this now and make it our priority to be prepared for our death.

I have been cognizant of my own mortality, but much more so since my Lord gave me an amazing glimpse of heaven several years ago. I knew with clarity that I was in heaven, and I knew this was where I belonged. I experienced more joy than I had ever imagined possible. I saw the Lamb of God who takes away the sins of the world, and I knew with immense delight and wonder that by His grace and infinite mercy, I was completely forgiven.

What great joy! I beheld such incredible beauty and enjoyed sweet fellowship with saints of God who have gone before. I sensed His love to the core of my being, and I knew I was welcomed in the glory and love of His presence and would live with Him for eternity. With all of my being, this was where I wanted to be. This was where I belonged.

That glorious glimpse of heaven has motivated me through the years. By His grace, my Lord has given me additional pictures of our heavenly home, where He dwells in the brightness of His glory, where love permeates everything, and where the saints of God know the richness of His love, joy, and glory.

Because of God's great love and mercy, everyone in heaven loves to worship Him and joyfully declare from the depths of our souls, *Worthy is the Lamb who was slain, to receive power and wealth and wisdom and might and honor and glory and blessing* (Revelation 5:12), and *Hallelujah! For the Lord our God the Almighty reigns. Let us rejoice and give Him the glory* (Revelation 19:6-7). When we are in God's Holy presence, we cannot help but give Him praise. Do you believe this? Do you long to praise Him now?

If we know and believe that the promise of God is true, that *to be absent from the body* is *to be present with the Lord* (2 Corinthians 5:8 KJV), how can we not want to praise Him? And how can it not affect the way we live our lives today? How could we not choose to worship Him from the depths of our soul with others who will be with us as His forever family? If we believe in the reality of heaven through faith in the Lord Jesus Christ, then don't we already long to love and serve Him with our whole heart?

When the apostle Paul wrote to Timothy from prison, he was very aware of his own mortality and that he would soon die. But did Paul give any indication that he was afraid or nervous about what was coming? Not at all. Rather, because he believed the sure promises of God, Paul looked ahead with joyful anticipation and confidence in what was coming for all who believe, know, and love the Lord Jesus Christ.

Shortly before his expected death, Paul penned these beautiful and triumphant words of faith: *For I am already being poured out as a drink offering, and the time of my departure has come. I have fought the good fight, I have finished the race, I have kept the faith. Henceforth there is laid up for me the crown of righteousness which the Lord, the righteous judge, will award to me on that day, and not only to me, but also to all who have loved His appearing* (2 Timothy 4:6-8). Amen! What a sweet promise for you and me.

How often I have read these inspired words at funerals of Christian brothers and sisters, for they are true. They were true for Paul the apostle, and they are true now for all who die belonging to the Lord Jesus Christ by faith.

Before my SCT, I wrote a version of this chapter to be included if I did not survive, for I knew that was a real possibility. I left instructions that if I was promoted to glory, that version of this chapter would conclude this book. I wrote it from the perspective of already being in heaven. I loved writing that version of this chapter, because I know that when I reach heaven, I will be where I belong and where I have longed to be – with our Lord in His heavenly glory.

But the Lord's answer to our collective prayers for His will to be done was to bring me safely through the SCT. I still face a prolonged season of recuperation as my bone marrow and blood rebuild, and the immunities that I will need to fight illness and infections are restored. I must be very careful. But I trust the Lord to see me through this and I look forward with rejoicing to more years of fruitful service for Him.

Because I have faced death on my cancer journey and I know that it could come at any time, I have joyful anticipation of what is coming by God's grace and the certainty of His promises. When death finally approaches for me, it may be hard to leave those I love. But in light of eternity, I know this separation will not be for long.

Yes, it will be painful to leave my dear wife Helen, our children and their spouses, our precious grandchildren, our sisters and brother and their spouses, our nieces and nephews, and so many family and friends that I love. This will be hard.

I expect that when I die many whom I have loved will grieve my passing. My earnest prayer is that the Lord of all who has conquered sin and death to give the sweet gifts of salvation and everlasting life will be their comfort, peace, and eternal hope.

I know that you have also experienced death, and you will again as your own death approaches. Let us remember in faith that as Christians we never really say goodbye to each other. Because of the wonderful grace of Jesus and His glorious promises to us, we can confidently say, "God be with you, 'til we meet again."

When my time of departure comes, and you hear that God has promoted me to glory, you can know that I am with my Lord in a most beautiful, glorious, and intimate way. There is no better place anyone can be. You may grieve my passing, for death, suffering, grief, and loss are the painful consequences of the horrible curse of sin.

But I hope and pray that you will be able to rejoice with me, for we have a Savior who has triumphed over sin, evil, and death. In Him we share His victory. So in seasons of despair and grief, may the Lord help you add His joy to your grief. And if you should grieve my passing or the passing of another of God's saints, I hope that you can be happy for me and for all who have died with faith in the Lord Jesus, for we are and will forever be alive in His presence.

And as you put your faith in the Lord, to love, trust, and follow Him, look forward with me to when we will see one another again in glory. And if we were not blessed to know one another personally while on our earthly journey, by God's amazing grace, we may yet meet in the eternal glory of His heavenly presence.

After my father died in August 2017, and I prepared for his funeral,

I found a box among his possessions that contained some of the readings he used at funerals, for he was a shepherd of God's flock. All the readings in my dad's box spoke of the true promises of God. I noticed that there was only one copy of most of the readings in this box. There was one reading, however, that had dozens of copies, which suggested to me that he often used this one and liked to provide copies for people to take home with them.

When I read this at my dad's graveside, it comforted me and others who mourned. This was my father's faith and my mother's, and by God's grace it was my faith too. I pray it is also yours. I share this with you because it describes what I so longed for and will soon be enjoying. It was written by Matthew Henry and discovered soon after his death.

Weep Not for Me

Would you know where I am?
I am at home in my Father's house,
    in the mansion Jesus prepared for me there.
I am where I want to be, where I have longed and often desired to be.
No longer on a stormy sea, but in a safe and quiet harbor.
My working time is done, I am resting.
My sowing time is done, I am reaping.
My joy is as the joy of harvest.

Would you know how it is with me?
I am perfect in holiness; grace is swallowed up in glory.
The top-stone of the building is brought forth.

Would you know what I am doing?
I see God; I see Him as He is;
    not as through a glass darkly, but face to face.
And the sight is transforming, it makes me like Him.
I am in the sweet enjoyment of my blessed Redeemer,
    my Head and Husband,
Whom my soul loved, and for whose sake I was willing to part with all.
I am here bathing myself at the springhead of

heavenly pleasures and unutterable joys.
And therefore weep not for me. . . .
I am here singing Hallelujahs incessantly to Him
    who sits upon the throne,
And rest not day or night from praising Him.

Would you know what company I have?
Blessed company, better than the best on earth.
Here are holy angels, and the spirits of just men made perfect.
I am set down with Abraham, and Isaac, and Jacob,
    in the kingdom of God;
With blessed Paul, and Peter, and James, and John, and all the saints.
And here I meet with many old acquaintances
That I fasted and prayed with, who got hither before me.
And, lastly, would you consider how long this is to continue?
It is a garland that never withers; a crown of glory that fades not away.
After millions and millions of ages, it will be as fresh as it is now;
And, therefore, weep not for me.[17]

To all of this, I can only say "Yes," and "Amen!" Billy Graham shared such faith, and he proclaimed it throughout the world. Regarding his own approaching death, he was quoted as saying, "Someday you will read or hear that Billy Graham is dead. Don't you believe a word of it. I shall be more alive than I am now. I will just have changed my address. I will have gone into the presence of God." Amen!

This will be my reality. I will be in heavenly glory. I will be welcomed into God's holy presence, not by my own merit, for I was an unworthy sinner, often disregarding obedience and choosing my own rebellious ways. But by God's great grace through the sacrifice of His perfect Son, the Lord Jesus Christ, my sins are completely forgiven. He has made me worthy to be in His holy presence for time and for eternity. For this I will forever adore Him.

And one day soon (1 Corinthians 15:35-58 and 1 Thessalonians 4:13-5:11), the Lord Jesus will return to this earth in heavenly glory

---

[17] Matthew Henry, *The Miscellaneous Works of the Rev. Matthew Henry, V.D.M.* (London: Joseph Ogle Robinson, 1883).

just as He promised that He will do (Matthew 24 and 25). On the day of His ascension into heaven, angels repeated the promise that the Lord Jesus will one day return in the same way that He ascended into heaven (Acts 1:6-11).

On the glorious day of our Lord's return, Jesus will call together all who remain alive and belong to Him through faith, and He will raise all from the dead who have been His by faith throughout history and give each one a new and glorious resurrected body, like His resurrection body. By His grace many whom we have loved will be among that throng. And oh, what a day that will be!

On the theme of this book, *Walking With God Through Deep Valleys*, perhaps there is no deeper valley than approaching our own death or dealing with the death of someone we love. The psalmist David referred to this as a valley when he penned these treasured words: *Even though I walk through the valley of the shadow of death, I will fear no evil, for you are with me; your rod and your staff, they comfort me* (Psalm 23:4).

Amen! My Lord who has always walked with me will be with me when I walk through this deep valley. He has already removed all fear of dying and exchanged it with joy. Throughout my illness and in my weakness, I always knew He was with me. I knew that He would lead me through the deep valley of death to a beautiful place of rest with Him in His heavenly glory.

For Christians, the hardest part is not the dying but the suffering that precedes the dying. Yet even in this, the Lord walks with us and teaches us to look beyond the struggles to see the sweet promises of God that we cannot yet fully see.

The apostle Paul made this point: *For this light momentary affliction is preparing for us an eternal weight of glory beyond all comparison, as we look not to the things that are seen but to the things that are unseen. For the things that are seen are transient, but the things that are unseen are eternal* (2 Corinthians 4:17-18).

Because of God's grace to me this was my faith decision in life, and because of all that Jesus Christ has done, I am forever blessed to behold Him in the fullness of His glory and to praise His Holy Name. I have prayed that all who read these words will know the blessing of trusting Jesus Christ as Savior and Lord and walking with Him in sweet, personal relationship through every day of the rest of your lives and then forevermore. This is God's created intention for us, for He made us in His image to be fully known and loved by Him and for us to know and love Him in return. There is no better way to live than in loving relationship with the living God.

If by faith in Jesus Christ you live your life in personal relationship with the One who made you and died for you, then you can be assured that through all of your life, God will be with you and walk with you, even in and through deep valleys. He is ever faithful, for time and for eternity.

FOR REFLECTION

How has reading this chapter affected you? To what extent have you accepted your own mortality, and why? On a scale of 1 to 10, to what degree are you at peace with it? What does it take to be able to approach your own death and be at peace with it, even to be filled with joy at the prospect of seeing the Lord in the fullness of His glory and being home where you belong? What effect does having such faith make when you grieve the death of someone you love who belongs by faith to the Lord Jesus Christ? If you struggle with facing your death, or if you remain stuck in deep grief over the passing of someone you love, ask the Lord to help you with this, and He surely will.

ACKNOWLEDGEMENTS

Everything we are able to accomplish while on our earthly journey is a team effort. Our God equips us to do whatever He has designed us to do but always with the help of others. This book is no exception. Beyond my complete dependence upon the Lord, my greatest blessing and encouragement is my dear wife, for in so many ways she loves and encourages me. When I think I cannot, she says, "You can." Thank you Helen!

I am also indebted to many family and friends who have walked with me through this long journey, loving me, encouraging me, and above all praying for me. It is to all who have prayed for me along the way that I dedicate this book and offer my deepest respect and gratitude. Though on this side of eternity we may not see the powerful effect of our prayers, God sees it.

By your prayers for me, as I have walked through the deep valley with my Lord, He has wonderfully sustained me, meeting my every need. For this I will be forever grateful to you. Please keep on praying, for every person and need the Lord sets upon your heart, for we are forever blessed to love and serve a prayer-answering, miracle-working God.

ABOUT THE AUTHOR

Dr. Stephen Gammon is a third-generation minister who has walked with God since early childhood. A pastor for 40 years, wherever and whenever God led him, he served in three local church pastorates, as a denominational leader of ministers and churches (Conservative Congregational Christian Conference), and as an Active Duty and Navy Reserve chaplain. Steve and his wife, Helen, now reside in Northfield, Minnesota. They have three adult children and four grandsons.

Connect with the Author
www.walkingwithgodforlife.com

Walking with God, by Dr. Stephen Gammon

Are you longing to walk closer to God, or wondering if it's even really possible? Would you and your sphere of influence benefit from being mentored for a lifetime of walking with God? Or, are you a minister leading people of various ages and in various seasons of life, but finding it difficult to relate to them?

God teaches priceless lessons through life, including some we may resist learning. Dr. Stephen Gammon shares timeless biblical wisdom and treasured personal insights learned through 14 successive chapters of life in *Walking With God: 101 Lessons for Life and Ministry.*

Available where books are sold.

www.ingramcontent.com/pod-product-compliance
Lightning Source LLC
Chambersburg PA
CBHW030441090526
44586CB00044B/459